Peace Research

Peace Research

Achievements and Challenges

EDITED BY

Peter Wallensteen

Westview Press
BOULDER & LONDON

Westview Special Studies in Peace, Conflict, and Conflict Resolution

Published in 1988 in the United States of America by Westview Press, Inc., 5500 Central Avenue, Boulder, Colorado 80301, and in the United Kingdom by Westview Press, Inc., 13 Brunswick Centre, London WC1N 1AF, England

Library of Congress Cataloging-in-Publication Data
Peace research : achievements and challenges/edited by Peter
    Wallensteen.
       p. cm.—(Westview special studies in peace, conflict, and
conflict resolution)
    Includes index.
    ISBN 0-8133-7474-X
    1. Peace—Research. I. Wallensteen, Peter, 1945–
II. Series.
JX1904.5.P423 1988
327.1′72′072—dc19   88-3788
                                                                                          CIP

Printed and bound in the United States of America

The paper used in this publication meets the requirements of the American National
Standard for Permanence of Paper for Printed Library Materials Z39.48-1984.

6   5   4   3   2   1

Contents

v

PART FOUR
Analysis of Armament Economics

PART FIVE
Challenges to Peace Research

Tables and Figures

Acknowledgments

This volume has been made possible through the support of the staff in the Department of Peace and Conflict Research, Uppsala University, Sweden. In addition, a grant was made available by SAREC, the Swedish Agency for Research Cooperation with Developing Countries.

Peter Wallensteen

Introduction

Peter Wallensteen

Peace research is coming of age. During the 1980s, some peace research institutions around the world will celebrate their twentieth and twenty-fifth anniversaries. The study of peace, which began at those institutions, can now be found as well in university curricula. The time seems most appropriate to pause and take stock, and it is to this task that the present volume is devoted. Peace research is analyzed in this book by some of those scientists who shaped the field as we know it. In their contributions, they explore the origins, the achievements, and the challenges of peace research.

Peace research is created by the intellectual challenge of historical traumas, critical thinking, and the search for alternatives. It has developed from a field employing simple models and crude statistics to one of increasing complexity with much theoretical innovation. The roots of peace research are in themselves complex, as is shown by Wallensteen in Chapter 1 and Wiberg in Chapter 2. On the one hand, there is a peaceful intellectual battle with Machiavelli and the realpolitik legacy for analysis and policy prescription. On the other hand, there is a tradition of making peace researchable and empirical by drawing on utopian thinking. Also, intellectually and sociologically, the diffusion of peace research throughout the world has affected its agenda. One significant development is that the issue of peace and development has become as important as the original issue of peace and war.

The central problem in peace research continues to be that of war. In Chapter 3, Russett discusses current trends in peace research. It is no longer sufficient merely to collect data, search for covariation, and test hypotheses. More complex models must be constructed. In the same vein, in Chapter 4 Väyrynen examines a special type of war—hegemonic war—that changes the entire system. To understand such an event more complex models are required. Thus, both Russett and

Väyrynen ask for models building on the interplay between internal and external variables, even transcending the difference between dependent and independent variables. Russett relies on quantitative investigations; Väyrynen is more interested in a systematic comparative analysis of specific historical events. Russett offers an interpretation of contemporary U.S. foreign policy; Väyrynen suggests a new way of understanding why World War I and World War II began.

Another field of importance to peace research is that of conflict analysis and conflict resolution, and perhaps this is the field that has progressed the least thus far. Conflict resolution analysis has remained in the hands of diplomatic historians, scholars of international law, and game experimenters. In Chapter 5, Wiberg points out some of the inadequacies of conflict theory, not the least of which is the difficulty of generating creative alternatives to current theories of conflict and conflict resolution. In Chapter 6, Wallensteen suggests that remedies might be sought by developing new concepts and by pursuing the intellectually challenging issues of asymmetric conflicts, i.e., conflicts between strong and weak, rich and poor. Rittberger (Chapter 7) demonstrates the utility of the international regime approach to issues of conflict regulation, whether dealing with negative or positive peace. Together, these three chapters argue for renewed efforts in a research area that has the potential to be an integrative element in peace theory.

Armament questions are also important to peace research, especially studying the twists and turns of the arms race as well as arms production, arms trade, and arms control and disarmament negotiations. Peace researchers have played an important role as informed observers. In terms of theory development, the relationship between armaments and the economy has probably drawn the most attention. Lindgren (Chapter 8) summarizes the results with respect to the impact of the arms race on economic performance. Many studies, attempting to uncover general patterns, are largely built on cross-sectional data and often have a mechanistic approach. Lindgren argues for comparative studies on a more disaggregated level. Gleditsch, Bjerkholt, and Cappelen (Chapter 9) focus on military research and development and its economic impact. Problems of availability of data impair research efforts, but the authors warn about the long-term effect of using some of society's best-qualified people for military R&D rather than civilian R&D.

Although future challenges to peace research are addressed in almost every chapter, Part Five is devoted specifically to this topic. The style and orientation of its two chapters appear divergent but are actually closely linked. Alker (Chapter 10) draws twelve personal conclusions from modeling and quantitative research. For him, research develops into a quest not only for more complex models but also for more complex data, and even the codebooks become information for analysis. Alker introduces the term *emancipatory empiricism* and argues for use of computerized knowledge in a way that contributes to empowering the public with the resources for peace building. Thus, he is not far from what Galtung suggests in Chapter 11. Galtung uses Buddhism and its eightfold path as a schematic metaphor for studying peace research in the future. Galtung does not give Alker's priority to data and emphasizes complex theory instead, but this is not necessarily something Alker would disagree with.

These chapters analyze peace research from various perspectives. All of the contributors are from Europe or North America, but their perspectives are global. The origin of this book was the symposium Peace Research: Retrospect, Prospect at Uppsala University, Uppsala, Sweden, November 15–17, 1985, with participants from all continents of the world. The occasion was the inauguration of the first holder of the Dag Hammarskjöld chair in peace and conflict research. In that same year, the Swedish government appointed two professors of peace research, and there are now two Ph.D. programs for peace and conflict research in Sweden in addition to basic courses on peace and conflict issues. Sweden was not the first country to encourage peace research in this way, and it is to be hoped that it will not be the last.

PART ONE

Origins of
Peace Research

1

The Origins of Peace Research

Peter Wallensteen

Two Traditions of Peace Research

"In the beginning was Machiavelli." This statement summarizes Western thinking on war, violence, and power. It also points out one of the roots of peace research: a continuous battle with Machiavelli and his legacy in the study of war and peace. Peace research grew as a critical and constructive analysis of some of the basic tenets of the "conventional wisdom" of violence, much of which was well formulated in the advice from the Florentine politician and diplomat Niccolo Machiavelli to the Renaissance rulers of sixteenth-century Europe. The same ideas do appear earlier—for instance, in Greek and Roman writings—and they are prevalent in strategic studies during the nineteenth and twentieth centuries, specifically within the so-called realist school. Peace research emerged as a criticism of these ideas. Its contribution is, however, not only criticism. Its strength has been in empirically testing whether Machiavellian ideas are in fact founded in reality. Peace research grew together with modern scientific methods of inquiry. What began as an intellectual struggle with Machiavelli developed into innovative approaches to the study of violence.

The battle with Machiavelli and his legacy is one important stimulus to peace research, but there is also another, one that is less easily captured but is still obvious and significant, and that is research drawing on utopism. There has been a considerable amount of peace thinking throughout history, some has derived from secular and philosophical traditions, some has built on religious, ideological, and other normative thinking, but all of it provides a rich pool from which ideas can be developed. Utopism is an input to peace research that is different from the one generated through the battle with Machiavelli and his legacy. The underlying idea of the former is not only to ask whether the world "really" looks and works the way some people argue it does but also

7

to say that the world has to be improved, no matter how we describe it today, because it is not close to a meaningful definition of peace. This type of peace research is in the tradition of peace philosophers, peace churches, war resisters, Tolstoy, Gandhi, and the advocates of nonviolence.

The critical and the utopist types of peace research can be distinguished analytically, but they are difficult to pinpoint with respect to particular fields of study, which means that the two do not necessarily contradict one another. They are complementary—one may provide the motive for involvement in peace research in the first place, and the other may determine the choice of research topics, methods of inquiry, etc.—and there is no broad division within peace research along these particular lines. The two appear as different sides of a prism. When looking through the prism from one angle, certain questions of violence are the most pertinent; when the prism is twisted, other issues appear. In this sense, peace research is an integrated whole. Still, when analyzing the growth of peace research, a distinction between the two types provides a useful approach for understanding what kind of research appears at what moment in time.

Peace research concentrates on the question of violence. In particular, it has come to focus on organized violence in societal conflicts. This concentration makes peace research unique. Although this aspect of society might also be considered in other fields of inquiry, it is not normally a central issue in theory building. The meaning of violence, consequently, is an important object of discussion and analysis in peace research. One obvious type is the instrumental, conscious use of violence by one actor on another in a conflict. It goes without saying that there is also a more structural type of violence, for instance, the latent use of violence that is inherent in situations of repression and deterrence. One actor does not need to use violence on the other, but the threat of it—whether explicit or implicit—still affects relations between the two. There is also another way of conceptualizing structural violence, namely, as a situation in which killing occurs not through the individual use of arms but through the organization of society—for example, humans dying from starvation in a country that is rich in food. It is significant, that discussions of this meaning of violence have taken place in recent years within the field of peace research rather than other disciplines (Galtung 1964, 1969; Schmid 1968; Gronow and Hilppö 1970; Derriennic 1972; Pontara 1978). In fact, the analysis of the links between direct and structural violence can be seen as a particular trait of peace research.

In addition to the focus on violence in peace research, there also seems to be a general preference for emphasizing empirical investigation.

Important theoretical contributors often explicitly invite empirical confirmation or suggest ways of such confirmation. This preference also unites the two traditions of peace research. The fact that criticism, sooner or later, requires empirical confirmation is quite obvious, but utopism also requires at least empirical exemplification.

This trend means that methodological innovation is of great interest and importance to peace researchers in order to pursue both criticism and utopism. For a traditional analyst, who largely is repeating what is already paradigmatically known, there is less need for methodological creativity as there is less expectation of finding something different or new. In contrast, peace researchers have been receptive to new methodologies and have been quick to take up natural science methods, quantitative data, behavioralism, game theory, future studies, and neo-Marxism. In terms of methods, peace research has been open and pluralistic, in short, interdisciplinary. Ideally, this situation would mean that results could be controlled through using different techniques, a possibility that has not been explored. In practice, peace research results have been subject to the same scrutiny as other research.

The interest in methods results from an additional ambition of peace researchers, namely, to be able to make generalizations and, in a certain sense, predictions about social realities. In this regard, peace research is part of a natural and social science movement to understand what is general and repetitive, to learn from reality something that is applicable and useful for society's development. There are obvious differences between the study of molecules and violence, of course, but peace researchers aspire to say something about the conditions that would favor the attainment of peace. The focus is on the conditions under which an equitable solution is likely to survive the tests of reality.

A consequence of this focus is that peace researchers have developed an awareness of values in research. Obviously, values will affect research—the more so the less conscious the researcher is of the value problems—but values are a major issue in peace research as the researchers are not simply interested in empirically understanding the extent of violence in the world but also hope to contribute to the *improvement* of the human condition. This is an ambition that significantly unites the researchers battling with Machiavelli and those drawing on utopism. For many peace researchers, the medical profession is an important analogy because the medical sciences are interested not only in understanding disease but also in developing methods to cure and eliminate "unhealth" (Galtung 1965). Other research fields, of course, have a similar ambition, for example, psychology. Indeed, value statements to guide research abound in many research fields, e.g., business administration and economics (studying efficient uses of resources for the benefit of firms or nations) and education (improvement of teaching practices to benefit the students). To want to contribute to the improvement of the human condition is not unique to peace research, but it is unique in wanting to do so in the field of violence. This emphasis means that peace research does not want to contribute to the improvement of a particular actor (be it a state or a movement) but to a system as a whole, to the benefit, for instance, of both opposing parties in a conflict. Peace research is not conducted to predict under what circumstances a war could be successfully launched; it exists in order to contribute significantly to the reduction of latent and manifest, present and future, uses of violence within and between societies.

The Battle with Machiavelli

Peace research raises a set of fundamental questions about violence and conflict. Machiavelli is interesting because he was among the first to describe violence without excusing or idealizing it. In *The Prince,* violence appears without camouflage or romanticism, but it does appear as a tool of power that can be rationally analyzed. Machiavelli's thoughts were not new or original, but they still have an educational content and motive: Questions of violence are opened for analysis. One might also mention that Machiavelli supported his general statements with historical examples, but his way of empirically "verifying" his statements has striking parallels with many present-day authors, and his selection of examples is often debatable.

The Prince gives many examples of how a leader can gain and maintain power, but another central theme is the uses of power for "higher" purposes. Machiavelli hoped to bring forth a prince that was strong enough to achieve the unification of Italy. He was not a detached analyst, and the semiconscious or unconscious mixture of detachment and involvement in *The Prince* was frequent in writings on international and national violence until this century.

Therefore, there are many traits in Machiavelli's writing that are general and appear in much of the work in the realist tradition, so that Machiavelli is a relevant starting point for an analysis of the roots of peace research. Machiavelli is not the founding father of peace research but the reverse, a foundation to be scrutinized and—perhaps— to be reversed.

Six Basic Issues

In the Machiavellian world, six basic issues appear to be fundamental, and they can all be documented from *The Prince.*[1] These are basic assumptions for realist analysis, within peace research they become issues of discussion. Thus, several ongoing intellectual battles over fundamental issues have emerged. In this battle, however, the weapons are pen and paper, the strategies involve methods and interpretation, and the goal is to find a common truth. These battles are models for a torn world of how conflicts could be carried out.

1. *Violence is omnipresent and inevitable:* "If I don't use it somebody else will" Machiavelli writes. "There is no avoiding war; it can only be postponed to the advantage of others" and "one should never tolerate having one's plans upset in order to escape war. Anyhow one does not escape: the war is merely postponed to one's disadvantage" (Machiavelli 1975, 40 and 43).

2. *Violence is instrumental* for a successful reign of power, but it should be used with judgement. "It is a question of cruelty used well or badly"; "cruelty is used well . . . when it is employed once and for all" (Machiavelli 1975, 65–66).

3. In politics, *violence is the ultimate source of power;* even if there are laws and popular support, control of military power will be the ultimate determinant. As a consequence, military matters are more important than other political questions. "That is why all armed prophets have conquered, and unarmed prophets have come to grief." "The main foundations of every state . . . are good laws and good arms" (Machiavelli, 1975, 52 and 77).

4. *Conflicts are resolved through power and violence;* this is the main theme of *The Prince* as a whole. Largely this principle is seen to be so because the victory of one is the defeat of the other. Only one can be the prince; the others are his subjects.

5. *The state and the government are the primary actors of importance;* this statement is the so-called unitary actor assumption that has played an important role in scholarly political analysis. In Machiavelli's case, the state is synonymous with the prince.

6. *The state is independent* vis-à-vis other states. This situation is at the same time the point of departure for analysis and the ultimate goal of a state. The assumption of sovereignty is discussed by Machiavelli, who points to the dangers of major-power behavior for Italy. The interests and goals are taken for granted; for instance, attaining and maintaining power, preserving independence, etc.—for states, often labeled "national interest."

The world that is described by these six assumptions is one in which violence is one of several means for the attainment of political goals. Machiavelli was not a prophet of violence. He did not see violence as the only possibility or as something that purifies, as twentieth-century fascists or Franz Fanon would. Rather, Machiavelli was searching for some principles that can limit the use of violence, as in the second basic assumption. In this respect, *The Prince* has many modern counterparts, notably the writings of the Prussian strategist Karl von Clausewitz and Herman Khan's thoughts on controlled escalation of a nuclear war. For peace research, however, these principles lead to six crucial battles with Machiavelli and his legacy. More or less systemically delineated, these battles have given rise to a set of different fields within peace research.

World War I and the Study of the Causes of War

The six assumptions concerning violence were dominant in Western thinking and political practices until World War I. Although many objections were raised by philosophers and pacifists—and by liberal, socialist, and Red Cross movements—they did not seem to affect the decision makers in the leading states. World War I began in the spirit of traditional thinking: "Violence is inevitable; if I don't strike first, I will lose. I control events sufficiently to know what the outcome will be; my country will support me." All centrally placed decision makers expected the war to run according to previously established timetables (see e.g., Tuckman 1962), but the war became devastating and took a course nobody anticipated. The initiators of the war were defeated, their kingdoms were overturned, and their states were reduced, without the victors being able to celebrate. The traditional thoughts on war and the reality of World War I contradicted each other. New thinking was required, and from this intellectual and moral trauma sprung what is today peace research.

Thus began the systematic historically oriented study of patterns and causes of war. During the 1920s and the 1930s several comprehensive projects were initiated. In effect they were directed to the two first elements of the six basic assumptions, those of the inevitability and instrumentality of violence. These were battles on fundamental questions, between pessimism and optimism, some would say. Some systematic studies of war in history had already been made before World War I (Bloch 1899), but the true pioneering efforts were made after 1920. Sorokin (1937) collected statistics on wars during Greek and Roman times as well as in the world after 1100, Wright (1942) studied the world from Renaissance times, and Richardson (1960) analyzed "deadly quarrels" since the Napoleonic age.

The statistics gave a different picture of history. Violence appeared to be not continuous or omnipresent but varied in time and space, and the researchers began to look for periodicities and correlations.

Some states have been more involved in wars than others. In other words, violence and war have causes and, in principle, it would be possible to influence and control them. These investigations also gave a picture of the destruction caused by the many wars before World War I, and it seemed apparent that many of those wars had also been more devastating than the decision makers had anticipated. This suggestion provided more material for the discussion on the instrumentality of war and violence.

The period right after World War I saw many peace efforts. The hopes for an effective international organization were high, and ideas from the nineteenth century were brought to bear on the actions of statemen and politicians. The League of Nations as well as international law were seen as possible roads to peace. A whole field of inquiry and practical implementation emerged, with a strong emphasis on law, and this type of investigation has remained a field of its own. Of the earlier peace researchers, Wright was probably the one most open to such influences, and he made suggestions about the effectiveness of the League of Nations. The ideas of world order had, of course, been around before, with a focus largely on the sovereignty of the states as the ultimate cause of war. International organization and international law would contribute to reducing this independence, in the interest of peace.

The tradition of studying the causes of war created during the 1920s and the 1930s is still vigorous. Today, the Correlates of War project at the University of Michigan, directed by J. David Singer, is perhaps the most determined manifestation of this field of inquiry. By using clear definitions and carefully collecting data, a widely used data base for further investigation has been created (Small and Singer 1982). The work initiated by Istvan Kende in Budapest also belongs to this tradition as is that by K. J. Gantzel in Hamburg (Kende 1971; Gantzel et al 1986).

The causes of war studies utilize a research approach that is fairly typical of peace research: Violence is the central issue, the approach is strongly empirical, and there is the hope that the research efforts will result in useful political proposals. This approach allows for analysis and methodological development, but the political impact of studies utilizing this approach has been limited. To show the amount of violence in the world has a strong educational effect but will not change the world. Also, some of the models suggested, for instance, Richardson's, appeared too crude to capture reality. Consequently, there was a need to sharpen the methodologies and raise more pertinent questions. Such improvements have been made in some of the post–World War II studies, for instance, the work by Michael Wallace (1979).

Also, we can now see that the causes of war studies addressed some fundamental assumptions of the traditional paradigm but left others unexplored. Further global traumas were to make these additional questions part of the peace research agenda.

World War II, Disarmament Research, and Conflict Theory

The devastation of World War II was even greater than that of World War I. The second war again underscored the inability of the powerholders to predict the effect of their actions: The initiators were all defeated; the victims became the victors. The need to understand the causes of war remained important. But World War II also gave rise to two new dangers: nuclear weapons and conflict among the victors. From these problems developed disarmament research and conflict theory.

The nuclear explosions over Hiroshima and Nagasaki were fundamental challenges to the research community, particularly to natural scientists and physicists. The basic civilian and humanitarian orientation of science was suddenly contradicted. Research, seen by its practitioners as theoretical and abstract, was suddenly and rapidly practical and concrete in the most devastating way. The political failure to control nuclear energy and to make it freely available, as well as the onset of the nuclear arms race, led to a movement among scientists to contribute to arms control and disarmament. Few political leaders mastered the technological questions involved, and too many of them depended on expertise that was motivated by other desires. In the Einstein/Russell manifesto of 1955, the need for scientists to work to prevent a nuclear catastrophe was expressed. One result was the international Pugwash movement, which drew together scientists from East, West, and South.

In the development of peace research, this problem resulted in disarmament and arms control research. In this field, study focuses on the twists and turns of arms technology, as well as on proposals for preventing further armaments. This tradition of peace research is now institutionalized, one example being the Stockholm International Peace Research Institute (SIPRI) founded in 1966. The basic premise of this type of research is the need to control (some types of) violence and to question the instrumentality of (some types of) violence and armaments. It relates to the second of Machiavelli's six basic issues.

However, nuclear weapons are not the only weapons to pose concern to the scholarly community. Equally important are the conventional, chemical, and bacteriological weapons as well as their production and trade. The nonnuclear arms questions have received attention but have not been strongly linked to arms control efforts, as international arms negotiators during most of the post-1945 period have concentrated on nuclear issues. Instead, this type of research has had a more important role in national debates, in which the purchase, transfer, and production of arms have often been contended issues. A related series of questions concerns the importance of armaments for economic problems such as unemployment, industrial profits, regional development, and inflation. Such questions have seldom received penetrating analyses among economic researchers, but in peace research, they played a role early on. Partly this interest has had to do with the battle concerning Machiavelli's assumption of the instrumentality of the use of arms (pointing out that armament decisions do not necessarily follow military logic), partly also with the battle concerning the role of the state (the military-industrial complex being a convenient label for complicated influences on a government, which contribute to a reduction of a government's influence over its own decisions).

A second consequence of World War II was the rapid polarization of the conflict between the victorious allies. After only a short period of time much of Europe was divided into East and West, and the joint interest forged during the war against Germany, Italy, and Japan was not sufficient to bridge all the issues of contention among the allies. The conflict was defined in general terms (democracy versus totalitarianism according to the West, socialism versus capitalism according to the East), and actions were explained in terms of historical lessons, in particular the fear of being deceived by the other and the danger of yielding to an opponent that had only one ambition, namely, to establish its own hegemony over the world.

The Cold War and the policies of deterrence—becoming nuclear deterrence during the 1950s—influenced the relations among the major powers. The frequent use of historical analogies, particularly Hitler and Munich, again served to underline the need for a historical study of the causes of war. Also, the generalizations made by the various parties suggested the need to understand how conflict works. Thus, *theories of conflict* emerged. Through the study of other conflicts and their dynamics, it was hoped that knowledge for understanding and bridging the contention between East and West would be gained. Much attention was placed on game theory, in particular its ability to illuminate situations in which two parties have difficulty reaching the optimal state of affairs (the so-called prisoner's dilemma game). Game theory seemed to suggest that conflicts do not necessarily have to be of the zero-sum type, according to which the victory of one is the defeat of the other (Rapoport 1961). Other approaches involved the use of sociological interaction theory, drawing on Homans and Parsons (Deutsch et al. 1957), and the social functions of conflict (Coser 1956). In the peace research journals and centers founded at this time (*Journal of Conflict Resolution* and the Center for Conflict Resolution, University of Michigan; *Journal of Peace Research* and the Peace Research Institute, Oslo) considerable attention was given to conflict theory and conflict analysis (Galtung 1959, 1964).

Part of the development of conflict theory and conflict analysis was the result of the great interest in integration issues. Integration was seen empirically in the developments in Western Europe, but it was also seen as a way of transcending conflicts between East and West. The concept of a "security community" was used to investigate how former rivals had been able to eliminate the danger of war among themselves (Deutsch et al. 1957). Various types of theories of détente were developed from these integration and conflict studies.

These new developments of peace research were part of a reaction to the narrow intellectual climate that existed during the Cold War years and the simplicity of the deterrence postures. The researchers worried that the origin of wars was to be found in the way the conflicts themselves worked, and it was feared that decision makers and public opinion would be trapped in the dynamics of conflict. Thus, deterrence would lead to an escalation of conflict rather than to the containment of it. Other ways of handling conflicts had to be found. In the models of integration, an underlying idea was that societies would become so strongly intertwined that violence and conflict could be "tamed"—an idea that involved battles with some other issues in Machiavelli's legacy, the view of violence as the "ultimate" determinant of power and as a way of resolving conflicts. Peace researchers suggested that the dynamics of conflict could be the ultimate determinant and that a state/government might not be in control of the forces released by sharp antagonisms. In addition, integration ideas pointed to ways in which economic, cultural, and social links could reduce the independence of the state, something that would reduce the likelihood of devastating conflict.

The peace researchers of this era and of these two approaches were closer to decision-making bodies in some of the leading countries than had been true previously, so the specialists on arms control and disarmament could hope to have an impact on the conduct of nego- tiations or on national decisions. The studies of conflict theory and cooperation were in line with the desire to reduce tension during the 1950s and the 1960s, and it was even proposed that there should be peace specialists, recruited from among the peace researchers, to advise the decision makers (Galtung 1967). To be the adviser was also Machiavelli's ambition; the role for the peace specialist would be the same, but the advice would be different.

The Vietnam War and the Asymmetric Conflict

The war in Vietnam changed the situation. Many of the peace researchers, as well as many social science researchers, had serious difficulty analyzing the Vietnam War.[2] In that war a superpower was in conflict with a very poor state, ostensibly for the sake of some not very clearly defined general principles of social order (anticommunism or prodemocracy) as well as for some general principles of social behavior (maintain credibility of commitments), neither of which had much to do with Vietnam itself. For peace researchers, the Vietnam War became an intellectual and a moral challenge. It was the most devastating war since peace research had become institutionalized, and it showed that many of the models of peace research were flawed. For instance, peace research theories often assumed that decision makers did not want wars but were drawn into them because of uncontrolled escalation and conflict dynamics. It was often taken for granted that decision makers were interested in solutions that would be satisfactory for all involved parties. Also, it was assumed that the parties (be they superpowers, alliances, states, or regional groupings) were about equal in strength and in causing the conflict. Such assumptions were probably largely correct for the East-West conflict, even in its coldest phases (e.g., the crises over Germany, Berlin, and Cuba), but the Vietnam War was different in all respects; for instance, both parties pursued the war to win, not to reach a compromise. Also, how could two unequal parties be treated equally? Perhaps this question was to have the most lasting effect on peace research as it revealed a theoretical emphasis on symmetry between contending parties in a world full of asymmetries. For many researchers the conclusion was not to pursue the development of peace research in order to improve its models; instead, the matter of importance was to influence the stronger of the parties, i.e., the United States, to change its goals. For others there was not necessarily a contradiction between these two positions.

With regard to the development of peace research, the Vietnam War gave rise to a whole set of new questions. How are parties shaped? How do the interests they pursue emerge? What are the relations between different types of interests, for instance, class versus nation? What does the international system really look like? What does sovereignty mean in a world of asymmetric economic dependencies? Studies were made on the links between economic dependency and war, military interventions, and other military actions. From neo-Marxism as well as classical Marxism, new ideas could be extracted and put to empirical test (Galtung 1971). In this way, the trauma created by the Vietnam War could be turned into a new phase of development for peace research. A lasting effect has been a widening of the agenda of peace research (Wiberg 1988) as the studies of dependence have led to inquiries into the possibility of creating more self-reliant and independent societies. Thus, issues of development theory have become linked to peace research, particularly with regard to questions about the role of the military in the development process and about conflict-inducing economic dependencies.

For conflict theory, asymmetric conflicts, conflicts between unequal parties, pose still unresolved problems. It is hard to determine how such conflicts could be separated from other conflicts or how they affect the analysis of conflict resolution. Even obvious cases like major-power interventions in Third World conflicts can cause theoretical problems because of (explicit or implicit) alliances. The study of asymmetric conflicts, such as issues between North and South, both supplement and contradict some earlier tendencies of peace research. The emphasis on economic factors takes integrationist arguments one step further. Not only are states and governments restrained by economic interests, as hoped for by integrationists, but in fact they are not even the ultimate determiners of power and influence. Rather, the ultimate power, in neo-Marxist analysis, is located in the economic sphere, and economic interests are the ones to be analyzed. What then does the state do? Does control over weaponry provide a state/government with an independence of its own, or does it only make it a more important target for others to control? This type of analysis of violence involves a new way of battling with Machiavelli's view of the state.

The question of sovereignty is another subject of debate for the peace researchers. In the study of international organization and integration, there has been an underlying assumption that the independence of the state is an important part of the problem. If only this independence could be restrained, devastating conflicts could be avoided. But the opposite conclusion emerges from studies of dependence and imperialism. Peaceful relations can be established only if states are more independent. According to this perspective, dependency results in imbalances that give rise to internal as well as to external conflict, revolutions and interventions. From a conflict resolution perspective, furthermore, independence could be a perfectly plausible solution to some conflicts, for instance, ethnic contention. Can this debate be solved simply by saying that integration promotes peace when the parties are equal and leads to conflict when they are unequal? How, then, do we distinguish between symmetric relations and asymmetric ones in a way that makes it possible to predict what solution will have what effect? We could also ask, What is the record? In contemporary Third World societies, which are supposedly very dependent, some

princes seem to behave in a highly independent way, in spite of the
cobweb they are supposed to be entangled in. Could it be that in
many Third World societies the superpowers are reactive rather than
active, that is, they might depose a leader if he or she becomes
embarrassing but not before the scandal is fully exposed? The sovereignty of a prince and, today a princess as well, continues to be a
pertinent issue.

Peace research, it seems, has been formed through a dialectical
process. One impetus has been the intellectual challenge posed by
Machiavelli and his legacy, a perspective that includes the utility of
violence against humans. Another factor has been the moral challenge
posed by the history of the twentieth century: the two world wars,
the rise of nuclear weapons, the danger of conventional military
technology, the inability to resolve conflicts. Together, the problems
have formed a set of traumas for humankind and for peace research.
Thus, peace research has developed dialectically, through struggling
with established thoughts and actions. But the growth of peace research
has also given rise to a continuous debate within the field of peace
research itself. This internal dialectic testifies to the strength of peace
research: its ability to change and to add to or challenge basic
assumptions.

The externally generated traumas and the internally developed dialectics that have formed one tradition of peace research are summarized
in Figure 1.1. This figure shows peace research developments during
the twentieth century, from questions posed by World War I and simple
attitudes to violence to the more complex structural issues raised as
a result of the Vietnam War. The development has been cumulative;
new elements have been continuously added, and old ones have been
challenged or reappeared in new forms. The figure also makes it
possible to see linkages, for instance, between the demands in the
1970s for a new economic order and the search for a global order in
previous periods. The figure gives an idea of the richness of peace
research, but it is still far from complete. Peace research in its entirety
cannot be understood unless we also introduce a second tradition:
peace research drawing on utopian ideas and reformulating them into
researchable topics.

Drawing on Utopias

Peace research cannot be described only as a continuous dialectical
process in which Machiavelli, global traumas, and peace research itself
are partners. Such a description might mean yielding the initiative in
formulating scientific problems to other than the peace researchers

Figure 1.1.   Traumas and the formation of peace research

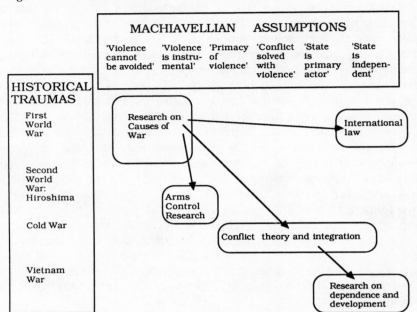

themselves. If the dialectical process were the only source of inspiration, peace research would face the danger of only being reactive, not initiating. In a way, Machiavelli would also be the ultimate determiner of what his critics are thinking. Consequently, there is a need to transcend the boundaries of dialectics and raise questions in a different way. In most scientific enterprises there is a desire to go beyond established confines and to explore what there is in directions without precedents. This is one reason why utopian thinking is important to peace research.

Second, some limits are imposed by an inquiry that is too empirical. In a statistical search for quantifiable generalities, there is the danger of verifying only what is stable and recurrent and underestimating nondominant developments, undercurrents, and counterdevelopments. Such undercurrents might illustrate the operation (or nonoperation) of typical peace ideas; they might be on the rise (thus, predictors of change), or they might be random, ad hoc, or badly reported but nevertheless of theoretical and practical interest. The danger of their neglect is a second reason for being interested in utopias and attempting to making them researchable—in part or as a whole.

A third objection to the dialectical and empirical development that has been described so far is that it makes peace research a science more of conflict than of peace. The hope that the analysis of causes of war would lead to conclusions about the operations of a peaceful society seems to be slow in being fulfilled. Researchers involved in studies of the causes of war might have very little to say about what a world without war would look like, although a fundamental idea for this type of research has been that if the "ultimate" causes of war are revealed, a recipe for removing war emerges. This idea is not necessarily true. Some skeptics argue that if some causes of war are removed, other causes might then become operative. Also this idea might imply that the world would be basically "sound" if only the war-producing factors could be eliminated. Is this a reasonable proposition? The problem not only afflicts studies of the causes of war but is even more obvious in arms control research. There are examples of how arms control agreements in one field have resulted in changes of the course of armaments rather than elimination of the phenomenon as such. The problem applies equally well in dependency studies, as empirical examples show that the mere removal of dependency does not improve human welfare and freedom (the case of Kampuchea, for instance).

The foregoing amounts to suggesting that there is a difference between a peace research tradition that has a "negative" orientation, critically and empirically analyzing the roots of repeated traumas, and one with a more "positive" orientation, drawing on utopias, in which violence in different forms is eliminated.[3] The distinction might appear sharper than it really is; it is more a way of turning the peace research prism to get a new look than a change of focus.

This second tradition of peace research might be called "utopist" rather than utopian, because it retains the empirical orientation of critical peace research. It is research, not speculation. Perhaps more precise labels could be developed to bring out the interest in alternatives, the future, and visions. To a large extent it is a tradition of a future-oriented study of the past and the present. In terms of research approach, there is often a preference for analysis of individual cases rather than of dominant patterns. In terms of growth and origin, it draws inspiration from hopes rather than traumas. This type of research is as powerful as the critical-analytical studies if consciously and strictly used.[4] The focus of this type of research is the realizability of utopias, whether partially or completely. Its political effect is to enlarge the scope of the possible alternatives that are open to public opinion and decision makers, illuminating directions that might not otherwise be seen. An additional reason for labeling this tradition "utopist" is its optimistic inclination: There is not only something "rotten" in the world, there is also something "ripening."

Overview

Since the focus is still violence, the topics raised within peace research drawing on utopias are similar to the issues already presented, but since a search for alternatives is central, the methods of inquiry are different. In a way, it becomes a study of historical "experiments," whether these were made consciously or not. Such research can be compared to the study of socialist and cooperative experiments of the 1840s that have been important to the emerging socialist movement, and thus of interest to historians; peace research investigates "peace experiments." Such investigation can be done on different levels of analysis: studying one particular actor and/or experiment; scrutinizing relations between pairs of actors, for instance, pairs in conflict with one another; and/or analyzing entire communities on a regional or global level (see Table 1.1). Much of the work consists of case studies of one particular actor or unit. The ambition is often to describe social events, which generally leaves considerable room for improvement of the analysis to include dyadic and systemic aspects.

It can be observed that many of the examples in Table 1.1 concern processes rather than states of affairs. Often these are studies of transformations of societies, for instance, turning away from a violent or military orientation and moving toward a civilian system. To this category belong studies of the elimination of military regimes, reductions of military production, and the elimination of military confrontation. It also suggests a major additional field for analysis, namely, studies of the developments that follow such transformations (e.g., democracy, civilian production, détente-type relations) as well as their durability. Very little seems to have been done on the regional level. Low-tension areas such as the Nordic and the Pacific areas need exploration, and a regional comparative approach might also illuminate the Latin American experience of the past fifty years, which has included considerable violence within nations and in relations to extracontinental actors but less among Latin American nations.

Thus, this tradition has not been fully explored, and there is a need for further exemplification. As a consequence, this tradition might well contribute to a change in perspective of what are dominant and nondominant traits in history and society. Perhaps there has been, in peace research and elsewhere, a premature emphasis on military conflictual relations in a world that largely is civilian and cooperative. After all, military research expenditures are much less than civilian

Table 1.1. Examples of empirical peace research drawing on utopian writings

Issue	Level of Analysis		
	One Actor	Interactions Between Actors	Social Systems and Structures
Conflict	Nonviolent actions	Nonviolent conflicts	Secure communities
Conflict Resolution	Peace Constitutions	Mediation Negotiation	International jurisdiction
Defense	Nonmilitary and/or nonprovocative defense strategies	Confidence-building measures Verification	X-weapon free zones, regional and/or global
Disarmament	Conversion of bases, industry Societies without military defense	Détente processes	Disarmament-development connections
Power	Democracy studies Demilitarization Civil control over the military Peace movements	Integration/ separation processes	Regional and global organization
Peaceful Societies	Societies in history and anthropology	Rivalries that ceased	Low-tension regions

ones,[5] and military expenditures in general are less than civilian expenditures for most governments of the world. Most conflicts do not become militarized, and most militarized disputes do not become war (Gochman and Maoz 1984).

This different emphasis could stimulate a most important debate, namely, the qualitative difference between civilian and military sectors of society. The impact of military violence on civil society is too strong to neglect. In peoples' memory, wars (as well as certain personal or natural disasters) stand out as highly important experiences, and they overshadow most civilian events. They even become ways of organizing memory ("before the war," "after the war"). Military violence, then, is an important research topic in its own right: What is the impact of the military sector on the civilian society today, how does it differ from the past, and what is the likely development of the future? To what extent do goals that can be achieved by military means actually form and direct the development of society as a whole? Do such goals actually contribute to the improvement of the human condition?

The real challenge to a peace research drawing on utopian writing is not to show that there is a large undercurrent (or even a dominant current) of civil, nonviolent, peaceful activity. Rather, it is to show that such alternatives are equally or more effective for the attainment of particular goals. This is a central problem for research on nonviolence. It should not only show that there are alternatives, it is also important to show that those alternatives can accomplish (some of) what military actions (allegedly) accomplish. This problem involves very complex research. It is more than comparing, for instance, economic sanctions to military actions, civilian defenses to military defenses, or international organizations to national ones. These actions, defenses, or organizations might be useful for different goals. Thus, goals are affected by the means chosen, which suggests a type of evaluation research that has rarely been tried, and it might result in an interesting debate on the burden of proof: Is it for the proponents of military action to show that such actions are more effective than civilian (nonviolent) ones, or is it—as it now seems—the other way around? If military actions have qualitatively different impacts, and form the memories of people, should it not be up to its proponents to explain why such actions should be undertaken at all?

What is presented in Table 1.1 are ideas and research projects inspired by utopian writings. However, they are all fragments of utopias rather than entire models. Possibly such fragments could be linked to form a whole, thus helping to verify more complete visions, but nobody has yet undertaken such a formidable task. From such fragments, would it be possible to respond to ideas on world government and its effectiveness? Obviously there is no historical example of world government, only examples of major-power dominance of regions and of governments ruling their own states. Can these examples be used to say something about world government? A final answer is, of course, impossible until we have such a government, but an educated estimate would be possible. After all, the situation is not too different from studies that make conclusions about the effectiveness of nuclear deterrence. Since there has been no failure, we cannot know whether nuclear deterrence is truly successful. We cannot know whether the absence of a major war between East and West is owing to nuclear deterrence, conventional deterrence, other development since 1945 or to a lack of ambition on the part of either side to attack in the first place. As a result, we can empirically study only "fragments" of the entire concept of deterrence, notably its effectiveness in particular crises. Peace research drawing on utopias is, thus, not the only field that has to face the problem of scarce empirical data for future-oriented conclusions. But the scarcity of such data means that such peace research shares the same vulnerability to methodological criticism.

Origins

We have seen how peace research has developed from a battle with Machiavelli because of some of the traumas of the twentieth century. Human, moral, and intellectual challenges have posed new problems for scientific developments. Peace research drawing on utopias seems to have a different origin. In this case, it has not been traumas that have challenged and forced fields of inquiry onto the scientific community but real world events. As a result, there are positive examples to build on, not just fears and disasters to avoid. But these positive examples might not be just hopes, they might, for many researchers, confirm expectations derived from theory. Research might have been done on these issues whether or not the examples occurred. Still, a real world event might make more researchers interested in the issues, and make a skeptical public aware of the utility of these particular studies.

Such events are perhaps less global and more local in nature than the traumas so far discussed. For instance, the study of nonviolence has been stimulated by the experiences of India and Mahatma Gandhi, which played a role for studies in Europe in the 1950s (Galtung and Naess 1955) and still continue to be important in India. During the 1960s, the civil rights movement in the United States gave rise to studies in many parts of the Western world (Sharp 1973). The Czechoslovakian resistance to the Soviet invasion in 1968 stimulated interest in the notion of civilian defense strategies (Roberts 1986), and in the 1980s, stimuli have come from, for instance, the experience of Solidarity in Poland (*Journal of Peace Research* 1982; Wehr 1985). These were all highly publicized events that directly or indirectly involved major states. Other examples come from smaller states or less tense circumstances. Cases of great societal transformation such as the reformist labor movement in northern Europe have seldom been identified as examples of nonviolence, and thus, such cases have not played the role they perhaps should in stimulating research.

Similarly, the development of the European Community stimulated historical studies of integration and led to the concept of "security communities" (Deutsch et al. 1957), an interesting case combining different traditions of peace research. Cases of mediation, such as the Camp David negotiations, might also have intensified interest in the possibility of negotiated endings to conflicts. The rise of the peace movements in the late 1950s and the early 1980s sparked interest in peace movement analysis. The public debate in the 1980s has also made nonprovocative defense an issue of peace research. These are but a few examples of the links between real world developments and the onset of peace research projects. General propositions in the public discussion have stimulated research on the theoretical and empirical issues involved.

Still, there are events and issues that could have been expected to give rise to more studies than they did, for instance, issues pertaining to the demilitarization of society. Several concrete examples have occurred during the 1970s and the 1980s, but researchers have been reluctant to investigate them deeply. Some of these situations are still volatile, some transformations are more partial than complete, other issues have been seen as more acute, etc. Some might even be dangerous to investigate, for the physical security of the researchers or for the maintenance of the "new societies." Still, they do provide an important field for comparative analysis, although the study might be better done at some distance from the object. The list of demilitarized societies is rather lengthy, and it constitutes a refutation of the widespread skepticism of the 1970s: Greece, Portugal, Spain, Peru, Brazil, Argentina, the Philippines, Haiti, and Guatemala. It is interesting to note that many of these countries have Mediterranean, Catholic and/or Latin cultures.

That list indicates that there are situations in which local or partial "peace" has been created and elements of utopias have been realized. These constitute legitimate and important objects of study for peace researchers. As we have seen, interest has often been related to events, but also, some events have not spurred as much research as could have been expected, and some studies might have been pursued no matter whether certain events occurred or not. Thus, there is a vast field of study still open for researchers interested in peace.

Traumas, Hopes, and the Future of Peace Research

Peace research has had its inspiration from two different sources. On the one hand, analyses of some of humankind's major disasters have prompted a reconsideration of some of the basic, traditional explanations. Conventional thinking has been challenged, and new sets of research topics have appeared. On the other hand, futuristic and utopian ideas—formed by thinkers, politicians, and researchers alike—have provided a pool of ideas for theoretical and empirical study. Thus, peace research now "walks on two legs," to cite a Chinese proverb. Increasingly, peace research is forming its own traditions and finding its own way to walk. Theories, data, and methods are being developed to increasingly sharpen the questions under investigation.

The traumas associated with the major wars have enlarged the scope of peace research by forcefully drawing attention to different types of conflicts. This attention has led to debate and a reconsideration of older propositions and assumptions of peace research. The widening scope means an increased awareness of complexity. A pertinent question is how wide peace research should become. Perhaps there is now time for a discussion on the limits of peace research. Should all types of violence be analyzed or only certain types?

The hopes provided by the positive developments in the world have given inspiration to another set of case studies, which have also developed into major and long-term research projects. Again, new traditions of scholarly inquiry are being created. In this case, the two traits might be suitable "correctives" to one another: to make sure that scholarly standards are kept but also that a larger perspective is maintained.

During these first decades of peace research, considerable developments have taken place. Still, many issues have not been penetrated at all, some have only been approached lightly, and research has concentrated only on certain fields. The need for peace research can no longer be questioned. One message has been clearly demonstrated: There were a number of researchable questions that were left untouched in universities and other research milieus throughout the world until the advent of the peace researcher. Therefore, for the future, peace research has a place within the universities and colleges. It is increasingly true that a modern university includes a special department for peace and conflict research.

Notes

This chapter has benefited from comments from all my colleagues at the Department of Peace and Conflict Research, Uppsala University. I am also indebted to participants of seminars held at Göteberg University and the University of Colorado, Boulder, Björn Hettne and Håkan Wiberg have provided very useful input. Needles to say, I remain solely responsible for the thoughts expressed.

1. All citations are from George Bull's translation into English (Machiavelli 1975). There are many interpretations of Machiavelli's work. Here, I am not interested in the "real" Machiavelli or in an analysis of his thinking in toto. *The Prince* has been selected for its eminent qualities in expressing some basic assumptions.

2. A case in point in Hans Morgenthau, who saw the need for a pathology of international relations to understand the U.S. desire to go into this war. Although he is a "guru" of realist thinking and the pursuit of national interest, he could see no threat to the national interest of the United States in Vietnam (see Morgenthau 1973, 7).

3. This difference in tradition might in fact be what is meant by references to "negative" and "positive" peace as different foci for peace research (see *Journal of Peace Research* 1964, 2).

4. A good example is the special issue on theories of peace (*Journal of Peace Research* 18:2 (1981).

5. See Nils Petter Gleditsch, Olav Bjerkholt, and Ådne Cappelen, Chapter 9 of this book.

References

Bloch, Ivan de. 1899. *The Future of War.* New York: Doubleday and McClure.

Coser, Lewis. 1956. *The Functions of Social Conflict.* New York: Free Press.

Derriennic, Jean-Pierre. 1972. "Theory and Ideologies of Violence." *Journal of Peace Research* 9:4, pp. 361–374.

Deutsch, Karl W., et al. 1957. *Political Community and the North Atlantic Area: International Organization in the Light of Historical Experience.* Princeton: Princeton University Press.

Galtung, Johan. 1959. "Pacifism from a Sociological Point of View." *Journal of Conflict Resolution* 3:1, pp. 67–84.

––––––. 1964. "A Structural Theory of Aggression." *Journal of Peace Research* 11:2, pp. 95–119.

––––––. 1965. "International Programs of Behavioral Science: Research in Human Survival." In M. Schwebel, ed., *Behavioral Science and Human Survival.* Palo Alto, Calif.: Science and Behavior Books.

––––––. 1967. "Peace Research: Science or Politics in Disguise?" *International Spectator,* vol. 21. Also in Johan Galtung, *Essays in Peace Resarch,* vol. 1, *Peace: Research, Education, Action,* pp. 224–243. Copenhagen: Ejlers, 1975.

––––––. 1969. "Violence, Peace, and Peace Research." *Journal of Peace Research* 6:3, pp. 167–191.

––––––. 1971. "A Structural Theory of Imperialism." *Journal of Peace Research,* 8:2, pp. 81–117.

Galtung, Johan, and Arne Naess. 1955. *Gandhis Politiske Etikk.* Oslo: Tanum.

Gantzel, Klaus Jürgen, et al. 1986. *Die Kriege nach dem Zweiten Weltkrieg bis 1984.* Munich: Weltforum.

Gochman, Charles, and Zeev Maoz. 1984. "Militarized Interstate Disputes, 1816–1976." *Journal of Conflict Resolution* 28:4, pp. 585–616.

Gronow, Jukka, and Jorma Hilppö. 1970. "Violence, Ethics, and Politics." *Journal of Peace Research* 7:4, pp. 311–320.

Journal of Peace Research. 1964. Editorial, 1:1, pp. 1–4.

––––––. 1981. Special Issue on Theories of Peace. Vol. 18, no. 2.

––––––. 1982. Special Issue on Poles on Poland. Vol. 19, no. 2.

Kende, Istvan. 1971. "Twenty-Five Years of Local Wars." *Journal of Peace Research* 8:1, pp. 5–22.

Machiavelli, Niccolò. 1975. *The Prince.* Translated by George Bull. Rev. ed. Harmondsworth, Eng.: Penguin Books.

Morgenthau, Hans J. 1973. *Politics Among Nations.* 5th ed. New York: Alfred Knopf.

Pontara, Giuliano. 1978. "The Concept of Violence." *Journal of Peace Research* 15:1, pp. 19–32.

Rapoport, Anatol. 1961. *Games, Fights, and Debates.* Ann Arbor: University of Michigan Press.

Richardson, Lewis F. 1960. *Statistics of Deadly Quarrels.* Chicago: Quadrangle Books.

Roberts, Adam. 1986. *Nations in Arms: The Theory and Practice of Territorial Defence.* 2d ed. Basingstoke: Macmillan.

Schmid, Herman. 1968. "Politics and Peace Research." *Journal of Peace Research* 5:3, pp. 217–232.

Sharp, Gene. 1973. *Politics of Nonviolent Action.* Boston: Sargent.

Singer, J. David, ed. 1979. *The Correlates of War: I. Research Origins and Rationale.* New York: Free Press.

Small, Melvin, and J. David Singer. 1982. *Resort to Arms: International and Civil Wars, 1816–1980.* Beverly Hills, Calif.: Sage Publications.

Sorokin, Pitirim A. 1937. *Social and Cultural Dynamics,* vol. 3. New York: Bedminster Press.

Tuckman, Barbara, *The Guns of August.* New York: Macmillan, 1962.

Wallace, Michael. 1979. "Arms Races and Escalation: Some New Evidence." In J. David Singer, ed., *Explaining War,* pp. 240–252. Beverly Hills, Calif.: Sage Publications.

Wehr, Paul. 1985. "Conflict and Restraint: Poland 1980–1982." In Peter Wallensteen et al., eds., *Global Militarization,* pp. 191–218. Boulder, Colo.: Westview Press.

Wiberg, Håkan. 1988. "The Peace Research Movement." Chapter 2 of this book.

Wright, Quincy. 1942. *A Study of War.* Chicago: University of Chicago Press.

2

The Peace Research Movement

Håkan Wiberg

By many criteria peace research is here to stay as a scholarly discipline. UNESCO lists 313 peace research institutions,[1] and the number of people who identify themselves as peace researchers by virtue of being members of peace research associations is in the four digits.[2] Even by the narrowest definition, we find more than twenty peace research journals, including one journal of abstracts.[3] Several bibliographies exist;[4] there are several books that try to give an overview of the field and its achievements;[5] and by now, there are biographies, or Festschriften, or both, about some of the founding fathers.[6]

Trying to write the history of the peace research movement will get any author entangled in the normal problems of writing the history of an academic discipline, and a few more. Many disciplines have had periodic acrimonious debates on how to define and delimit the subject matter, but peace research more so than most. There is no unanimity on how to define "peace," or on what it means to juxtapose it with "research"; it is unusual, even if by no means unique,[7] to find the term *movement* added to the name of a discipline.

At this juncture, there is the risk of circular reasoning: To delimit the object of historical study requires taking a stand on definitions, both of "peace" and of "peace research," that are still contentious within the field. I have attempted the following solution: The debate on the definition of "peace," as well as on the limits of "peace research" (more or less synonymical expressions), is presented in later sections of this chapter. My criterion on what is "peace research" depends on

From G. Heiss and H. Lutz, eds., *Friedensbewegungen: Bedingungen und Wirkungen*, Wiener Beiträge zur Geschichte der Neuzeit, 11 (Vienna: Verlag für Geschichte und Politik, 1984), pp. 165–185. Reproduced with permission.

time: For an older period, it refers to research on the causes and functions of war and the necessary and sufficient conditions for abolishing it; for a more recent period, it also includes other research carried out by significant groups of people who identify themselves as "peace researchers." In this way, it may be possible to avoid both making too inclusive a delimitation of its older history and excluding by definition parts of its recent history.

Another crucial decision concerns the "research" part of "peace research." War and peace have been topics for publications for millenia, and specialists can probably go far beyond Thucydides, Kautilya, and Sun Tzu. Hundreds of peace plans with arguments have been produced in Europe since the fourteenth century.[8] To cut the millenia down to decades, or at least generations, we have added a criterion that might be myopic in other contexts: To qualify as "research," a treatise has to present either theory formation with some rigor or systematic data analysis, or both.

One choice remains: Whether to write a history of research on peace or to write one on the "peace research movement." In the first case, definition would be—comparatively—simple; the second one adds the complexity of defining what a "movement" is and by what criteria we can recognize the "peace research movement."

There are both classic[9] and modern standard works[10] on social movements that never make a nominal definition of the term. The following elements of definition would seem to be sociologically essential. First, there is some kind of social organization in it. This may be more or less formal, more or less rigid, more or less unified. For example, the "labor movement" antedates both parties and unions and cannot be identified with any particular one of them. Second, it is engaged in diffusion of ideas, at least some of them being normative, to some target category. The ideas may be of many kinds and may or may not include common material interests. The target category may be universal ("Go ye out . . .") or limited (small peasants, women, Germans).

How can one have movements around theories, disciplines, and methodologies? In particular, what distinguishes such movements from the more normal phenomenon of schools and paradigms? It appears to be common to the peace research movement and the others mentioned (see note 7) that they have all seen themselves as at least value relevant, even value oriented, and that they have all had extra-academic target groups, in addition to the intra-academic ones, to which they have tried to communicate proposals or thoughts about how to improve society. Earlier movements found this "double" existence difficult to maintain for long, tending either to change into "normal" academic disciplines or to leave (or be sent down from) the academic community altogether, sometimes transforming into sects.

We must distinguish the "peace research movement" from the "peace movement": The relationship between them is an empirical question. Only a limited part of the peace research movement, as we define it, has had its roots in the peace movement, not all of which is convinced that peace research makes sense.

How, then, do we define the "peace research movement"? It is necessary to confess that no simple operational criterion can be given. The ideal typical member would seem to have the following properties: self-identification as a "peace researcher" (except for the purposes of making a pun or getting a chair); acceptance of the definition of peace research as "value oriented" and "applied"; intending the research to contribute to the "peace" of a whole system, rather than furthering the particular interests of some state; placing "peace" very high up in the value hierarchy. These are obviously several dimensions, none of which are dichotomous. The easy way out of the problem is to largely identify the history of the movement with the history of its infrastructure: institutions, associations, and journals. I shall therefore start with precursors and founding fathers; then present the development of the infrastructure; and finally discuss the academic trends in the movement in different periods, including the future.

Precursors and Founding Fathers

When somebody believes that he or she comes with something really new, that only proves how little he or she has read. The history of peace thinking is very old indeed. By modern criteria of what constitutes research, it has been customary to see the works of three men— Richardson, Wright, and Sorokin—in the interwar years as the beginnings of peace research. Closer inspection, however,[11] reveals that the history of empirical, and even quantitative, research on war and peace is older, by decades and even by generations. As early as 1817–1819, the Massachusetts Peace Society (which was itself one of the first in the world) carried out studies on the losses of human life through war since Adam and Eve, as well as estimating military expenditures and what civilian purposes they could have been used for. Several scholars in the late nineteenth and early twentieth centuries published encompassing statistics on battles and wars and the ensuing human and economic losses. Hardly any of these precursors appear to have had any influence on the later peace research movements, except for their figures being used by later scholars with more of a theoretical foundation.

Pitirim Aleksandrovich Sorokin was one of the first professors of sociology in czarist Russia. After a public controversy with Lenin, he left for the United States in 1922. His first major sociological works were "The Sociology of Revolution" of 1925 and "Contemporary Sociological Theories" of 1928, of which some parts deal with the sociology of war. After founding the Department of Sociology at Harvard in 1930, he published the four-volume *Social and Cultural Dynamics* in the late 1930s. The third volume of this deals with war, containing also his statistical survey over battles and wars since the sixth century B.C.

Sorokin's grand sociological conception in this work is focused on how patterns of meaning (including values, norms, epistemologies, etc.) are established, disseminated, and dissolved. He sees history as consisting of very long-wave movements between what he calls sensate and ideational cultures, creating a multiplicity of empirical indicators.[12] One main empirical result is that neither type of culture is inherently more belligerent, internally or externally, than the other. The peaks of wars, as well as of internal disturbances, occur in periods of transition from one type to the other, due to the upsetting of various equilibriums. Wright quotes this work extensively, and Richardson occasionally. Otherwise, his influence on the first generation of peace researchers appears to have been limited. Somewhat later, his ideas have influenced scholars as diverse as Paul Smoker[13] and Rudolph J. Rummel.[14] After retiring in 1949, Sorokin devoted the rest of his life to his creation, the Harvard Research Center for Creative Altruism, contributing to the nonviolence tradition.[15]

Lewis Fry Richardson (1881–1953), of a Quaker family, graduated in physics and in psychology and was most famous as a meteorologist in his lifetime.[16] In 1919, he wrote *The Mathematical Psychology of War,* printed in 300 copies at his own expense; revised parts of it were published much later. After 1940, he devoted himself full-time to peace research, publishing a score of articles in various scientific and statistical journals. His two main works, *Arms and Insecurity* and *Statistics of Deadly Quarrels,* were completed many years before being found after his death. They were then shown by his son to the early "invisible college" around Kenneth and Elise Boulding, where they were of great importance. Anatol Rapoport wrote a lengthy presentation of Richardson's theory of war,[17] and in 1960, both works were published, the former edited by Rapoport's teacher Nicolas Rashevsky, and the latter by Quincy Wright.

The immediate, and perhaps most important, results of these two works was that they demonstrated by example that *it was possible* to investigate the causes of wars and of arms races with rigorous scientific method, limiting the influence of the personal convictions of the researcher to a minimum. Both books carry the dedication that they were "Written in memory of the insistence by Professor Karl Pearson, F.R.S., that popular beliefs ought to be tested by statistics." Richardson had collected statistics on a number of variables for hundreds of "deadly quarrels" between 1820 and 1949, and this served as a data base for testing many popular beliefs (including those of statesmen, political scientists, and his own) as translated into statistical hypotheses. The great majority of them turned out to be unfounded, and later quantitative studies have largely borne him out in this: Where correlations have been found, they have mainly been multivariate.[18]

In *Arms and Insecurity,* he formulates interactive hypotheses on arms races by means of various sets of differential equations, testing them against data from a few case studies. In this, too, he was a path-breaking pioneer, followed by a vast number of later scholars.[19]

Alfred North Whitehead pointed out that a science that hesitates to forget its founders is lost. Later scholars have improved much on Richardson's models, statistical methods, and substantial conclusions. The lasting value of his works is that they provided something to improve upon.

In conventional terms, Richardson's epistemology was positivist (although considerably more sophisticated than most of his contemporary social scientists). He takes great pains to not allow his own convictions to bias his results, seeing this as a major weakness with most pacifism. In this, too, his major works served as paradigms (in the narrow and more original sense of that word). At the same time, much of early peace research defined itself as value oriented, seeing little contradiction. It took many years before this was seriously questioned, in the eruption of 1968.

Quincy Wright (1890–1970) alternately taught international law and political science. He was professor, first in the latter and then in the former, at the University of Chicago from 1923 until his retirement in 1956, after which he remained active as a teacher and researcher for many years. His main contribution to the early development of peace research is *A Study of War,* which appeared in 1942 after sixteen years of project work by him and a number of associates. Although some of the data collection was parallel with Richardson's, this book is of a very different character. From one point of view, it contains a vast compendium of what scholars from a rich variety of disciplines, from biology to law, had previously contributed in attempts to understand various aspects of war, as well as the creation and maintenance of peace. The way in which the material is organized, as well as the further development by Wright, also make the book a vast research plan, relating different levels of conflict to each other and to sets of background factors. His collection of statistics on, e.g., modern wars since 1480, primitive cultures, and historical civilizations, appear in various appendixes and have also provided a valuable data base for many later researchers; at the same time, his own analyses make him one of the pioneers in quantitative methods in this field.

Theoretically, one of his main concerns lies in the study of how balance-of-power systems can be transcended and superseded by supranational integration. His work on this has been a source of inspiration to several later scholars, like Kenneth Boulding, Anatol Rapoport, Amitai Etzioni, Ernest Haas, and Karl Deutsch.

Whereas Sorokin and Richardson were not members of the early peace research community, Wright was. In fact, he was asked to write the very first article in the *Journal of Conflict Resolution* in 1957. There was also another reason for this request: Wright, who had just retired but remained a prolific writer,[20] had great prestige and influence in the fields of international law and international relations. He may therefore be seen as a link between a "founding father generation" and another generation, who still had their main works before them and who are still alive and active. These, however, we will gradually present in the course of writing peace research history from an institutional perspective. A new discipline has become established when it has built up an infrastructure consisting of a considerable number of institutions, as well as a spectrum of professional journals and a network of professional associations to link them together. How did this happen in peace research?

Peace Research Institutions

Those who like having the impression that peace research as a discipline was established long ago and has been growing rapidly since then will do well to consult the surveys made by UNESCO in 1965, 1972, and 1978.[21] We find 81 institutions at the first time point, 149 at the second,[22] and no fewer than 310 at the third, hiring several thousand researchers.[23] The picture gets much more modest when we read the text of the surveys and add a few reservations of our own. First, if we limit ourselves to the subcategory "peace research institutions" (omitting "engaged in peace research" and "promoting or supporting peace research"), the figure for 1965 sinks to a more realistic 17, and closer inspection puts some doubt even to that. A more restrictive source for 1970 gives the number as 60,[24] and that, too, is clearly somewhat inflated by the inclusion of peace councils and associations.

Second, the impression of growth must also be exaggerated, since much of increase has to be accounted for by redefinition or increasing visibility. Where the first survey lists 70 institutions founded before 1964, the second gives 85, and the third no fewer than 133 of them, as compared with 152 that were founded in 1965–1978. (There are some missing data.) Since the subcategorization had been abandoned by 1978, closer inspection is impossible as to whether the first trend was prolonged: Between 1965 and 1972, 25 new "peace research institutions" were founded.[25] Depending on what assumptions we make about proportions and trends, the estimate of the number of institutions in the world that exclusively or primarily occupy themselves with "peace research" will range between 50 and 100, and the number of institutes that "engage in peace research" somewhere between 100 and 200.

These two estimates can be used to make a third: How many peace research milieus are there, if by such a milieu we mean an institute, or a part of an institute, in which at least a few self-defined peace researchers work and interact intellectually? If we assume that a majority of the first category and a minority of the second category belong there, positing that the total number of peace research milieus in the world is a bit over 100 probably will not be too wide off the mark.

A similar vagueness is inescapable when it comes to assessing the number of peace researchers, this, too, being heavily dependent on definitions. If we use the most narrow definition—people who identify themselves as peace researchers—the 1972 data would make us add some 400 researchers working at institutes in the first category (practically all of whom identify themselves in that way), a minority of those (1,700) working at institutes in the second category, and an unknown number of people working elsewhere (which will rarely be in peace research milieus). In all likelihood, 1,000 will be in the right magnitude.[26] Allowing for (at least some part of) the growth seen between 1972 and 1978, the magnitude 2,000 might be better in 1983. More inclusive definitions, by excluding self-definition from our criterion or by making a wider delimitation of the subject than "(negative) peace and war," may multiply that by two, or four, or even more.

Let us make a few more calculations with the UNESCO data,[27] bearing in mind all the reservations already made. If we disregard the international institutions, of which only a small minority are research institutions, as well as those for which there are no data on the foundation, we are left with 245 of them, divided as shown in Table 2.1.

We may assume that the density of such institutions that are identified with the peace research movement is much lower in the pre-1964 institutions than in the later ones. That makes it particularly interesting to compare these figures. We see that the period of major growth

Table 2.1. Peace research institutions

	To 1964 (%)	1965–1971 (%)	1972–1978 (%)	Sum (%)	N
North America	49	36	14	99	77
W. Europe	36	48	16	100	100
E. Europe	67	33	0	100	18
Asia	50	33	17	100	24
Africa	33	0	67	100	3
Latin America	32	23	45	100	22
Oceania	100	0	0	100	1
Total	44	38	17	99	245

appears to have been in the years around 1970, the only important exception being Latin America where it came several years later.[28]

This fact can be interpreted in several ways. The first is a purely methodological one: Very young institutions may be less visible. Disregarding that, we may also hypothesize that the growth pattern observed is a ramification of a more general trend: the rapid growth of social sciences in the 1960s, followed by stagnation or contraction in the 1970s, where that faculty tended to be first hit by increasing parsimony. Furthermore, it may also be the case that there *was* a turning point in the years around 1970, after which the network had become so widely spread, at least in the North Atlantic core areas, that new "converts" to the peace research movement to an increasing degree may have seen it natural to join already existing milieus rather than to spend a great deal of energy and resources in building new ones.

The 1972 study contains the most detailed analysis of institutions and thus permits us to make some generalizations as to what a typical peace research institute looks like.[29] It is of recent creation and is rather small: some ten researchers, including a few assistants. It is about as likely to be independent as to be part of a university. It is high on disciplinary pluralism, more than half a dozen disciplines being represented. International relations, political science, and sociology are probably represented, and it is about as likely as not that we find economics, international law, social psychology, psychology, and statistics. These disciplines, together with anthropology, are also those that are most frequently indicated as desirable to add to the institute. It is rare that any discipline (even physics or biology) is seen a priori as being outside peace research. The predominant opinions are that peace research should deal with both intra- and international conflicts, working with case studies or a combination of these and statistical analysis. Very few think that peace research should concentrate on theory to the exclusion of policy advice or that peace researchers should abstain from being active politically—mostly, no contradiction is seen (which leaves open what are the adequate combinations).

The Spread of Peace Research: From Diffusion to Fusion

For a historian of ideas or sociologist of science, the quantitative data we have presented or summarized above are insufficient: They tell about sizes and trends but only remotely and superficially indicate how the discipline was born and what were the crucial factors of its success. For this, we have to turn to other sources.[30]

I have already hinted at the intellectual origins of early North Atlantic peace research and will return to how these came to merge or clash with other traditions in a later phase. Another question of interest is where we find the organizational midwives of the movement; the answer varies from phase to phase. In the early history, we find many Quakers represented among the initiators and promoters in the Anglo-Saxon world.[31] Others came from the Pugwash movement, which also contributed to the creation of IPRA.[32] In many cases, peace research can be described as an (academic) grass-roots movement: Individual or small-group initiatives were decisive for the creation of institutes, which only gradually managed to obtain legitimacy, status, and resources from universities, funds, or political bodies. In a few cases, interventions by leading politicians have been decisive,[33] and in a few countries, notably the Nordic ones, peace research has managed to get political support from a wide range of parties.[34] Such support has normally been ex post facto rather than initiating, and in many countries, the powers that be have been more of an obstacle to overcome, e.g., by skillful naming.[35]

Among the IGOs, UNESCO has played the greatest midwife role, having taken an interest in peace research even before assisting in the creation of IPRA. Its repeated surveys of peace research institutions have signified interest and have also contributed to strengthening the network. It has supported the infrastructure of peace research for a long time, and several of the institutes in the Third World in later years have relied on support from UNESCO for their creation.

A midwife has no function without parents. We will therefore concentrate on the social process among intellectuals by which the peace research movement has originated and spread. Three early growth poles can be pointed out in the North Atlantic area: Ann Arbor, Oslo, and Groningen.

Ann Arbor housed several members of the early "invisible college" inspired by Richardson's works. They set up the Center for Research on Conflict Resolution in 1956[36] and started the *Journal of Conflict Resolution* (*JCR*) in 1957, which for several years remained the only journal in the field. Apart from serving as a training ground for many of the North American peace researchers, emissaries from the center and its surroundings were active in getting peace research started in many other places, from Oslo to Tokyo, in the early years as well as playing a prominent role in the setting up of the international infrastructure.

The creation of PRIO in Oslo in 1959 had a prehistory of several years in the Institute of Social Research there. That institute had a number of leading American social scientists as guest professors and had an early interest in peace. A prize contest was set up in 1954 for the best paper on "The Relevance of Research to the Problems of Peace,"[37] and among the winning essays we find one by Quincy Wright.[38] It also set up a seminar on conflict research in 1957, with Daniel Katz from Ann Arbor among the participants.[39] There was, however, another source of inspiration: In 1955, Arne Naess and Johan Galtung had published a book on Gandhi's ideas.[40]

PRIO took a few years to get off the ground and started issuing the *Journal of Peace Research* (*JPR*) in 1964. From about that time, it also served as a training ground for the first generations of peace researchers in the Nordic countries (as well as for visiting young researchers from several other countries). Galtung has been instrumental in promoting peace research and setting up institutes all over the world, through both his prolific writings[41] and his nomadic itinerary.

The Polemological Institute in Groningen was set up in 1961 by Bert Röling, an international lawyer who had, inter alia, been a judge in the Tokyo war crime trials. This institute hosted the inaugural conference of IPRA in 1965, and Röling was secretary-general of that organization until 1971. The institute has served as a training ground for many of the Dutch and Belgian peace researchers and has also influenced peace research in Germany.

Much of the history in the North Atlantic area, as well as in Japan,[42] can be seen in terms of diffusion from these early growth poles, and intellectual inspiration from the founding fathers, and from these growth poles. This goes for British peace research, whose early phase was inspired by Sorokin and by Richardson. It also goes for West German peace research, which started late but then grew rapidly, with American, Scandinavian, and Dutch inspiration.[43]

In other cases, the growth of the peace research community is better seen in terms of fusion than of diffusion. For example, France has a long tradition of *polémologie*[44] and of *études strategiques,* but with some exceptions, there have been few contacts with the international peace research community, and the community that is now growing there can be seen as more indigenous than imported.[45] The involvement of Eastern Europe is more a matter of existing research traditions on development and imperialism there having come to be defined as relevant by the peace research community than of diffusion. India and Latin America may be said to constitute cases in between. Even before the bringing together of the Indian and non-Indian peace research communities at the IPRA conference in Varanasi in 1974, there had been exportation of Gandhian thinking as well as importation of North Atlantic peace research.[46] Likewise, the incorporation of Latin America in later years is partly based on the *dependencia* tradition's being defined into peace research, partly by spreading, e.g., the peace research tradition of studying military institutions to Latin America.[47]

Peace Research Periodicals

A crucial role in the emergence and dissemination of a new discipline is played by the growth of periodicals, journals, yearbooks, conference proceedings, etc. One swallow makes no summer, but when we find many periodicals issued from several countries and in several languages, we may regard the takeoff phase as over.

In the case of peace research, unambiguous identification is more than normally difficult, depending on how one draws disciplinary lines (e.g., vis-à-vis international relations), distinguishes professional journals from those targeted at the "general reader," differentiates peace periodicals from peace research periodicals, and separates association newsletters from professional journals. This problem grows over time. There can be little controversy about seeing *JCR* as the nestor, followed by the *JPR* and a few others in 1964. The first non-English journal appears to have been *Études polémologiques,* from 1966.

Today, however, the number of periodicals depends on what source we consult. Among those with stricter delimitations, Chatfield lists twenty periodicals,[48] and van den Dungen includes twenty-six.[49] Scharf-fenorth enumerates twenty-eight periodicals of peace research and forty-eight "with contributions to peace research" as well as several yearbooks and similar publications.[50] Most inclusive is Boulding, who includes eighty-three periodicals and several more annuals.[51]

If we make a strong criterion, counting only periodicals that are issued or sponsored by some peace research association or institute, then we can make the following generalizations. In the last twenty years, just over one new journal per year has been started, and almost all of them have survived.[52] The great majority are published in English, but we also find journals in—at least—German, French, Dutch, Japanese, and Finnish. More than one periodical is issued from the United States, Canada, West Germany, Norway, Finland, India, and Japan. About half of the periodicals are edited in North America, almost as many in Western Europe, and a few elsewhere, mainly in Asia. The non-English, as well as a few of the English, journals almost exclusively serve as outlets for peace researchers in a single nation. Even among the major English journals, there are hardly any that can be characterized as truly transnational in their publishing. The North American journals are all strongly dominated by North American authors.[53] The most transnational one may be *JPR*, in which the majority of authors are usually non-Scandinavian, and now and then even non-European.[54]

Does this also mean that there are separate North American and West European profiles in peace research, and that this can be discerned by inspection of the major journals? That depends on how we formulate the question, since all journals cover a wide range of topics and approaches.[55] On the one hand, some types of articles may be over-represented in some journals in comparison with others, such as case studies in *JPR*, gaming and game theory in *JCR*, and abstract mathematical models with no empirical tests in the *Journal of Peace Science* (*JPS*). On the other hand, this does not mean that they are typical: It is probably true for a majority of the articles in all the journals that they might just as well have been published in one of the others. The difference is more one of emphasis. One difference in declaratory policies concerns positions on the value orientation of peace research. This is clearly greater in the European journals. How it is translated into practice is another matter. Thus, in the early years, *JPR* encouraged authors to include a section on policy implications; but little came out of that, since many authors did not, and when they did, the relationship between the results and the alleged policy implications was often remote.

We would therefore give the following overall impression. Judged by the number and variety of journals, peace research had become internationally established somewhere around 1970. It may be more transnational and value oriented than other disciplines but is less so than many peace researchers claim. It is difficult to define any clear mainstream.

Peace Research Associations

The third essential aspect of the emergence and establishment of a new discipline is that of professional associations. In this respect, peace research exhibits three peculiar features. There are two parallel international organizations, both of which were established long before national and regional associations, and in some areas where peace research is relatively strong, there are no associations.

The International Peace Research Association (IPRA) and the Peace Research Society (International)—PRS(I), later PSS(I), having changed Research to Science—were both created in 1963–1964 and both held their inaugural conferences in 1964–1965. Since then, both have held regular conferences, developed their associational networks, published their periodicals—and had very little to do with each other in spite of there being at least some overlap in membership and authors. This is not absolutely unique, but in the few other cases, it has signified either ideological cleavages (East versus West), linguistic barriers (Anglophone versus Francophone), or the emergence of a subdiscipline; and none seems to apply here. Tradition has it that it was more a matter of personal disagreements between the founding parents of IPRA and Walter Isard, the founding father of PRS(I).

The two organizations differ in several ways. In sheer size, IPRA is the bigger one everywhere. PSS(I) has from the beginning been more predominantly North American. IPRA is the one that is represented in the International Social Science Council (ISSC) and UNESCO. IPRA has a number of national and regional associations as corporate members whereas PSS(I) is organized in sections.[56] IPRA is also the organization that has more "movement" character—it defines itself as an organization of "researchers and educators" whereas PSS(I) addresses itself only to "scholars." IPRA's *International Peace Research Newsletter* (*IPRN*)[57] contains much material about relations to the peace movement and about policy issues. PSS(I)'s newsletter contains nothing of that, and its statutes state that it "does not participate in activities involving carrying on propaganda, or otherwise attempting to influence legislation or domestic or international deliberations."

This more "scientistic" position was also reflected in the change of the name of the organization and its publications from "peace research" to "peace science" about 1971.[58] By exaggerating what in reality is only a tendency, it could be said that IPRA engages scholars and milieus that *do* define themselves as "peace researchers" whereas PSS(I) is more attractive to peace researchers who prefer not to use that label.

The fact that international organization preceded national may be interpreted as an indicator of the transnational movement character of peace research. To some extent, the dates of the creation of national and regional associations support our description of a combined pattern of diffusion and fusion.[59]

There are important exceptions, however: areas that are conspicuously absent (Norway, Sweden, the Nordic area, and Europe) or late (Netherlands). For example, the Nordic area has had regular biannual conferences since 1966, and a great number of seminars and symposia in addition. It may be precisely the fact that the network has functioned quite well, both in social[60] and economic[61] terms, that has made a formal association appear unnecessary. Something similar may apply to (Western) Europe. As long as IPRA's secretariat was in Europe[62] and most of the biannual conferences were held there,[63] little need was seen for a specific European network; it was only after the "de-Europeanization" of IPRA that regular European peace research conferences started. It should also be pointed out that the history of peace research infrastructure is not coterminous with the history of peace research associations; other networks have been used, too. ISA and IPSA, as well as some of their regional and national associations, have long had commissions dealing with peace research or subareas. The same applies to the history community in the United States, where a peace research subcommunity with its own journal developed.[64] In the Nordic area, much of the early network (1962–1965) was formed inside a much broader interdisciplinary organization called the Nordic Summer University.

The 1960s: From Expansion to Controversy

The history of the peace research movement will look different when written from inside and outside. In the preceding sections, this difference may not be so great, since they have dealt with remote history and with—to some extent—quantifiable data on infrastructural growth. In attempts to write the more recent history of the intellectual development of the movement, the idiosyncracies of the author play a greater role.[65] In addition, there is always the risk of reading history backward, of interpreting earlier developments in the light of later facts.

To an external observer, the budding peace research movement would not have been visible in 1960, unless he knew exactly where to look and whom to ask. In 1970, he could hardly have missed it, given its rapid growth, but he would have found it more difficult to decide what peace research was about. What had happened in the latter respect?

The first decade, say from the late 1950s to the late 1960s, of the peace research movement may crudely be characterized as further development of the agenda set by the founding fathers: What are the causes of war and similar types of manifest conflict behavior? How can they be averted? How do arms races develop, and how can they be reversed? How is it possible to build peace: by integration of the international—and other—systems, by the creation of institutionalized mechanisms for conflict resolution, by making popular and political culture more peaceful?[66]

In this period, the intellectual growth of the movement took place in at least three different ways: by further development of the models and methods of the founders; by the existing peace research community bringing in new models, e.g., from economics,[67] game theory and its experimental applications,[68] sociology,[69] etc.; and by recruiting scholars from various disciplines to see what they had to add to the agenda.[70]

A summing up of the first decade may look thus: Some general conflict theory had emerged, but on a high level of abstraction. Some large empirical projects were under way, but had still yielded few results.[71] The original agenda was still rather uncontroversial, but there was a multiplicity of theories and models, with little unifying theoretical framework across the movement. Journals, proceedings, and anthologies published a plethora of articles, ranging from programmatic essays and abstract verbal or formal theorizing about case studies and quantitative international relations to laboratory experiments. What was, and what was not, relevant to peace research could be debated—and was—but at least the same agenda served as reference point. Positivism, but not in the crudest versions, was still the predominant epistemology in the movement (and often not seen as an epistemology at all—it was uncontroversial).

If the spectacular events of the early 1960s were the Cuban crisis and the Partial Test Ban Treaty, those of the late 1960s were the Vietnam War and the invasion of Czechoslovakia. The first set of events demonstrated the dangers of the Cold War, and the possibilities of reversing it. They were perfectly interpretable in terms of the old agenda and demonstrated its relevance and salience. Not so with the second set: They were clear cases of asymmetric conflict (unless one believed in the propaganda from the perpetrators). Even if they did not "cause" the emergence of a new agenda, they made its formulation easier and its position stronger.

A set of new questions were articulated in debate articles and anthologies of "critical peace research."[72] What are the mechanisms of dominance and exploitation between and within nations? What are the objective, even if often latent, conflicts defined by them? How can these conflicts be made manifest so as to make it possible to resolve them? How can liberation be achieved? Can peace researchers avoid taking sides in these conflicts, and what is their proper role?

These agenda items were bound to clash. What one saw as "integration," another would see as "institutionalized domination"; "conflict resolution" could also be viewed as "mystification"; what was the difference between "preaching revolution" and "solution of conflicts through adequate polarization"? The major showdowns occurred at the PRS(I) European conference in Copenhagen and the IPRA conference in Karlovy Vary, both in 1969. In the first case, the result was polarization and separation: The protagonists of the new agenda largely left, and the association marked its distance from them by changing its name.

The development of IPRA was more complex. A major split was avoided, thanks, inter alia, to Röling's enjoying the confidence of both camps and agreeing to serve another period so that a similar successor could be found. The eventual result was one of peaceful coexistence: Some of the exclusivist protagonists of both agendas left. Some of those associated with the original agenda stated their objections to the reorientation, but stayed, whereas others reoriented their theorizing so as to integrate the agenda.[73]

One important result of the adoption of both agendas, rather than settling for one of them, was that some of the fusion processes came about by the inclusion of, e.g., the Marxist research tradition on imperialism, the Latin American dependencia school, and the emerging "peace education" movement.[74] This meant that new types of institutes (e.g., development research) as well as new geographical areas were brought into contact with the peace research movement.

The 1970s: From Confusion to Diversity

As we have seen, the 1970s saw considerable horizontal growth of the peace research movement, as well as some vertical growth. In 1970, the directions of both types were still difficult to anticipate in the middle of the controversy. By now, we have some *facit* ("answers"). As for diversity, the published proceedings of the IPRA conference in 1979 are divided into six parts: political economy of food (three articles); social consequences of the new international division of labor (four); world information order (four); world military order, militarism, and disarmament (seven); ideological confrontation and transnational communication (four); and peace education (five).[75] Most of these categories correspond to a number of standing commissions that came into existence in IPRA in this decade, and this may also have affected the selection. Only a minority of the articles in, e.g., *JPR* or *JCR,* could easily be put into these categories, at least not without stretching them considerably. The *JPR* articles in 1979, however, show approximately the same proportions as the proceedings in another respect: The "old agenda" and the "new agenda" are approximately equally represented, whereas *JCR* almost exclusively publishes articles addressing the former.

There is, however, also some order in the diversity. As the standing commissions exemplify, the peace research community has increasingly come to consist of a number of "subdisciplinary" networks, whereas the networks in the 1960s (apart from that of the initiators) were more linked to geographical proximity. Within these networks, there are sometimes more common perspectives and research orientations than within peace research as a whole.

For ordinary disciplines, this has been a normal development (e.g., "hyphenated sociology"), whether hailed or deplored. It has sometimes been counteracted by the emergence of new macrotheories (like Marxism) or new methodologies (like causal modeling) that have spread widely. Peace research, however, is not normal, because of its interdisciplinary and (at least professedly) normative character. Both of these traits may have contributed to the process of spreading the intellectual boundaries of the movement wider and wider, until one leading peace researcher complains that "peace research has become what a black hole is in astronomy. There seems to be no social problem which in the final analysis does not have its legitimate place within peace research, and therefore is absorbed by the definitional processes in peace research."[76] In peace research, as elsewhere, rapid growth causes its own problems, e.g., in terms of integration. Extremely few, if any, of those who define themselves as "peace researchers" today have an overview of the entire field,[77] and hardly any peace research institute has more than some parts of it represented. To many peace researchers, it is a source of embarrassment that a field which prides itself on its transdisciplinarity should become so compartmentalized.

To some extent, this process can be seen as an inescapable result of the transition of peace research from being essentially North Atlantic in the 1960s to having become more truly international in the 1970s. Since primary concerns are not the same in different parts of the world,[78] the transnationalization has had to be accompanied by a widening of the normative agenda, and hence a wider range of topics. It has also had to accommodate a wider spectrum of culture-bound epistemologies, in addition to the intra-Western debate.

Increasing diversity has also exacerbated the problems that peace research has in common with other intellectual movements. Some critics maintain that it has already become fairly sectarian, whereas others think that it has become too much of a normal academic discipline and is losing its normative relevance.[79] The rapid growth according to several criteria should not hide the fact that peace research has had limited success in getting into academia as a full citizen. We find lots of courses in peace studies, and many small institutes at universities, but extremely few chairs with complete departments.

The 1980s: Weathering the Storm?

A Chinese scholar some decades ago, when asked about the impact of the French revoluiton, replied that it was still too close to be seen clearly. This is much more true for the threats and challenges that peace research faced in the 1980s. Some of these are of the making of the movement itself, such as how to cope with the increasing diversity and the problems of integration and disciplinary identity entailed by it, or how to balance between the "research" and "movement" facets. Others are indirect effects of the growth of peace research, and the increasing attention and political support it has received. Established disciplines have therefore increasingly come to see it as a threatening competitor for scarce resources or for the status of defining reality,[80] and this may in several places force peace researchers to choose how to define themselves in relation to the rest of academia.

Other problems have large external components. The temporary resurgence of international tension and a Cold War atmosphere has also put peace research under increasing attack, both in UNESCO and in countries like Norway[81] and West Germany.[82] This, of course, is not a new experience for the peace research movement, and one of the reactions to it has been to give increasing stress to what we called the "old agenda."[83] In addition, the economic crisis has widely meant an end to the expansion, or even considerable cuts, for the social sciences, including peace research, but most peace researchers are used to operating with meager resources.

It is difficult to prophesy about the future. The following scenario, however, appears likely. The process of diversification is largely over, and may even be somewhat reversed. This will give better possibilities for consolidation and for integration. The old agenda will be vitalized, but not to the exclusion of the new agenda. Professionalization will increase, leading to some tensions in the movement. The position of peace research at the universities will solidify, but probably more through peace researchers in established disciplines and only to a limited extent through the creation of new chairs. There will still be an intense debate among peace researchers about the definition of the discipline.

Notes

1. *World Directory of Peace Research Institutions,* Reports and Papers in the Social Sciences no. 49 (Paris: UNESCO, 1981).

2. Less vague estimates are impossible to give (see also note 23).

3. *Peace Research Abstracts Journal,* started by the Canadian Peace Research Institute in 1964.

4. The best general Anglo-Saxon bibliography is E. Boulding, J. R. Passmore, and R. S. Gassler, *Bibliography on World Conflict and Peace* (Boulder, Colo.: Westview Press, 1979). Those who plan undergraduate courses will have much help from *Peace and World Order Studies: A Curriculum Guide* (New York: Transnational Academic Program/Institute for World Order, 1981). English, French, and German literature are covered in G. Scharffenorth et al., *Neue Bibliographie zur Friedensforschung* (Munich: Kösel, 1973).

5. H. Newcombe and A. G. Newcombe, *Peace Research Around the World* (Clarkson, Ont.: Canadian Peace Research Institute, 1969) is an early overview. J. Dedring, *Recent Advances in Peace and Conflict Research: A Critical Survey* (Beverly Hills, Calif.: Sage Publications, 1976) covers Anglo-American peace research better than European peace research. For the latter, see H. Brauch, *Entwicklungen und Ergebnisse der Friedensforschung* (Frankfurt am Main: Haag & Herchen, 1979). For a comparison, see E. Boulding and R. Väyrynen, "Peace Research: The Infant Discipline," in S. Rokkan, ed., *A Quarter Century of International Social Science* (New Delhi: Concept, 1979), pp. 245–272.

6. For example, *The Search for World Order: Studies by Students and Colleagues of Quincy Wright,* ed. A. Lepawsky et al. (New York: Appleton-Century-Crofts, 1971); C. E. Kerman, *Creative Tension: The Life and Thought of Kenneth Boulding* (Ann Arbor: University of Michigan Press, 1974); *Liber Röling: Declarations on Principles,* ed. R. J. Ackerman et al. (Leiden: 1977); *Social Science—For What: Festschrift for Johan Galtung,* ed. H.-H. Holm and E. Rudeng (Oslo: Universitetsforlaget, 1980); and *Frontiers in Social Thought: Essays in Honour of Kenneth Boulding,* ed. M. Pfaff (New York: North-Holland, 1976).

7. One may find the term used in the "positivist movement" around Comte in the mid-nineteenth century (one trace can be found in the flag of Brazil), the "sociology movement" in United States in the late nineteenth century, the "evolutionist movement," and the "psychoanalytical movement."

8. A 1966 joint project on the part of peace researchers in Groningen, Oslo, and Warsaw collected 450 items since 1306 and sorted them into thirty main categories on the basis of the underlying conceptions.

9. H. Cantril, *The Psychology of Social Movements* (1941; 2d ed., New York: John Wiley and Sons, 1963).

10. A. Oberschall, *Social Conflict and Social Movements* (Englewood Cliffs, N.J.: Prentice-Hall, 1973).

11. P. van den Dungen, "Varieties of Peace Science: An Historical Note," *Journal of Peace Science* 2:2 (1977).

12. To give one imaginative example, the weight of popes.

13. Smoker has been working on a volume about Sorokin for several years (personal communication).

14. R. J. Rummel repeatedly asserts his indebtedness to Sorokin in his five-volume work, *Understanding Conflict and War* (Beverly Hills, Calif.: Sage Publications, 1975–1981).

15. His major works from this period are *The Ways and Power of Love: Types, Factors, and Techniques of Moral Transformation* (Boston, Mass.: Beacon Press, 1954) and *Power and Morality* (Boston, Mass.: Porter Sargent, 1958).

16. A short biography and bibliography appear in L. F. Richardson, *Statistics of Deadly Quarrels* (Chicago: Quadrangle Books, 1960).

17. A. Rapoport, "Lewis F. Richardson's Mathematical Theory of War," *Journal of Conflict Resolution* 1:3 (1957).

18. In Appendix III of vol. 4 (*War, Power, Peace*) of *Understanding Conflict and War,* Rummel lists 317 quantitative international relations studies that he has used and indicates in his text how they bear on his theoretical propositions.

19. For an overview, see J. Rattinger, *Rüstungsdynamik im internationalen System: Mathematische Reaktionsmodelle für Rüstungswettläufe und Probleme ihrer Anwendung* (Munich: Oldenbourg, 1975).

20. Bibliography in A. Lepawsky et al., *The Search for World Order* (New York: Appleton-Century-Crofts, 1971). For appraisals of Wright's contributions in various areas, see "In Memoriam: Quincy Wright, 1890–1970," *Journal of Conflict Resolution* 14:4 (1970), pp. 443–554.

21. The 1965 survey is reported in M. Holmboe Ruge, "Present Peace Research," in *Proceedings of the IPRA Inaugural Conference* (Assen: van Golcum, 1966), p. 293. The 1972 survey is analyzed in Ph. Everts, "Developments and Trends in Peace and Conflict Research, 1965–1971," in *Proceedings of the IPRA Fourth Conference* (Oslo: IPRA, 1973), pp. 137–168. All surveys are reported in UNESCO, *Reports and Papers in the Social Sciences,* no. 23 (1965), no. 28 (1972), no. 43 (1978, with some analysis), and no. 49 (1981; updating of the directory in no. 43).

22. The 1972 survey identified 264 addresses; it received data from 149 of them, and that figure is more comparable with the 1965 and 1978 figures.

23. Of the 310 institutes, 99 reported a total of 1,327 researchers. When the authors estimate the peace research community to include 5,000 researchers, they obviously make inclusive definitions of "peace" and of "peace research" and do not use individual self-identification. These circumstances imply that the figure may refer to an objectively defined *category* but the *community* must be considerably smaller.

24. Scharffenorth et al., *Neue Bibliographie,* pp. 53 ff.

25. On the other hand, several of the 1965 institutes were no longer listed.

26. One way of cross-checking these estimates lies in the membership of associations and attendance at their conferences.

27. Based on the data reported in UNESCO, *Reports and Papers in the Social Sciences,* no. 43 (1978).

28. The visibility factor is probably of importance here; the 1977 conference of the International Peace Research Association was held in Oaxtepec, Mexico.

29. Based on the analysis made by Everts, "Developments and Trends," using the most narrow category of "primary" peace research institutes.

30. The following narrative is based partly on histories and biographies, such as those cited in notes 5 and 6, and partly on my recollections and conversations with many colleagues over time.

31. P. van den Dungen, *Foundations of Peace Research* (London: Housmans, 1981), p. 49, citing C. H. Michael Yarrow's chapter "Quaker Conciliation and Peace Research" in his book, *Quaker Experiences in International Reconciliation* (New Haven: Yale University Press, 1978).

32. Ackerman, *Liber Röling,* pp. xxii–xxiii, citing J. Rotblat, *Pugwash: A History of the Conferences on Science and World Affairs* (Prague: Czechoslovak Academy of Sciences, 1967).

33. Premier Erlander's announcement of the creation of SIPRI; President Heinemann's initiatives to get DGFK started (see note 82); President Carazo's initiative for the Universidad para la Paz.

34. This support does not mean that the parties have agreed on what peace research is, or should be.

35. Whereas the word "peace" was not politically controversial in, e.g., India and Japan, it definitely was in the North Atlantic area during the Cold War era. Several of the early institutes avoided the word in the naming of institutes and journals (see K. Boulding, *Stable Peace* [Austin: University of Texas Press, 1978], and Ackerman, *Liber Röling,* p. lvii). Many of the Nordic institutes combined "peace" and "conflict," gradually dropping the latter as peace research became more respectable. Most of the German institutes still combine the two. *Polémologie* has been widely used in the French and Benelux areas. For an overview of concepts and connotations in various cultures, see J. Galtung, "Social Cosmology and the Concept of Peace," *Journal of Peace Research* 18:2 (1981), pp. 183–200.

36. For the history of the center until its demise in 1971, see K. Boulding, "An Epitaph: The Center for Research on Conflict Resolution 1959–1971," *Journal of Conflict Resolution* 15:3 (1971), and Kerman, *Creative Tension.*

37. *Journal of Conflict Resolution* 3:1 (1959), pp. 2 f.

38. His essay, and those by W. Cottrell and Ch. Boasson, were published in *Research for Peace* (Amsterdam: North-Holland, 1954).

39. *Journal of Conflict Resolution* 3:1 (1959) contains the main papers from this seminar, written by D. Katz, I. L. Janis, J. Galtung, and G. Sharp.

40. J. Galtung and A. Naess, *Gandhis politiske etikk* (Oslo: Tanum, 1955). Parts of this work appear in A. Naess, "A Systematization of Gandhian Ethics of Conflict Resolution," *Journal of Conflict Resolution* 2:2 (1958), pp. 140–155.

41. N. P. Gleditsch et al., *Johan Galtung: A Bibliography of His Scholarly and Popular Writings, 1951–1980* (Oslo: International Peace Research Institute, 1980). Many of his articles and papers are collected in Johan Galtung, *Essays in Peace Research,* 5 vols. (Copenhagen: Ejlers, 1975–1980).

42. For its development, see G. Hook and H. Kan, "Peace Research in Japan," *International Peace Research Newsletter* 21:2 (1983), pp. 10 and 41–45.

43. See Brauch, *Entwicklungen,* chap. 1.

44. *Polemos* may mean both "war" and "contradiction." Gaston Bouthoul used the word to name his institute in 1945. It later spread to the Netherlands.

45. For a short presentation of French institutes, organizations, and journals, see *Paix et conflits* (January-February 1983).

46. Apart from Galtung, Gene Sharp has been much inspired by Gandhi. See his work *Gandhi as a Political Strategist* (Boston, Mass.: Porter Sargent, 1981).

47. For a programmatic presentation of the Latin American Council for Peace Research (CLAIP) and an overview of research projects, see *La investigacion para la paz en America Latina* (Mexico City: CLAIP, 1979).

48. Ch. Chatfield, "International Peace Research: The Field Defined by Dissemination," *Journal of Peace Research* 16:2 (1979), pp. 161–178.

49. van den Dungen, *Foundations,* pp. 25 ff.

50. Scharffenorth et al., *Neue Bibliographie,* pp. 57 ff.

51. Boulding, Passmore, and Gassler, *Bibliography,* pp. 145 ff.

52. Among some thirty journals mentioned in Chatfield and van den Dungen, only *War/Peace Report* from the United States, *Science et paix* from Belgium, and *Études polémologiques* from France have ceased publication, and the last is now reborn.

53. With few exceptions, even those issues of PSS(I) papers that have been published after European conferences have a majority of U.S. authors.

54. The main economic sponsor of *Journal of Peace Research,* a joint Nordic research fund, insists that the Nordic authors are too few and has asked for an increase in their number to continue the funding.

55. For overviews of the major journals, see E. Converse, "The War of All Against All," *Journal of Conflict Resolution* 12:4 (1968), pp. 471–532, and H. Wiberg, "What Have We Learnt About Peace?" *Journal of Peace Research* 18:2 (1981), pp. 111–148.

56. IPRA's regional associations are COPRED (Consortium on Peace Research, Education and Development) in North America since 1970, Consejo Latinoamericana de Investigacion para la Paz (CLAIP) since 1977, and Asian Peace Research Association since 1980. The PSS(I) newsletters indicate four sections of the organization in the United States, one in Britain, and one in Japan.

57. *IPRN* was started in 1963 as the newsletter of the Peace Research Committee of the Women's International League for Peace and Freedom, founded in 1960. Since 1965, it has been the organ of IPRA.

58. The explanation given to me was that "peace research" had gotten a bad name in the United States, making it more difficult for graduate students

to get grants. No institutions, except those with which Professor Isard is associated, have adopted the new term, however.

59. Canada (1970); Japan (1967, 1973); West Germany (1968, 1970); Britain (ca. 1970); India (1971); Netherlands, Flemish Belgium, and New Zealand (1975); Denmark (1977); France, Chile, and Madagascar (1980); Brazil (1981). Some are professional, others are of a support character; West Germany and Japan have both.

60. Most of the older peace researchers know each other.

61. Conference funding has mainly come from the intergovernmental Nordic Cooperation Committee for International Politics, Including Peace and Conflict Research, created in 1967.

62. Groningen (Bert Röling) until 1971; Oslo (Asbjörn Eide) 1971–1975; Tampere (Raimo Väyrynen) 1975–1979; Tokyo (Yoshikazu Sakamoto) 1979–1983; United States (Chadwick Alger) 1983.

63. Netherlands 1965, Sweden 1967, Czechoslovakia 1969, Yugoslavia 1971, India 1974, Finland 1975, Mexico 1977, West Germany 1979, Canada 1981, and Hungary 1983.

64. *Peace and Change,* since 1972; subsequently issued by COPRED.

65. To indicate them briefly: Swedish, male, forty-one years old, Social Democrat; originally mathematician and philosopher, later sociologist; peace activist before joining the peace research movement about twenty years ago.

66. See, e.g., the editorial in the first issue of *Journal of Peace Research* in 1964. At that time, "positive peace" was still equated with integration rather than seen as the antonym of structural violence.

67. E.g., K. Boulding, *Conflict and Defense: A General Theory* (New York: Harper and Row, 1961).

68. E.g., A. Rapoport and A. M. Chammah, *Prisoner's Dilemma: A Study in Conflict and Cooperation* (Ann Arbor: University of Michigan Press, 1965).

69. E.g., Galtung's use of rank disequilibrium theory.

70. Anthologies like *War: Studies from Psychology, Sociology, Anthropology,* ed., L. Bramson and W. Goethals (New York: Basic Books, 1964; 2d ed. 1968); *International Conflict and Behavioral Science,* ed. R. Fisher (New York: Basic Books, 1964); and *The Nature of Human Conflict,* ed. E. B. McNeil (Englewood Cliffs, N.J.: Prentice-Hall, 1965). More integrated is *International Behavior: A Social-Psychological Analysis,* ed. H. C. Kelman (New York: Holt, Rinehart and Winston, 1965).

71. For example, Rudolph J. Rummel and others around the Dimensions of Nations project in Honolulu, J. David Singer and others around the Correlates of War project in Ann Arbor, Michigan, and SIPRI before the yearbooks.

72. *Proceedings of the International Peace Research Association Third Conference,* vol. I (Assen: van Gorcum, 1970), has the subtitle *Philosophy of Peace Research* and contains attacks by Herman Schmid, Lars Dencik, Ib Martin Jarvad, and Ole Jess Olsen as well as replies by Bert Röling, Kenneth Boulding, and Johan Galtung. A representative anthology is *Kritische Friedensforschung,* ed. D. Senghaas (Frankfurt am Main: Suhrkampf, 1971).

73. In the former category, we find B. Röling in the revised third edition of his *Polémologie* and K. Boulding in "A Program for Justice" (Paper presented

at the IPRA conference, Varanasi, India, 1974). Johan Galtung is a good example of the latter category, even if he did start articulating the "new agenda" before 1969 and did not abandon the "old agenda" after 1969. His bridging concept between the two agendas is "structural violence." For a good example of early integration of the agendas, see P. Wallensteen, *Structure and War* (Stockholm: Rabén & Sjögren, 1973).

74. For the relations between the two movements, see M. Borrelli and M. Haavelsrud, "The Development of the Concept of Peace Education in the IPRA Archipelago" (Paper presented at the IPRA conference in Györ, 1983).

75. *Elements of World Instability: Armament, Communication, Food, International Division of Labour,* ed. E. Jahn and Y. Sakamoto (New York: Irvington, 1982).

76. Hylke Tromp in his introduction to UNESCO, *Yearbook on Peace and Conflict Studies* (1980), p. xxvii.

77. I cannot make such a claim.

78. This is a statement of how they are seen, not of how they ought to be seen.

79. That both criticisms are voiced may be an indicator of "balance."

80. This feeling of threat may particularly be true for political science and international relations.

81. The conservative government has appointed a committee to evaluate the activities of PRIO. On the other hand, the Swedish government has just created two chairs in peace research, and the Danish parliament has decided to use more than a million dollars for the promotion of peace research.

82. The DGFK (German Society for Peace and Conflict Research) was initiated by President Heinemann in 1970 and has been the most important financial source for research since then. In the last few years, several *Bundesländer* with conservative governments have left the society, and it is now about to be dissolved (*DGFK-Informationen,* no. 1 [1983]).

83. Thus, even *JPR* had a predominance of "old agenda" articles in 1982.

PART TWO

The Study of War

3

Peace Research, Complex Causation, and the Causes of War

Bruce Russett

The publication of this book seems to be, to a substantial degree, a reunion of middle-aged peace researchers. As such it is a good time to take stock of our intellectual enterprise, to evaluate its successes and failures in light both of our early expectations and of our current understanding of its possibilities. We can look back on the accomplishments and development of the enterprise over recent decades. As a reference point, it seems as reasonable as any to begin from the establishment of the *Journal of Peace Research* in 1964.

"Solving" the War and Cancer Problems

It is apparent that we have not "solved" the war problem. Of course there was no reason to expect we would. Sometimes people make an analogy between the war problem and the cancer problem. Among other things that analogy implies a value judgment about the undesirability of both, and that is a value judgment I share. There are several other ways in which the analogy is appropriate. One is in highlighting the difficulty of "solving" either problem, in the sense either of understanding the causes of the phenomenon or of eradicating it. Only some of the environmental agents that can produce cancer have been identified, and to only a limited degree are the genetic processes by which normal cells are changed into malignant ones by those agents now understood. Once malignancy occurs and is detected, medical practitioners are able to eliminate it in only about half the instances; the success rate varies widely for different types and sites of malignancy. The judgment of professionals seems to be that whereas they have achieved great improvement in the ability to cure certain kinds of cancer, the overall success rate has not improved markedly over the past decades, despite the work of tens of thousands of scientists and tens of billions of dollars of research funds. As an analogy for the enterprise of peace research, with its much more modest human and financial base, these results are sobering. Few of us would claim that social problems are intrinsically easier to understand or solve than are medical ones. In Walter Bagehot's famous aphorism, "Politics is harder than physics."

To understand why the war problem should be so intractable, it will help to pursue the analogy. We are now well aware that cancer is not simply "caused" by a simple action and reaction but rather by a complex set of conditions. For example, a given malignancy may arise because an individual has been exposed, not to a single environmental agent (e.g., a dangerous component of tobacco smoke), but also to another (e.g., asbestos or a virus), and the two interact with a much greater likelihood of carcinogenesis than would be produced by either one alone. One agent (tobacco) is associated with deliberate choice by the individual; the other (asbestos or the virus) is in the larger environment about which the individual has some, but less, degree of control over his or her exposure. Moreover, even the two together do not produce a malignancy with anything approaching certainty. Rather, genetic (inherited) predisposition seems also to matter—some people simply are much more susceptible than others—and thus many scientists now advocate highly controversial procedures for genetic screening to exclude susceptible individuals from occupations in which they will be subject to high exposure. Susceptibility of any individual may also vary over time. It becomes greater with a longer history of sustained environmental insults and a diminished ability of the body, with age, to repair the damage caused by those insults. Possibly even personality characteristics play a role. But despite all these variables, there remains some degree of indeterminacy to this predictive model, attributable to other influences still not identified and, perhaps, to some degree of true randomness in the phenomenon.

Understanding the causes of war is not a fundamentally different enterprise.[1] If we take the decision of a particular government to wage war as the object of our analysis, we recognize that the decision is partly affected by the international environment (the distribution of power in the international system; the principles and rules governing international trade and finance; the content and binding nature of international law; the power of international and transnational insti-

tutions; the level of international technological achievement for transportation, communication, and weaponry; etc.). The particular policies—
acts, threats, promises—of other states constitute relevant external
stimuli. A variety of conditions within the nation in question similarly
are important. These include the history and personality characteristics
of individual government decision makers, the decision-making process
within the government, the economic and political structure of the
nation, its changing conditions of economic prosperity, how its history
has structured contemporary institutions and individual expectations,
etc.

The list is familiar in its basic outlines, and it could be modified
and extended by every reader.[2] The point is simply that the occurrence
of war is the consequence of a variety of conditions and these conditions
interact in complex, often multiplicative, ways so that the explanatory
utility of any single variable is likely to be very limited. Furthermore,
no single condition or variable can be expected to always lead to any
particular outcome, such as war, nor is any single outcome always the
result of one particular causal variable.[3]

Complex patterns of causation of course imply the need for complex
theory, with the consequent strain between complexity (completeness,
for understanding or "treatment") and parsimony (for analytical tract-
ability or a manageable research enterprise). Increasingly we learn to
tolerate complexity. We quite correctly dismiss single-cause "theories"
and have developed analytical tools such as large-scale simulations or
applied mathematical models to deal with complexity.[4] I can illustrate
one way of treating this problem by referring to my own research.[5]

Economic Decline as a Cause of International Conflict

I began with a condition that can perhaps be termed *environmental*
in that it is external to the decision makers of a state: the condition
of the national and international economy. My hypothesis was that
conditions in the economy so affect and constrain the political choices
available to leaders that they are more likely in periods of economic
downturn to engage in risk-taking behavior in the international political
arena. That is, I hypothesized that individual acts can be explained,
in part, as a response to choices presented by environmental conditions.
The model was thus an implicit one of individual rational choice.

Many conditions other than economic ones affect the choice, however.
One is the state's position in the international political system; as an
approximation, whether it is a major power or not. Major powers are,

because of a combination of their capabilities and extended interests, much more likely to be involved in international conflict than are minor powers. Another condition is a state's military capability: I hypothesized that a state is more likely to engage in the threat or use of force internationally if its military establishment has been recently expanded. Expanded military forces would provide the means for assertive international action, and perhaps would imply a strengthened role in the domestic political system for those whose interests would be served by military action. Finally, I hypothesized that the leaders of democratic states are under more immediate political pressure from unfavorable domestic economic conditions than are the leaders of nondemocratic states (traditional autocracies, military dictatorships, and Communist states). Because of the necessity of facing frequent elections, democratic leaders are especially concerned with maintaining favorable economic conditions or, if that is not possible, seeking to divert domestic hostility toward other adversaries, often external ones.

What we have then, as with the cancer example, is an interaction of several causal or aggravating influences: conditions external to the "organism" (the state), such as position in the international system and conditions in the world economy (which to some degree affect conditions in the domestic economy); internal conditions, such as nature of the political system and changes in militarization; and— unlike the medical example—some opportunity for conscious choice by the state's decision makers as they consider their constraints and opportunities. The last implies that by no means all instances of economic distress will result in a decision to initiate international conflict and, as well, that some decisions to initiate international conflict surely will occur quite independently of economic conditions. Indeed, the decision to initiate international conflict may stem from elsewhere in a state's environment; that is, from another state acting as aggressor. Still, "it takes two to make a quarrel" (a deadly one, at least), and how one responds to another's aggression (by appeasement, tit-for-tat, or escalation) is a matter of choice that may be strongly conditioned by domestic political considerations.

I investigated this problem using data on many countries' economic and political characteristics, information on annual changes in per capita income for twenty-three industrial countries over an average span of nearly a century and for virtually the entire universe of nation-states since 1950, and the COW (Correlates of War) compilation of militarized international disputes.[6] The results did confirm a rather complex pattern of causality. Major powers were indeed much more likely to be involved in disputes than were minor powers, and recently increased levels of militarization were associated with dispute involvement. Dispute involvement tended to follow, with a two-year time lag, declines in per capita income—in democratically governed states. In nondemocratic states, by contrast, involvement in international disputes tended to follow periods of economic advancement. Perhaps economic improvement created a mood of optimistic readiness to embark on foreign adventures, or perhaps the economic expansion marked only one aspect of generally activist and interventionist government by assertive authoritarian leaders. Whatever the mechanisms at work, it is clear that the responses of democratic governments to changing economic conditions differ significantly from those of nondemocratic governments.[7]

These results are among the very few that show systematic differences among states distinguished by regime type. This fact alone would make the findings of some interest, because previous, largely inductive, investigations have proved so thoroughly unproductive in finding differences. For my success, I credit the role of an explicit theory, in this instance, the rational-actor perspective attributing deliberate choice, in the face of economic threats to electoral viability.

It is also worth noting that although some variables (particularly militarization) may contribute independently to the likelihood of involvement in international disputes, others contribute only in combination. Thus, in general, democratic governments are neither more nor less dispute prone than are nondemocratic ones, and there is little or no overall relationship between economic conditions and dispute involvement. But the combinations of democratic government and economic decline, and of nondemocratic government and economic expansion, produce greater dispute involvement. Finally, the role of major-power status is mixed. Major-power status makes an independent, positive contribution to dispute involvement, but a careful further examination of my data shows that the combination of regime type and economic conditions becomes, by and large, dangerous only in major powers, which have wide-ranging interests and capabilities. Minor powers are little affected by this combination, probably because they have so much less control over their international fate, including the fact and the timing of involvement in militarized disputes. As Thucydides' orator put it in the Melian dialogue, "The strong do as they will, the weak do as they must." Thus for major powers, the hypothesis of deliberate, willed involvement in international disputes is strengthened.[8] Dispute involvement is to some notable degree a consequence of choice, not environmentally determined or random accident.

All of these variables together account for only a rather small proportion of the variance in dispute involvement that we would like explained. Crudeness in categorization of some of the variables (e.g., democratic versus nondemocratic states, where of course a sensitive understanding of regime differences would be much more subtle and multidimensional) and unavoidable data error doubtless account for some of the unexplained variance, but much more is surely owing to other variables that are not included at all. A more comprehensive explanation certainly would include such other elements as characteristics of the dyadic relationship (if leaders of an economically distressed state are tempted to initiate a militarized dispute, are they especially likely to choose an economically distressed state as the target, and is such a target readily and plausibly available?) and the range of policy alternatives available to a nation's leaders. Leaders may first try to deal directly with the economic conditions and turn to foreign distractions only after that effort fails. Or their legitimacy in the eyes of their populace may be sufficiently high, perhaps on the basis of a record of past success, that they do not feel impelled to pick a foreign quarrel. Or the timing of an economic downturn may be sufficiently distant from a forthcoming election that the leaders may feel they have adequate time to weather a spell of temporary discontent. Or they may respond to manifestations of domestic dissent directly, by repressing it. (This temptation and possibility may be stronger for nondemocratic than for democratic governments; if so, that may be another reason why nondemocratic governments do not show a greater frequency of international dispute involvement subsequent to periods of economic decline.) And of course, international dispute involvement may have many causes other than those I have so far specified; any sophisticated observer of international affairs would surely believe so.

Some of these variables are ones I was able to include in further analyses. First, focusing on the United States, I looked at the interaction of election years and economic change over a century-long period. It became apparent that U.S. participation in international disputes is most common in those election years that followed a decline in per capita income, and least common in nonelection years following an increase in per capita income. Furthermore, disputes are more common in years when a president is to be elected than in years when the only national election is for Congress. These results follow nicely from my initial theoretical perspective: The temptations to engage in international conflict as a means of deflecting discontent about economic conditions are greater in those political systems in which the leaders are held accountable to the public and at times (of elections) when the accountability is most immediate. These may be the least auspicious times for concluding international agreements, like arms control treaties with adversaries.

Second, I looked directly at the role of domestic conflict—protest, rebellion, and state repression—in all countries of the world since World War II, a period for which good data on domestic conflict are available. In this analysis, economic decline per se is no longer statistically significant, but participation in international disputes is strongly associated with protest in the same year or the preceding year. For the democratic countries, international disputes are also associated with repression in the preceding year. That is, domestic protest, and especially domestic protest that cannot be contained by the relatively mild repressive actions available to democratic governments, is likely to result in those governments becoming engaged in international conflict. International conflict thus emerges as an important consequence of internal political conflict, which in turn may arise from economic difficulties or from other causes.

It is also important to make a distinction between involvement in international disputes, defined as any threat or use of military force between states, and involvement in interstate war, as defined, for example, in standard COW terms as battle fatalities. It is one thing to say that leaders will more or less deliberately, partly in response to domestic economic/political conditions, involve their countries in international disputes and another to say that they will deliberately take on the high costs and risks of war. Whereas dispute involvement usually produces a short-term increment in a leader's support, attributable to the phenomenon now widely known as the "rally round the flag" effect, war involvement regularly produces a long-term decline in national cohesion and in leaders' popularity. War involvement is distinctly hazardous to the electoral health of leaders, and in direct proportion to the length and intensity of the war.[9] Decisions to escalate disputes to the level of actual warfare thus are much more likely to stem from the dynamics of international bargaining and negotiation—including, very definitely, the decisions of the adversary state—during the course of the bargaining than from considerations of domestic political advantage.[10] Domestic circumstances, and leaders' responses to them, may be one of the conditions that brings a country to the edge of war, but to understand why its leaders go over the edge, we must look much more closely at the decision-making process than at the kinds of largely environmental variables identified above.

Some Implications for Quantitative Research

One lesson of the exercise just described is, as I suggested, the need for complex theory to cope with a complex reality. Additional kinds of complexity would recognize the difficulty of always speaking of dependent and independent variables, as was implied above. Just as economic downturn may, in certain kinds of political systems, raise the propensity for involvement in international crisis, involvement in crisis, and especially in war, of course affects the economy. The immediate response will likely be economic expansion to meet the military demands of external conflict, with the longer-run effect being economic contraction induced either by the end of the conflict or by the destruction of productive capacity brought about by the conflict. Economic downturn caused by a recent international conflict, however, is less likely than other kinds of economic downturn to stimulate incentives for another immediate round of international conflict. Memories, and domestic and international consequences of that conflict, are likely to condition strongly decision makers' choices of how to respond to this particular phase of domestic political unrest.

A second lesson concerns the danger of treating our familiar verbal concepts, war, for example, as covering fully comparable phenomena. The COW operational definition, which depends on casualty levels, entails serious limitations as well as advantages. Its major virtue is its elimination of minor intrusions, clashes, border skirmishes, and substantially unopposed occupations. Events such as these, which may be undertaken for limited goals and be subject to control by those who initiate them, should not be lumped together a priori for the purpose of causal analysis with the more substantial conflicts we call wars.[11]

But the definition's fault lies in the use of the familiar encompassing term in a way that suggests that all wars have similar purposes, and therefore similar causes. Some wars have their origin in domestic political weakness, others in a secure domestic political domination that allows free rein to an adventurous leader. Some are fought to establish domination over a weaker neighboring country, others to establish widespread hegemony, and still others to defend oneself or to defend one's existing hegemony over others against a vigorous challenge. To treat these as the same kind of social phenomenon, arising from the same kind of internal or external "cause," is as silly as we now know it is to consider that all cancers are produced by the same cause or are subject to the same treatment. Instead, we have an emerging understanding that "hegemonic" wars—wars fought between major powers for dominance over the international system—have a very different timing, and a very different structure of causation, than do many lesser violent conflicts that, nevertheless, fall within the COW casualty definition. In fact, this problem is so complex that there is as yet no agreement among analysts as to precisely which wars should be characterized as "hegemonic."[12] Again, precision and clarity of theory, rooted in a thorough familiarity with the empirical phenomena, are essential.

Both of these lessons are part of the larger lesson that good quantitative empirical analyses must follow, and not precede, the construction of theories and their constitutive hypotheses. There was a time in the development of our discipline when quantitative analysis of large-scale international political phenomena was new, and there was a role for rather inductive exploratory exercises designed to find some simple generalizations and to lay the basis for some tentative, empirically based typologies. I contributed some of those efforts, as did others.[13] But whatever use such studies may have had at that stage, our understanding has now progressed to the point at which such inductive fishing expeditions have lost any utility, and statistical analysis must follow, not precede, theory construction. Most of us, indeed, would substantially accept the Lakatos injunction that empirical analysis must be used to test *alternative* hypotheses.

One conference participant said that nonwar outcomes of certain processes, as well as those outcomes that we call wars, need to be studied. By one understanding of this statement, it is too obviously true, merely an exhortation to ensure that there is some variance in one's dependent variable (nonwar as well as war) and so avoid the most basic of research design flaws. A more serious meaning for the statement emerges, however, if one makes the further distinction—familiar to all current peace researchers—between different kinds of nonwar conditions. If peace is not merely the absence of war—that is, if we wish to use the term *peace* to describe a state of "positive peace" involving large elements of reciprocity, equality, and joint problem-solving capabilities—distinctions must also be made among "nonwars." Nonwar as negative peace may be rooted in a variety of different conditions, such as mutual deterrence, one-sided dominance, or even mutual irrelevance. Under conditions of positive peace, war is not only absent, it is unanticipated and essentially unthinkable.

Nonwar as positive peace is a phenomenon we still do not well understand. It may be attributable, in different degrees, to high levels of communication and interaction, to common attachment to similar political values and institutions (especially pluralistic ones), or perhaps to unity against a perceived "external" enemy.[14] The phenomenon of positive peace among the developed industrial countries of the contemporary world is especially interesting, and an instance where at least one prominent alternative theory—Lenin's about imperialism—certainly predicted just the opposite. The passage of advanced capitalist countries from the alleged "last stage" of capitalism (i.e., imperialism) to a stage where they are able to suppress their mutual competition requires explanation whether one observes it from a Marxist or a non-Marxist perspective.

Understanding the distinction between quantitative analysis for theory construction and quantitative analysis for theory testing would help to dispel a common criticism of quantitative analysis as a rich person's way of doing research. Certainly quantitative analysis as a way (often misguided) of theory construction, with a very heavy component of induction, is a rich person's way of doing research. The initial data gathering is extremely time-consuming, and the inductive data crunching of large bodies of information often has required large amounts of time on large computers. This latter problem, however, is rapidly changing as microcomputers, which are cheap, equipped with re-markable storage capacity, and quite easy to learn to use, become readily available. They are becoming common in the offices of individual researchers and of small, far from rich, research institutes around the world. Allowing for inflation, they are not much more expensive than electric typewriters were a decade or so ago. Although they are not available to everyone, they are far more than a rich person's work instrument or toy.

Equally important are the readily accessible crossnational data bases produced by international organizations like the United Nations and its agencies, nongovernmental international organizations like SIPRI and the International Institute for Strategic Studies, national govern-ments, individual research projects like COW, and private institutes like the Wissenschaftzentrum in Berlin with its third edition of the *World Handbook of Political and Social Indicators* and associated data bases needed for its world model simulation (GLOBUS). The reliability and comparability of these data bases have improved markedly in recent years. If they are used in moderation for theory testing—that is, after careful theory construction rather than as a substitute for it—they offer something of value to virtually any serious researcher. One need not feel that in advising the use of such material one is furthering an exclusionary, elitist enterprise.[15]

Values and Data

All peace research, whether quantitative or nonquantitative, draws its strength from its tradition of independence and skepticism toward the established wisdom of the elites. Most of us are not advisers to the prince, but rather critics of the ways of power practiced by the prince. Our vitality comes from a determination to challenge established wisdom and established interests. The role of the intellectual must always be to question whether those in power are pursuing their goals in the most effective manner; more important, whether those goals are being pursued in a normatively desirable manner; and especially, whether the goals themselves are normatively desirable from some viewpoint broader than that of the elites themselves.

Quantitative materials cannot provide us with the proper norms, but they can tell us how effectively the normative goals are being approached, at what cost, and what alternatives may be available. In such a way they provide essential information to popular critics and counterelites, breaking the monopoly of information that governing elites would like to maintain. They provide the means we need to convince others, whether they be those who are already sympathetic to our viewpoint or merely those who retain an open mind. And, not to be forgotten, quantitative materials can provide us the evidence we need to convince ourselves of the correctness of a proposition before we move to persuade others.

Similarly, quantitative evidence can be important in persuading those among the governing elites who may have some sympathy for our arguments. I recall an instance involving President Richard Nixon, a man who is not exactly a hero among peace researchers today. He was at least a man who read, and who was interested in evidence. He read an article about malnutrition in pregnant women and infants, one that suggested that malnutrition caused permanent brain damage and mental retardation. Disturbed by this article, he asked someone on the White House staff to investigate whether it was correct so that if necessary, he could initiate policy to provide preventive nutrition. The answer came back that the article was erroneous, and so nothing was done. We now know well, however, that it was the staffer's answer, rather than the article, that was wrong. Perhaps the staffer was too ideologically blinded to recognize the correct evidence, or even to care. But perhaps if the quantitative evidence were then as strong and convincing as it later became, the staffer would have been persuaded. It seems that he would then have had a reasonably open-minded listener in the Oval Office.

A health professional, immersed in day-to-day contact with the poor and malnourished, might not have needed systematic quantitative evidence to believe that poor early nutrition causes mental deficiency. He or she might simply say, "open your eyes." But elites are, by their nature, isolated from the personal experiences of nonelites and are unlikely to have the kind of qualitative information and intuitive understanding to persuade them. Moreover, most elite individuals take some pride in being "hardheaded" realists, persuadable only by concrete and often quantifiable evidence. Quantitative evidence, with the power of numbers, may therefore be the most effective means by which to reach them. This is one of the ways in which Johan Galtung's "marriage between values and data" can be productive.

As can be inferred from the previous example, research and action are hardly mutually exclusive pursuits—which is not a call for inaction while we do "more research." The threat of war is urgent, and time may well be short. We do know enough to prescribe some courses of action and to proscribe others. There is also much we do not know. Those who seek to cure a disease like war or cancer need evidence for the effectiveness of the cures they advocate. A candid evaluation of the effectiveness of peace movement activism of the past few decades would, I believe, necessarily provide very modest cause for self-congratulation. The reasons for failure are themselves complex, but certainly they include the resistance of established elites to proposed courses of action that would damage their own entrenched interests. Other reasons surely would include both the insufficiency of the knowledge base behind our recommendations and the insufficient knowledge of the political processes in which we operate. We have yet, for example, to do much careful research on the reasons why our peace activism efforts have failed. We are long on regrets and recriminations and short on research into the matter. In this sense, a necessary dimension of knowledge for peace research is "know thyself."

Notes

1. Elsewhere I have likened the causes of war to the multiple causes of an automobile accident—a useful analogy so long as one does not imagine that all wars are "accidental" (see Bruce Russett, "Cause, Surprise, and No Escape," in Russett, *Power and Community in World Politics* [New York: W. H. Freeman, 1972]).

2. For one such classification see Bruce Russett and Harvey Starr, *World Politics: The Menu for Choice,* 2d ed. (New York: W. H. Freeman, 1985), chap. 1.

3. See Benjamin Most and Harvey Starr, "International Relations Theory, Foreign Policy Substitutability, and 'Nice' Laws," *World Politics* 3:3 (April 1984), pp. 383–406.

4. Still relevant is Hayward Alker, "The Long Road to International Relations Theory: Problems of Statistical Nonadditivity," *World Politics* 18:4 (July 1966), pp. 623–655.

5. Bruce Russett, "Economic Change as a Cause of International Conflict," in Christian Schmidt and Frank Blackaby, eds., *Peace, Defence, and Economic Analysis* (New York: St. Martin's Press, 1987), and Bruce Russett, "Economic Decline, Electoral Pressure, and the Initiation of Interstate Conflict," in Charles Gochman and Alan Ned Sabrosky, eds., *Prisoners of War* (forthcoming). I am

grateful to the World Society Foundation of Switzerland for support of this research.

6. Charles Gochman and Zeev Maoz, "Militarized Interstate Disputes, 1816–1976: Procedures, Patterns, and Insights," *Journal of Conflict Resolution* 28:4 (December 1984), pp. 585–616.

7. Russett, "Economic Change as a Cause," and Russett, "Economic Decline, Electoral Pressure."

8. It is worth noting that an effort to distinguish between those states that initiated disputes and those that were mere noninitiating participants did not improve the explanatory power of my equations; on the contrary, the explanatory power declined. Part of the reason may derive from difficulties the COW compilers had in adequately identifying initiators (they coded the dispute participant that first threatened or used force as the initiator regardless of any earlier diplomatic or political origins of the dispute), and part probably stems from my observation that states have some freedom in deciding whether and when to provoke, as well as whether and when to respond, to a dispute.

9. This point is well documented by Timothy Cotton, "War and American Democracy: Voting Trends in the Last Five American Wars," *Journal of Conflict Resolution* 30:4 (December 1986). A recent sophisticated variant of the "rally" effect is found in Charles Ostrom and Brian Job, "The President and the Political Use of Force," *American Political Science Review* 80:1 (June 1986), pp. 541–566.

10. Paul Huth and Bruce Russett, "After Deterrence Fails: Escalation to War?" in Michael Wallace, ed., *Accidental Nuclear War: A Growing Risk?* (London: Butterworth, 1988).

11. On the other hand, as I have suggested, the element of control should not be exaggerated, and a key element of causal analysis must be why some militarized disputes escalate to war and others do not.

12. See Jack Levy, "Theories of General War," *World Politics* 37:3 (April 1985), pp. 344–374.

13. Bruce Russett, Hayward Alker, Karl Deutsch, and Harold Lasswell, *World Handbook of Political and Social Indicators* (New Haven: Yale University Press, 1964), esp. pt. 2; Bruce Russett, *International Regions and the International System* (Chicago: Rand McNally, 1967); and Rudolph Rummel, *The Dimensions of Nations* (Beverly Hills, Calif.: Sage Publications, 1972).

14. Most readers will recognize allusions here to the familiar work of Kenneth Boulding, Karl Deutsch, and Johan Galtung. I have tried to treat their work in Russett and Starr, *World Politics,* chap. 15.

15. It should be apparent that I do not see large-scale quantitative analysis as the only relevant method of empirical research, but rather as integrated with case material (see "Case Studies and Cumulation" in Russett, *Power and Community*).

4

Domestic Crises and International Wars

Raimo Väyrynen

War: An Act of Violence or a Systemic Shock?

Definitions of war abound. War is usually considered a large-scale, organized use of military force between political collectivities of which at least one is a nation-state. This definition is, historically speaking, a restrictive one as it applies to only the last two centuries, when nation-states have been the only major actors conducting wars.[1] Reliance on the nation-state criterion is, however, helpful because it makes it possible to distinguish wars from various acts of aggression, such as riots and terrorism, which are primarily initiated by subnational actors.

Wars have customarily been divided into limited and total wars. Limited wars were typical of the pre-Napoleonic era, when warfare was constrained both by the restricted nature of technology and by political objectives. War was subordinated to diplomacy, which was conducted in the framework of flexible alliances. The new military dynamism of the nineteenth century introduced an era of total wars. The deployment of nuclear weapons in the arsenals of great powers has made the notion of a limited war again relevant, however, as continued reliance on the use of military force has necessitated the prevention of its escalation to the level of nuclear weapons. A Clausewitzian marriage has been concluded between nuclear weapons/nuclear deterrence and limited conventional wars (Osgood and Tucker 1967, 70–78, 185–191).

Limited wars between two states (dyadic wars, Vasquez 1986, 319) are examples of warfare as a specific act of interstate violence resulting from a given combination of global, regional, and local factors. Such military acts can usually be explained by intranational conditions of the participating states or by their mutual relations. They can be investigated as isolated cases of collective international violence or as statistical generalizations developed from a sample of wars. Such statistical studies often disaggregate even complex wars into the underlying bilateral relations of warfare. A common feature of studies dealing with wars as specific acts of interstate violence is a lack of interest in long-term and systemic consequences. This situation is true for both historical narratives and statistical exercises. The focus is on the act of war itself and on its proximate causes. In terms of explanatory power, such approaches leave much to be desired. Still, they can be useful in developing prescriptions on how wars can be avoided. Case studies and statistical generalization can help to point out conditions in which crises may or may not escalate into wars. This possibility gives a pragmatic quality to the studies of limited, dyadic wars.

In contrast, the studies dealing with the systemic effects of warfare more often have theoretical ambitions. In such studies, major wars (which are usually complex, involving several states and unlimited in character) are regarded as a cause or a consequence of transformations in the international power structure. Seen as a cause, the systemic war contributes to the breakdown of an international system and to the emergence of a new system. Seen as a consequence, such a war results from the redistribution of power and the erosion of international institutions. The systemic perspective is directed to the most extensive, enduring, and destructive wars called—scholarly tastes tend to differ in this respect—global, general, or hegemonic wars. A common denominator is that such wars are considered to be systemic shocks to the prevailing international order. The number of systemic wars is necessarily limited, which means the case study approach is the only viable one.

The distinction between wars as specific acts of violence and as systemic shocks is less rooted in methodological differences than in divergent theoretical, and sometimes practical, objectives. The interpretation of wars as goal-oriented acts of violence leads to the use of organizational and decision-making models to explain the forces, motivations, and objectives that result in a decision to start a war. The analysis of interstate wars as mechanisms of system transformation leads to a more comprehensive historical perspective, to functional macrosociology. These two approaches do not necessarily exclude each other. For instance, in the study of systemic wars, the decision-making approach is important because the decision to launch a general war is based on estimates of future power relations and the role of war in a process of power transition. Systemic features such as the distribution of military power, geopolitical realities, and diplomatic alignments are pertinent in accounting for the origins and the logic of limited wars. The origins of limited wars may too often have been explained by organizational factors and military plans while relevant external factors have been neglected. The omissions of either of these two sets of factors may lead to spurious inferences (Levy 1986).

Explaining Interstate Wars as Specific Acts of Violence

The study of war as an act of violence is, of course, legitimate as each war has its specific aspects resulting from national decisions and background conditions. Empirical evidence from such study suggests that domestic factors are, as a rule, poor predictors of interstate violence. One of the few exceptions is the empirical finding that a simultaneous consideration of domestic conflicts and domestic attributes adds to the understanding of the causes of war.[2] Previously, only capability attributes, directly related to the hierarchical nature of the international system, have been able to provide an explanation. The reason has to do, among other things, with the fact that great powers historically have been involved in a disproportionately high share of interstate wars.

One deficiency in the resort to domestic attributes as explanations of warfare is their static character. This problem can be alleviated, in part, by a focus on domestic political processes and decisions, which provide a more dynamic perspective. Such processes, in order to be meaningfully understood, require that initiatives and reactions of the adversary must be taken into account. A dyadic perspective has to replace the reliance on domestic factors for explanation. For instance, the expected-utility theory of war does not sufficiently take this need into account. According to this theory, leaders decide to go to war if the expected utility of this action is greater than that of continued peace. The expected-utility theory has empirical support, but it largely fails to consider the dyadic nature of decision making.[3]

One of the problems in the explanation of wars by domestic attributes is that those attributes spell out necessary but not sufficient conditions for the outbreak of war (Most and Starr 1983, 138). That is why the systemic, structural aspects have to be incorporated into the analysis. They specify the context in which wars are started, waged, and terminated, and they tie the study of war to major theories of international relations such as polarity, balance of power, and collective security. It is possible that systemic factors provide sufficient reasons for the outbreak of, or for that matter, the avoidance of, major wars.

This assertion can be elaborated by utilizing Midlarsky's distinction between structural and mobilization interstate wars. A structural war is an outcome of an accumulating and escalating crisis between opposing coalitions of states. The existence of a crisis between such coalitions is a necessary precondition for the onset of a systemic war. A mobilization war is not preceded by a political crisis but is the result of unilateral aggression. It has been argued that the Napoleonic wars and World War II were mobilization wars while the Thirty Years' War and World War I were structural (Midlarsky 1986, 127–128). A related distinction has been made between wars of rivalry and wars of opportunity. Rivalries occur between symmetric states; available opportunities are used by great powers in their relations with weaker states. These two types of wars are distinguished by different capability relationships between the warring parties (Vasquez 1986, 317). In empirical terms, wars of opportunity and mobilization are preceded by similar escalatory dynamics.

A mobilization war results from the inequitable distribution of power among states, which fuels a military quest for hegemony. In this analysis there is the danger of regarding system structure as both a necessary and a sufficient cause for the outbreak of war. This viewpoint is misleading, however, as domestic decisions are always needed to unleash the forces of war. A mobilization war presupposes the existence of propitious international structure, but also the determination of a government to exploit the situation. Also, in a structural war, the polarized structure of the international system is a sufficient, but not a necessary, condition of war. Such a necessary reason is provided by the national decisions to escalate the crisis leading, inadvertently or not, to war. This situation means that power transitions can be peaceful. For instance, a proper international arrangement can alleviate structural pressures on governments to launch a war. Midlarsky has tested a theory of hierarchical equilibrium, characterized by two or more alliances and a large number of small powers, and suggested that such an arrangement provides a sufficient precondition for avoiding interstate wars (Midlarsky 1986, 93–126). Other international arrangements, such as a free-trade regime or a system of collective security, may also provide sufficient preconditions. Even in the absence of an international arrangement to regulate power transition, war is not inevitable. But in this case, the prospects for peaceful change are dependent on the prudence and pacifism of the leaders of the major powers.

Domestic attributes and decisions are necessary, but not sufficient, conditions of war. The attributes of two or more nations can be related to each other, and incompatibilities can be used as independent variables. It has been shown empirically that wars between liberal capitalist countries are rare, vindicating the Kantian recipe for peace (Doyle 1986). This finding should not be stretched too far, however,

as has obviously been done by Rummel (1983), who concludes that
"libertarian" political systems in general are more peaceful than other
types of systems. Several empirical studies arrive at more cautious
conclusions. Liberal capitalist countries appear to have been peaceful
only in their mutual relations (Chan 1984; Weede 1984). Often peace
between these countries has prevailed at the expense of interventions
and extrasystemic wars in the peripheries of the world.

Dyadic attribute measures are still static, however, and hence they
do not allow the construction of a dynamic process model to capture
the accumulation of tensions and grievances that may erupt into war.
The escalation of disputes into arms and hostile behavior, and ultimately
into a war, is not an uncommon event in international relations. Yet
interstate wars have been surprisingly little studied empirically from
such a perspective, in contrast to the popularity of formal models of
escalation processes (Singer 1981, 14). A similar concern seems to lie
behind Dina Zinnes's emphasis on environmental conditions as the
operative causes of wars: "Environment has an important bearing on
the violent behavior of nations."[4] In the unit-to-system relationship,
the structure of the international system is the decisive factor, although
having different meanings for states with different capability endow-
ments. However states operate primarily through unit-to-unit relations.
Their relationship to the system structure boils down to the problem
of constraints and opportunities in external policies.

The necessary background conditions are connected to the war
outcome by bargaining strategies. Leng and Gochman (1982) have
singled out three aspects of bargaining strategies for closer attention:
the militarization of disputes, the extent of escalation, and the degree
of reciprocity in hostile behavior. By splitting these variables, eight
combinations of different bargaining strategies, ranging from "fight" to
"prudence," can be generated. A "fight" strategy, characterized by
militarization, escalation, and reciprocity, leads most probably to war.
War is less probable, yet occurs in half of the cases, when the dispute
is militarized and escalated by one party but not reciprocated by the
other. The probability of war decreases if the nonreciprocating, weaker
country is able to obtain support from a third party.

That finding suggests the importance of the power dimension in
accounting for warfare. The relevance of that dimension becomes even
more obvious when the analysis of bargaining strategies is explicitly
placed in their international structural context. The analysis of within-
group variances allows Leng and Gochman (1982) to conclude that
"disputants with relatively unequal military-industrial capabilities tend
not to go to war with one another unless the stronger party, in a
premeditated manner or provoked by popular pressures, pursues the

war option." On the other hand, the relative equality of capabilities between adversaries is conducive to wars "unless powerful third parties intervene or unless the dispute pits great powers against one another." This point might mean that particularly in the wars of opportunity by the strong against the weak, the necessary domestic conditions for the outbreak of war are important. This possibility is consistent with the conclusion that risk acceptance and risk aversion, rather than differences in national capabilities, are the critical factors in accounting for war and peace (Bueno de Mesquita 1981; Vasquez 1986, 314–315). Furthermore, the findings by Leng and Gochman suggest that in certain cases the role of the third parties may be critical.

Theories of Hegemonic War

Several empirical studies show that static domestic attributes are not capable of accounting for warfare, with the exception of national capability. The importance of this power dimension for the initiation and conduct of wars has been discerned also in dyadic interstate relations and in the structure of the entire international system. A caveat has to be added, however: Often the risk-taking behavior and the strength of the political resolve are at least as important as the balance or imbalance of capabilities (Maoz 1983). This problem underlines again the need to study decision making as a necessary precondition for the outbreak of wars. Domestic reactions to environmental challenges seem to make a difference. Such reactions alter the structure of international action, affect costs and incentives, and in that way create a new context for national decision making.

These observations seem to call for a theory that combines the systemic explanations of war with intranational conditions. One obvious candidate for a systemic explanation is the theory of hegemonic war. Such a war is defined, as a rule, by its functions in the process of international change and not independently of its causes and consequences. This *Eigenart* ("peculiarity") of hegemonic, or global, wars becomes clear in Thompson's distinction among imperial, interstate, and global wars. Imperial wars are waged by the leading powers in the peripheries, and interstate wars are those military confrontations between leading powers that are not global. Global wars are defined functionally as "the end-of-cycle succession struggles for the system leader role" (Thompson and Zuk 1986, 258–259). Gilpin has, in turn, defined hegemonic war as "a direct contest between the dominant power or powers in an international system and the rising challenger or challengers." In such a war "the fundamental issue at stake is the nature and governance of the system." As a consequence, "a hegemonic war is characterized by the unlimited means employed and by the general scope of warfare." For Gilpin, "hegemonic war historically has been the basic mechanism of systemic change in world politics" (Gilpin 1981, 186–210).

Theories of hegemonic war postulate a pivotal role for some wars in resolving a disjuncture between the old political organization of the world and the new distribution of power. Hegemonic war amounts to the violent reorganization of international relations. It resolves the dilemma created by the decreasing capacity of the leading power to maintain its privileged position, owing to the law of diminishing returns, and its ambition to uphold existing global institutions. The relative decline of the leading power is the most important single symptom of the "increasing disjuncture between the existing governance of the system and the redistribution of power" (Gilpin 1981, 186). Such a situation fosters a hegemonic war, which is unique not only in terms of its scope, duration, and destructiveness but also in terms of its systemwide consequences. It leads to an extensive restructuring of international relations in favor of the winner, that is, the new leading, hegemonic power.

The theories of hegemonic war are parsimonious and, in many ways, valid efforts to account for violent structural changes in international relations. A major problem is, however, that the functional character of these theories precludes, for all practical purposes, their empirical falsification. "All general wars confirm the hypothesis by definition; if wars do not have the expected consequences, they cannot be general wars and hence do not disconfirm the hypothesis" (Levy 1985, 359–361). This critical remark is justified to an extent. The concept of hegemony implies motivation and goal orientation; hence wars associated with it cannot easily be defined by such objective and independent criteria as their scope, duration, and lethality. Before carrying the theories of hegemonic war to the ash heap of historical macrotheories, however, one should recall that they do not aim at explaining wars but the process of international structural change. Hegemonic wars are, indeed, theory specific, deriving their meaning from a particular theory. It is also true that they "are best understood if seen in the framework of the modern world system in terms of their consequences rather than their causes" (Modelski and Morgan 1985, 400). The stress on consequences rather than causes further illustrates the fact that theories of hegemonic war are not specific in relation to the theory of war but in relation to the theory of international change to which they subscribe. The specificity of these theories can hardly justify, however, a solution in which only three out of the total five hegemonic, or global, wars were included in a master list of 114 great-power wars from 1495 to 1945 (Modelski and Morgan 1985, 394–403; Levy 1985, 357–359).

The credibility of the theory of hegemonic war hinges upon historical interpretation, not upon empirical confirmation. The functional and teleological character of the theory can be relaxed by introducing an element of uncertainty into the outcome of a hegemonic war as far as its systemic consequences are concerned. Thus, Levy defines a general war as one in which "there is a reasonable probability of a decisive victory by at least one side that could lead to the emergence of a new dominant or leading power, and hence to the structural transformation of the system" (Levy, 1985, 364–365). Another, more radical, departure from the functionalism of the theory is to distinguish a set of general wars by objective, empirical criteria and check how they correlate with the long economic cycles and international power transitions (Väyrynen 1983, 406–414). Levy's definition is a halfway solution between functional-historical interpretation and empirical measurement.

A critical question in the theories of hegemonic war is how its systemic and structural aspects can be integrated with the decision-making and bargaining processes of the major powers. The main issue is how these processes reflect, and bring about, changes in the international distribution of power and in the international political order. To express the matter otherwise: How can the systemic and national levels of analysis be linked in the study of hegemonic wars? In trying to solve this riddle, it is useful to recall the distinction between mobilization wars and structural wars. The mobilization war may be initiated either by the challenger in its quest for world power or by the hegemonic state in a preemptive fashion in order to stop the downward slide of its relative power. These possibilities suggest that the initiation of mobilization wars is based on a calculation of the present and future development of international power relations. The structural wars, on the other hand, are more probably the result of symmetric interstate dynamics (bipolar tensions, breakdown of deterrence, alliance dilemmas, etc.). National decisions are, of course, also needed to initiate structural wars, but they are based more on the dynamics of interstate interaction than on the calculation of interests in the context of power.

Theories of hegemonic war have, to a surprising degree, neglected the problem of national decision making, partly because of a focus on the consequences of global wars rather than on their causes. Thus, in one study it was concluded that "global war must therefore be considered one of the more important sources of the growth and expansion of the modern state" (Rasler and Thompson 1985, 504). Another example is Rosecrance (1987) who, in exploring the relationship between economic cycles and war, hardly mentions the decision-making processes preceding the outbreak of wars. Yet the theories of hegemonic war have an inbuilt, often implicit, systemic conception of the causes of war that reverberate into the domestic systems of major powers. According to this conception, the process of power transition alters the domestic balance of costs and incentives, and this balance differs among declining and rising powers. The declining powers become more reluctant to initiate, barring extreme conditions, a war on their own and seek to maintain the status quo by a policy of appeasement or by the formation of coalitions. Rising powers might be more risk acceptant and hence prepared to launch a war. The strategic interaction associated with power transitions is usually tense and hence prone to misperceptions. As a rule, rising powers have been inclined to military overconfidence and to overestimate the hostility of the adversary. Declining powers have probably overestimated the hostility of the challengers but may have had underconfidence in their own military capabilities (Levy 1983).

Power transitions and the dynamic international environment in general transform the context of national decision making. These changes are more drastic at turning points of the national cycles of relative capability, which is why the decisions made at these turning points are more prone to overreaction, misperception, and the use of force (Doran and Parsons 1980). Obviously, these problems become even more serious when the turning points of national cycles in two adversarial states coincide. This point suggests a link between domestic crises and the outbreak of hegemonic wars. The rapid growth of catch-up countries leads to a profound transformation of their economies and societies. New leading industries, underpinned by technological innovations and new patterns of capital accumulation, emerge. Socio-economic dislocations become stronger because of class and urban-rural cleavages. Political mobilization and confrontation destabilize the society and pit the establishment and opposition against each other.

In the rising powers, the old society which has immense staying power, clashes with the new society, which is moved by social and economic dynamism. The army and other coercive organs of the state are more often than not enlisted to ensure the old social order. Their pivotal role is disclosed in an acute crisis in which the shift of the military to the side of the opposition may tilt the balance in its favor and seal the demise of the old society. In the rising powers, the main dividing line is between tradition and modernity, but this demarcation does not exclude internal divisions that may create unexpected coalitions. In the declining powers, the domestic divide most probably runs within the old society. One potential clash is between groups that are reluctant to give up old institutions but have resigned themselves to managing their decline and groups advocating regeneration and revival, whether right-wing or left-wing.

Thus, one can argue that domestic crisis and instability in a major power, in particular if it is challenging the prevailing international order, is an important factor in the outbreak of a general war. In such a situation, a rational, utilitarian model may not be able to capture the essence of the national processes that lead to war. Obviously, decision makers also make calculations under conditions of domestic strain and conflict. For instance, they may count on having the new national capabilities at their disposal, but there is no guarantee that calculated policies can be rationally implemented. In a rapidly changing society, domestic battles easily spill over into external relations. Alternatively, foreign policy may be used by the government to manage domestic relations and contradictions. In other words, the *combination* of domestic social, political, and economic strains in major powers and international power transitions is conducive to war; not because of the precise power calculations involved, but more because of the ungovernability of the expansive economic and military forces by the available political resources. A structural crisis of society in the aggressor nation is a necessary condition for the outbreak of a general war, and the existence of an international power transition is a sufficient condition. This formulation says that international power transitions do not lead per se to general or hegemonic wars. They greatly enhance, however, the probability of war if a catch-up country experiences a domestic crisis that places old and new orders against each other. Let me explore the validity of this formulation by focusing on the two general wars of this century, World War I and World War II.

World War I

World War I, the Great War, was preceded, without any doubt, by a power transition that was global in scale. In Europe and Asia, a dominant trait of this transition was the growth and expansion of two continental powers, Russia and Germany. The Russian expansion in Asia, although overextended because of the country's inadequate resources, put British imperialism to a severe test. Great Britain could not meet this test without establishing an anti-Russian alliance with the rising power in Asia, Japan. Germany was determined to catch up with England as the dominant industrial and maritime power and in the beginning of the twentieth century, was well on its way to this target. The most rapidly growing power of all was, however, the United

States, whose economic growth was accompanied by external expansionism (Kennedy 1984).

The expanding industrial and military capabilities of Germany and its *Weltpolitik* ("world policy") were interpreted by some, but not all, circles in the British establishment as a threat to British dominance. The main source of conflict in Anglo-German relations was economic and commercial rivalry, amplified by geographical proximity and ideological differences between German authoritarianism and British liberalism. Such dyadic factors were important (Kennedy 1982, 464–466), and they suggest that World War I was not, in the first place, caused by the naval arms race between Germany and England, even though the dynamics of that race exacerbated mutual suspicion. The United States entered as a supporter of the declining hegemonic power, England, because of an interest in maintaining a multilateral balance of power in Europe and Asia, which would assure the United States the most freedom of action. Alone, the United States was unable to establish a new political order; thus it preferred, as an alternative, a flexible balance of power. Such a balance would not commit it to underwriting overly heavy political obligations in European or Asian politics but would allow it to utilize commercial and political niches opened by the very flexibility of the balance of power.

The United States did not commit itself unequivocally to British activities in Asia or in Europe. Rather, the United States freed itself from a variety of imperial commitments in the Western Hemisphere, which helped it to reallocate resources needed in a leadership role. According to a standard power-transition theory, World War I should have been waged between the United States as the challenger and England as the hegemonic defender. That such a conflict did not occur suggests some complementarity of U.S. and British imperial interests, which, indeed, was the case. The calculation of power relations was not mathematical. The commonality of U.S. and British interests was reinforced by ideas of common destiny and the solidarity of the Anglo-Saxon "race." The idea of racial affinity across the Atlantic was short-lived, but it had considerable influence at the turn of the century (Anderson 1981).

To be able to explain the outbreak of World War I, the standard theories of power transition and hegemonic war have to be modified. The war has to be accounted for by a combination of the balance-of-power theory and the arguments of domestic crisis. As a bottom line, it is useful to recall that in the beginning of the century, the ruling classes of Europe, with the partial exceptions of France and England, were controlled by the landed and service nobilities. Mayer argues that their position was "solid and awesome . . . because their immense capital was not only symbolic and cultural but also economic" (Mayer 1981, 127). In Europe, the rising industrialists, Mayer continues, were not able to subvert the old elites and "doubting their own legitimacy . . . decided to imitate, cajole and join them." On the other hand, the position of the traditional elites was threatened by the pace of capitalist modernization and the rise of radical workers' movements. The socioeconomic pressures were manifested, in particular in the German case, by the increase of the urban population, conflict between landed and industrial interests, and strikes and other forms of political turmoil. The domestic pressures were also intensified by the expansion of new technological industries (Langhorne 1981, 39–45).

Apart from its political consequences, the technological revolutions in transportation, communication, and production paved the way for technical rationality in war planning. The Schlieffen Plan with its two-front strategy, for example, relied on swift military mobilization by means of the extensive German railroad system. Rapid mobilization and the fast movement of forces were intended to secure the German industrial strongholds of the Rhineland and Silesia, located near the borders. At the same time, France would be thrown off balance by being deprived of its industrial heartland and forced to rely on the resources of Great Britain. The Schlieffen Plan had, thus, industrial elements based on Germany's newly acquired capabilities, which were exploited by the military to implement its favorite knockout strategy (Pearton 1982, 126–131). German war planning became a function of Germany's capitalist industrial development as Eckart Kehr (1977, 53–55) has observed. From Moltke to Tirpitz and Schlieffen, the German industrial planners understood that the vulnerability of the new industrial capitalism required a short war, a blitzkrieg.

In Germany, the navy and the army were integrated in different ways into the Wilhelminian society. Steinberg (1965, 35–37, 39–41) has argued that the navy was a product of a liberal, industrial tradition and that its building program had antiagrarian implications. Naval officers were mostly drawn from the middle class and were thus linked to commercial interests. German naval policy was, in spite of its association with international commerce and the industrial state (*Industriestaat*), mercantilistic in its economic orientation. The sociopolitical contrast between the navy and the army is well summarized by Kehr: "The navy was part and parcel of a world policy oriented towards capitalist interests, while the army remained a pillar of the continent-oriented policy, which was conceived in the same vein as the agrarian-oriented constitution" (Kehr 1977, 7–8). The agrarian elite, the Junkers, went to great lengths to preserve its control over the army through the officer corps. The social composition and the structure of authority in the army were inextricably linked to the landowning class. The army was directed against the rising working class and had the task of preventing internal disturbances (Wehler 1973, 159–165).

The technological and industrial development created tensions between the new technical rationality and the political function of the army. The latter did not remain an instrument of the agrarian class interests but began to acquire an identity of its own. In the process, the old Prussian military virtues of obedience, discipline, and loyalty were not dropped, but they were integrated into the new armaments ideology, bred by the right-wing radicalism of patriotic organizations. This ideology was, in turn, linked to the international arms race, which was fueled by the process of power transition. Both in the industrial and the military spheres, demands for greater national efficiency emerged. They called for stronger societal and administrative organization, tariff barriers to protect the society against external economic rivals, and social compensation to silence the radicalism of the workers' movement. The policies of national efficiency and *Sammlung* ("unity") aimed at making the state an arbitrator in the class conflict and imposing a unity of interests on heavy industry and agriculture. The military was also integrated into this *Herrschaft* ("dominance") system (Geyer 1984, 83–95; Stone 1983, 96–107, 129–143).

Domestic social conflicts and the efforts to manage them linked external policy, and even war, more closely to the intranational conditions.

> War ceased to be the continuation of diplomacy to become the extension of politics, Europe's governors becoming even more prone to resort to foreign conflict to further domestic objectives. As the realignment of home politics became the principal end-purpose of foreign policy, war was called upon to serve ever more arbitrary, ill-defined and unlimited diplomatic aims. In sum, internal conflicts of class, status and power charged external war with absolute and ideological impulses. . . . This mutation of war into an instrument of domestic politics involved a heightened predilection of governments to launch or accept external conflict despite enormous hazards. [Mayer 1981, 304–305]

In such a political atmosphere, the acceptance of risks became, in a sense, functional in the conduct of external relations. The threats to use force were not only a part of foreign policy but served domestic objectives as well.

Recent historical research has shown in a convincing way that by the 1890s, the German empire was confronted with a domestic "danger zone" created by the tensions between the rapid rate of heavy industrialization and the archaic traits of society. In order to avoid domestic explosion, the Bismarckian policy, and later on the *Sammlung* strategy, aimed at imposing from above a new coherence on German society. This domestic-crisis strategy comprised protectionist economic policy, antisocialism, colonial expansion, and militarism. This new militarism appeared first in the ambitious naval program that challenged England and strengthened the basis of domestic liberal-conservative unity. The naval bills, effectively propagated, appealed both to the commercial middle class and to heavy industrialists and, as a symbol of Germany's search for *Weltgeltung* ("world standing"), to agrarian interests as well. In terms of material interests, *Sammlung* was based on a combination of agricultural protection and promotion of industrialization, including naval construction. In terms of values, the unifying thread was heady and expansive nationalism fostered by neomercantilist colonial and commercial policies (Berghahn 1973, 12–18; Wehler 1973, 172–179).[5]

The domestic-crisis strategy sought, in other words, to contain the social and political instability of the country by a combination of social imperialism and military strength. Social imperialism assumed contin-ued economic growth and expansion under protectionism. In the political sphere, *Sammlung* and missionary nationalism figured most prominently. These factors were interwoven into a national political totality that still retained its explosive character. One way of defusing it was by enhancing material interests and satisfying people's minds by external expansion and efforts to climb higher in the international power hierarchy (Berghahn 1973, 8–27; Gordon 1974, 205–209). This strategy meant that Germany became involved in the international power struggles in the pre-World War I period; in fact, it became a pivot in these struggles on the European continent. Germany's role in challenging the hegemonic power made its naval bills have anti-British implications. Yet Germany's main adversaries were the other two land powers, France and Russia, not England (Berghahn 1971, 424–428).

A major dilemma in Germany's foreign policy, motivated by domestic instabilities, was the tendency to convert all the leading powers, except Austria-Hungary, into enemies. In the decades preceding World War I, Germany vacillated between England and Russia as the major enemy. In both cases, domestic interests precluded closer economic and political cooperation. The Junkers wanted a protective tariff against grain imports from Russia and were suspicious of the British liberal, industrial model of society. Kehr has summarized the outcome of this dilemma: "The social structure of the Bismarchian Reich, combined with the crisis of the debt-ridden but politically powerful landholders east of Elbe, permitted only one harmonious solution: a foreign policy directed against both England and Russia" (Kehr 1977, 26–29; see also Gordon 1974, 206–207).

Militaristic values were fostered to bridge existing social and political cleavages. Especially in Germany, but also in the other major powers of Europe, "war was seen as a great restorer of sense; action itself, in whatever direction, could solve problems and restore proper values" (Stone 1983, 151–153). At the same time, the bureaucratic and political autonomy of the military increased, and new industrial capabilities were converted into unprecedented peacetime military power. These developments were opposed by socialists and some liberals but supported by right-wing nationalists, who were politically reorganized into a populist-nationalist movement (Eley 1980, 330–334). The weight of military organization and ideology was enhanced by the domestic crisis, which called for a political intervention "from above." New military technologies, and competitive interstate relations, gave the military more professional self-confidence. Such an *Eigendynamik* ("self-generated drive") contributed, in turn, to the decline of civilian control over the military and reduced the ability of foreign policy makers to direct strategy and war planning. Thus, these influences "seriously limited opportunities for diplomatic accommodation and, once they had been put into effect, virtually assured general war" (Osgood and Tucker 1967, 53–56).

In order to explain the genesis of World War I, the transformation of the European balance of power and the development of the domestic situation in Germany after 1910 have to be linked. In Germany, the emphasis on the numerical increase of battleships produced internal imbalances in the navy and made, with the conversion of the naval arms race into a qualitative competition, the Tirpitz Plan an outdated conception. A further problem was the change in the international premises of the plan as a consequence of Britain's alliance with France in 1904. The final blow to the German naval program was the country's deepening fiscal crisis. The threat of growing direct taxation turned the debt-ridden agrarians against the expansion of the navy, which was a major source of fiscal imbalance. This protest undermined *Sammlung* and reduced the value of the expansive naval policy as a method of domestic integration (Berghahn 1971, 469–475; 1976, 76–79). The naval arms race led, in 1909, to financial crises for Germany and England, and both took some tentative steps toward political détente. The German objective was to reduce the number of its enemies by extracting from England a commitment to remain neutral in a European war. In return, Germany contemplated reducing the pace of its fleet increases, thus recognizing de facto British supremacy at sea. Such a deal was resisted by the German naval lobby and was received with shivers in the British foreign policy establishment (Kennedy 1982, 446–447; Berghahn 1976, 79–81).

By 1912, the German Navy had outlived its domestic and international usefulness, and the military emphasis shifted to the army. A number of steps were taken, especially in 1912, to strengthen the army and to restore its position in the Wilhelminian politics of domestic order. This reorientation also vindicated the traditional agricultural and bureaucratic elites, but did not restore their previous control of the army. Rather, the army expanded its control over the rest of the society (Geyer 1984, 84–91). The shift of military priorities from the navy to the army was accompanied by an increase in anti-Russian and anti-Slavic sentiments, fueled for instance, by the Deutsche Wehrverein (German Defense Association), an organization established in 1911 to support the expansion of the army. These internal changes in Germany resulted in a redefinition of the country's geopolitical and imperialist orientation. *Weltpolitik,* supported by the naval program, was converted into a Lebensraum strategy emphasizing expansion to the east and southeast (Smith 1986; Eley 1980, 321–322). *Weltpolitik* had combined a continental European and a maritime orientation, based on the analysis that the possession of continental power was a precondition for global colonial and commercial expansion. The Lebensraum strategy devalued the importance of the maritime dimension and directed attention and energy to the establishment of a *Mitteleuropa* ("Middle Europe"; Berghahn 1971, 598–600).

The redefinition of the German military and imperialist priorities was rooted in domestic politics, but it was not isolated from the international developments in Europe. It has been argued that without the independence of Serbia, German hegemony would have replaced the European system of balance of power (Gasser 1973, 331–332). Germany was, however, adamant in continuing its policy of expansion in the Balkans as part of its new geopolitical and economic orientation. The objectives of this policy, and ultimately the aims of war, were functional for the German society. The true rationale was "the need to stabilize a world of aristocratic and monarchical tradition which had outlived its time" (Wehler 1973, 207–209). This priority did not contradict an international concern in Germany's expansionism, that of maintaining Austria-Hungary as a great power. This policy attempted both to further German expansion in the Balkans, thus weakening Russia's influence, and to deter any Russian attack on Austria-Hungary (Lambi 1984, 381–382). Germany's commitment to support Austria-Hungary's attack on Serbia raised the specter of a three-front war. England had made it known as early as 1912 that it would not remain neutral if Germany resorted, under cover of a war between Austria-

Hungary and Serbia, to a preventive war against France (Gasser 1973, 315–316).

The offensive aspects of the Austro-German dynastic alliance made, in other words, British neutrality and the localization of a Franco-German war impossible. The military and political leadership in Germany did not realize this fact, however, and calculated, mistakenly, that a war between Austria-Hungary and Serbia could be kept limited. In such a case, Germany could have achieved its objectives in the Balkans without sliding into a general war with the Triple Entente. In reality, the destruction of Serbia would only have exacerbated the Russo-German rivalry in Eastern Europe and consolidated Russia's relations with France and England (Lebow 1981, 119–122; Lambi 1984, 361–362). In shifting the direction of German expansionism to the east and southeast, the Wilhelminian government challenged the prevailing balance of power in Europe. Trapped in an inflexible military plan (the Schlieffen Plan) and in an inflexible alliance structure, the inability of the German leadership to reevaluate its strategy considerably increased the probability of war. In this sense, World War I was a consequence of the cognitive closure of the German political system (Lebow 1981, 105, 119).

Such a closure, contributing to an unrealistic strategy, was a result of Germany's internal conditions. In July 1914, those conditions were characterized by an odd combination of *Siegesgewissheit* ("certainty of victory") and uncertainty. On the one hand, the traditional elites were unable to solve, by diplomatic means, the problems of Germany's foreign relations in an increasingly democratic world. More and more a successful war was considered a means to salvage the old societal order. The accumulation of weapons and troops led to some confidence of military success. On the other hand, the German elites were not able to cope with the complexity of their own society and the external environment. The political leaders were filled with anxiety and uncertainty in the immediate prewar period, a condition that amounted to the abdication of political control over military moves (Wehler 1973, 198–200; Lebow 1981, 146–147). There is indeed "as much evidence of confusion and pessimism about the future as there is of desire for expansion and conquest." This state of affairs had drastic consequences because in July 1914, "virtually all the tangled wires of causality led back to Berlin" (Kennedy 1982, 457).

The history of World War I suggests that the socioeconomic structures and political processes in a hegemonic challenger are important and necessary preconditions for war. The positive link between domestic conflict and war preparation in Germany can be contrasted with the negative link between them in another hegemonic power, England, in which foreign policy remained moderate and largely defensive in spite of that country's decline (Gordon 1974). The internal conditions in Germany, and to a certain degree in Austria-Hungary, can be seen as the root cause of Austrian bellicosity; they paved the way to a limited dyadic war in the Balkans. These acts of violence would not have escalated into a complex and structural war of rivalry in the absence of a rigid alliance system, technological arms race, and interstate competition for power. These characteristics of the international system were sufficient to allow for the escalation of a limited war, motivated by domestic factors, into a general military confrontation in Europe.

The role of unintended consequences should be one of the most central ingredients in political analysis. Its pertinence in the case of World War I can easily be seen. Instead of stabilizing the domestic order in Germany, or in Austria-Hungary or Russia for that matter, the war sparked revolutions and reshaped the map of Europe, as Bethmann Hollweg had anticipated just before the outbreak of hostilities. "Men seldom determine or even anticipate the consequences of hegemonic war. Although in going to war they desire to increase their gains or minimize their losses, they do not get the war they want or expect; they fail to recognize the pent-up forces they are unleashing or the larger historical significance of the decisions they are taking" (Gilpin 1981, 202).

World War II

The role of unintended consequences presupposes that political actors pursue well-defined objectives. It is to be doubted, however, whether Germany, or any other revisionist power, has had a coherent view of the international order to be established by war. In any case, World War I was unable to produce hegemonic stability, and by the 1930s, both the Versailles system, based on the 1919 peace treaty, and the Washington system, established by the 1922 naval-limitation agreement, had broken down. In addition, the League of Nations proved to be incapable of establishing a viable system of international collective security and of deciding on meaningful arms limitations. The United States and Great Britain were inclined to provide some *Spielraum* ("margin") for German revisionism in Europe to reduce the danger of a violent explosion, but this policy was resented by France and the Soviet Union, both of which regarded Germany as a threat to their security. There were, thus, no coordinated international efforts to efficiently contain the rising power of Germany and Japan. Not only was this failure a result of the "unwise" foreign policies of the Anglo-

Saxon powers, it also reflected the prevalence of economic interests and objectives in their external relations.

The acceptance of some German and Japanese expansionism by the Western powers was intended to help stabilize the world economy. Such stability was achieved during the second half of the 1920s, but because of corporatist arrangements in major European economies rather than international political strategies. This domestic stability allowed a temporary truce in interstate conflicts and, thus, gave rise to stabilizing agreements under the aegis of the Locarno system created in 1925. The Great Depression and the resurgence of domestic political revisionism, fueled in Germany and Japan by U.S. economic predominance, opened the explosive decade of the 1930s (Maier 1975; Ziebura 1984).

German and Japanese economic and territorial expansion signified a departure from the Versailles and Washington systems as well as opposition to them. This expansion was underpinned by vigorous rearmament programs. The economic, organizational, and technical preparations for war were well under way by the middle of the 1930s. International relations were increasingly polarized between the aggressive revisionist group of countries—Germany, Japan, and Italy— and the accommodating status quo group—the United States, Great Britain, and France.

In both groups, military spending played a role in overcoming the economic depression. Eugen Varga perceptively predicted, in the middle of the 1930s, the outbreak of the coming general war as well as the economic crisis of underproduction in productive sectors of the aggressive group of countries. In their search for autarky and through the ensuing international conflicts, which destroyed the international division of labor, Germany, Italy, and Japan overburdened their own economies by huge investments in war preparations (Varga 1935, 122–138; Kerner 1981, 34–44).

The march to World War II was not, however, necessarily a straightforward movement in which the aggressive revisionist powers deliberately prepared for a major confrontation. The German economic and military preparation for war, for instance, was a complex and controversial process. This process has been explained in several different ways.

One explanation is that Germany did not have a coherent policy of military preparation before 1936. Even later, it would have been able to use a much greater share of its national product for armaments and other military purposes (Klein 1948; 1958). Despite the growth of the military outlays, they represented an average of 17 percent of the total government spending and only 1.3 percent of GNP in 1932–1935. These figures reflect Hitler's desire to restore domestic sociopolitical stability by increasing employment, in particular in agriculture and the building industry (in his two-track policy, Hitler also smashed the anti-Nazi opposition). Heavy military spending would have jeopardized the goal of domestic stability by threatening the state-directed recovery of the civilian economy.

Until 1936, these policies were, in essence, liberal and guided by the private profit. The economy was directed by the Ministry of Economics under the leadership of Hjalmar Schacht, who had been the candidate of the army and heavy industry for this position (Overy 1985, 314–315). The state supported construction, transportation, and industrial investment, and through a spin-off process, private economic activity benefited from these public economic programs as well. The Great Depression had been so deep in Germany that state intervention was probably the only way of stimulating the economy.

In addition, the depression had reduced Germany's dependence on the world economy; a fact welcomed by the National Socialists. Schacht's New Plan of 1934 moved further toward autarky. This policy was supported by some industries, such as the chemical industry, and opposed by others, including the consumer-goods industry. The trend towards autarky was not to be stopped, however, and the reduction of foreign trade continued. In Germany's foreign trade, bilateral trading arrangements became more common (Petzina 1977, 117–124; Overy 1982a, 28–53). Germany was dependent on several vital raw materials, such as nickel and iron ores, and in order to reduce this dependence, domestic resources were mobilized. Also economic expansion became a central ingredient in Hitler's strategy. This expansion was to occur primarily toward eastern and southeastern Europe, and to a lesser extent, toward northern Europe. Germany's economic diplomacy very explicitly aimed at building an autarkic base, a *Grossraumwirtschaft* ("large-space economy"), to satisfy the raw-material needs of the country's civilian and military economies (Kaiser 1980).

Germany's economic strategy from *Machtergreifung* reflects Hitler's political plans. His imperial plans were predicated on the subjugation of the German society to fascist ideology. Their implementation required the recovery of the German economy before the rearmament program was set in full motion, and recovery assumed tactical concessions to private industry. The imperial agenda included the establishment of a military-economic core comprising, in addition to Germany, Austria, Czechoslovakia, and parts of Poland. This autarkic core was to be built by a series of political maneuvers and small wars. Hitler personally was averse to the idea of a "total war" and favored the construction of an impressive array of military weapons instead of building up reserves for a long war. Hitler's aim was to demoralize the opponent from inside and then win by massive but swift military actions. Such a blitzkrieg was not conceivable, however, before the economic core region in central Europe was established (Carroll 1968, 93–105; Overy 1982b).

Hitler's strategy also had a domestic economic rationale. A massive rearmament program and preparations for a long war would have created bottlenecks in the availability of raw materials and other inputs for production, undermined financial stability, and weakened the private capital market. The avoidance of heavy armament burdens in 1933–1936 made too drastic cutbacks in civilian consumption unnecessary. These considerations were negated, however, in 1936, and a switch toward the rearmament program was given priority. The critical policy decision was the approval of the Four-Year Plan in October 1936. The German economy had to be made self-sufficient and prepared for war in four years—two unrealistic aims. After 1936, contrary to Burton Klein's argument, the share of the German economy devoted to arms was substantial in comparison to any other industrial power (Geyer 1984, 144–149).

In the political sphere, the introduction of the Four-Year Plan started the perfection of fascist control of state and society. The public control of the economy was taken away from the Ministry of Economics and handed over to the National Socialist party (NSDAP), and to Hermann Göring. Heavy industry made efforts to resist the Four-Year Plan and the increasing Nazi control of the economy to retain autonomy and preserve the market mechanism, but the industrialists failed and had to retreat in the face of party power (Overy 1985). The state- and party-controlled rearmament program created economic imbalances and social repercussions that contributed to external expansion.

The implementation of the Four-Year Plan and the rearmament program gave rise to a major crisis in German civilian industries. The allocation of almost all available resources to the military industry damaged the ability of the civilian sectors to earn foreign exchange. The stockpiles of raw materials had been reduced by early 1936 to meet only two months' consumption, and basic foodstuffs had to be rationed. The Four-Year Plan was a stopgap measure intended to make the intensification of the rearmament program and the policy of economic revival commensurate until the establishment of a *Grossraumwirtschaft* would provide an autarkic economic base for a "new Germany." The Four-Year Plan was to be a temporary measure also in that a renewed emphasis on civilian development would follow after the conquest of the necessary Lebensraum (Petzina 1977, 124–134; Carroll 1968, 122–139).

However, the Four-Year Plan did not prevent the deterioration of the civilian economy but instead contributed to it. An underproduction crisis followed and led to the push toward external expansion. The lack of raw materials and foreign exchange made the economic situation almost unbearable. The political control of empire building was by 1937–1938 firmly in the hands of the NSDAP and the army. The domestic economic base could not support an empire building that also militated against the narrower financial and political interests of German capitalism (Overy 1985, 332). The financial stalemate and the underproduction crisis moved the country to an expansionist solution to gain raw materials and foreign exchange. This solution was also deemed to be useful in generating domestic support among an increasingly skeptical public. The Anschluss with Austria and the attack on Czechoslovakia were based on less than promising forecasts of future international power relations.

By 1937, it had become clear to the Nazi leadership that the rearmament program would not be able, under existing economic constraints, to generate sufficient military power to allow Germany to prevail in the long run. This realization increased the temptation to move before Germany's adversaries were able to strengthen their military apparatuses by drawing upon their superior economic resources. At the Hossbach meeting in November 1937, Hitler predicted that the German position would start declining after 1943–1945 when Germany's adversaries would have completed their military preparations. Hitler was adamant that the rearmament program be continued even though it posed a threat to the standard of living and, as a consequence, to the popular support of the National Socialists. Logically, as William Carr (1972, 71–88: Murray 1984, 27–29, 134–137) observes, this left expansion as the only way out of a self-imposed dilemma. The international situation in the late 1930s also tended to favor an expansionist policy.

The occupations of Austria and Czechoslovakia revealed considerable weaknesses in the operational capabilities of the *Wehrmacht* ("armed forces"). However, in strategic and economic terms, the Anschluss yielded some benefits. The foreign exchange reserves of the Austrian Central Bank became available, and private Austrian capital also started flowing toward Germany. As a result, Germany was able to secure raw materials for its industry. The German state appropriated the spoils of the Austrian economy, and later on those of the Czechoslovakian and Polish economies, without sharing them with private business (Overy 1985, 325).

In a long-term perspective, Austria turned out to be an economic burden to the German government after its relatively limited raw-material resources had been exploited and its sources of foreign exchange had been depleted. The occupation of Czechoslovakia produced more tangible strategic and economic benefits, as its industrial potential, supply of raw materials, and ability to earn foreign exchange through exports were all considerable. On balance, the costs of Germany's political and military overextension increased, but the invasion of Czechoslovakia still consolidated Germany's military and economic influence in eastern and southeastern Europe (Murray 1984, 149–151, 290–294; Kaiser 1980, 244–246, 259–262). In Germany, autarky of the military industry became the main objective rather than general economic self-sufficiency, and the labor force was increasingly coerced to serve the interests of military production (Carr 1972, 98–99; Carroll 1968, 176–178).

Hitler's grand strategy was to gain control of the European continent to the Urals and to acquire the material basis necessary for the hegemonic struggle with England. The conquest of eastern Europe was to be achieved by a combination of blitzkrieg and political intimidation. According to this strategy, a lightning attack on eastern Europe could be accomplished with only limited military capabilities, which would not strain Germany's economic resources. Blitzkrieg was, thus, a military strategy formed by limited economic resources and by the political need to maintain support for the National Socialists—in particular, among the German middle class.[6] The lightning strategy, which was not militarily coherent, was also predicated on the assumption of weak enemies that could be rapidly defeated. This expectation was reinforced by the German military successes against Poland and France.

England was a different matter, however. The National Socialist leaders did not believe that England, which had started an impressive rearmament program in 1938, could be defeated by swift military action. In 1938, the share of military spending of Britain's central government expenditures was 38 percent compared to 15 percent only three years earlier. The rearmament program kindled an economic and social crisis that strengthened the arguments for the policy of appeasement as a complement to the military buildup (Kennedy 1981, 298–299, 302–304). The National Socialists believed that in order to emerge victorious from the great contest with England, they had to secure control of continental Europe, and Hitler believed that the allied powers would allow the political and military *Drang nach Osten* ("longing for the East") to continue without serious resistance. This belief was strengthened by the behavior of the allied powers in the crisis precipitated by the German. occupation of Prague (Carr 1972, 94–97, 112–117).

These observations support a strategic explanation of Germany's policy leading to World War II. Such an explanation is, in turn, consistent with the hegemonic theories of war, and they are also supported by a variety of explanations of the German attack on Poland. In one interpretation, the attack was propelled by the British rearmament policy, which threatened to reduce decisively the military edge enjoyed by Germany in short-term capability calculations (Carr 1972, 106–107; Carroll 1968, 183–189). In the case of World War II, the explanation centering on the theory of hegemonic war has to be complemented by the persistent German underestimation of Soviet military resilience. In general, Germany overestimated its long-term military capabilities in relation to the allied powers.

The strategic-hegemonic explanation does not exclude, however, the role of domestic factors in the German decision to go to war. Economic difficulties increased from 1935 on. Financial problems, inflationary pressures, and an acute shortage of raw materials pushed the leadership to the expansionist policy to preserve the fascist political system and its mode of production. In a deeper sense, the Nazi system experienced in 1938 a *Herrschaftskrise* ("a power crisis"), which was alleviated by the policy of external expansion (Geyer 1984, 151–161; Carr 1972, 96, 118–120). Earlier compromises—often tenuous right from the beginning—between the Nazi elite, generals, and big business started to break up, and the crisis became manifest in the 1938 struggle for control of the rearmament programs. Until 1938, the military commanders had advocated their weapons programs solely on the basis of military criteria, without giving consideration to their economic requirements. The programs of the individual services were justified by Hitler's general exhortations to increase military power. As a consequence, "German rearmament was not . . . a comprehensively planned, systematically organized and centrally directed process" (Deist 1981, 93–96).

In the 1930s, the German military was as determined as ever to retain its tradition of autonomy in the decisions to acquire arms and to use them. The quest for autonomy was crystallized in so-called deployment plans, introduced in 1935. They provided guidelines and military rationale for the use of force, which had to take place under military control. The available military resources defined the political objectives that could be instrumentally pursued by force. In order to expand these objectives, the General Staff and the individual services relentlessly demanded new and more weapons, which had an increasingly offensive character (Geyer 1985, 139–144). The link between resources and objectives was undermined, however, by serious economic problems. The rearmament program suffered from setbacks and delays because of "limited economic resources and the inadequate organization of the armaments economy" (Deist 1981, 108–109). The military was not, in other words, to make ends and means meet.

The rearmament program isolated Germany both economically and politically from the international system. This isolation tended to lead to a push for expansion into eastern Europe, in part to obtain new resources for the military buildup. Domestic economic problems and the policy of autarkic isolation had made the idea of a militarily rational and instrumental war a chimera by 1938 (Geyer 1985, 145). The military strategy of the General Staff had become the victim of its own incompatibilities and disregard for economic realities. As this failure became obvious, Hitler restored a heavy-handed Nazi control over the military. The potent and offensive military force became, more than before, a tool of politics to serve Hitler's short-term intentions (Deist 1981, 99–100; Geyer 1984, 158–159). The German military had prepared for a limited and politically instrumental war in Europe. Instead, the Nazis took control of the German military machine, in particular after 1938, and directed it according to politics and ideology rather than according to professional military standards. Hitler's expansionist plans were implemented by a new generation of officers who counted, in lieu of risk calculations, on the efficiency and firepower of their weapons (Geyer 1985, 146–147).

The German invasion of Poland in 1939 and the expansion of the war in 1941 were the results of a combination of Hitler's expansionism, domestic socioeconomic disjunctures in Germany, and the technocratic offensiveness of the miltiary. The underestimation of the political intentions and long-term economic and military capabilities of the adversaries underpinned the German attack. Such a miscalculation assured, at the same time, its ultimate failure.

Concluding Observations

Both World War I and World War II can be accounted for by the theory of hegemonic war as long as it posits that war is started by a rising rather than by a declining power. Gilpin observes correctly that such wars are preceded by "an important psychological change in the temporal outlook of peoples" (Gilpin 1981, 239). One of these changes is the "fear of ultimate decline and the perceived erosion of power" in the hegemonic state. Gilpin's statement that this fear has caused such states, fearing decline, "to precipitate great wars" is not universally valid, however. On the contrary, most general wars have been launched by a rising power in its quest for more power and control. This was certainly the case in both world wars, which were started directly or indirectly, by Germany in order to increase its territorial, economic, and political control in eastern Europe.

The validity of the hegemonic war theory is enhanced by the conclusion that the power transition theory, its main ingredient, does not "contain any internal consistencies and thus is not theoretically false." Its main weakness is the neglect of alliance formation as a means of aggregating capabilities (Bueno de Mesquita 1980, 376–380). The hegemonic war theory is also parsimonious, and hence a succinct way of accounting for the major military convulsions of international relations. On this basis, one would conclude that the theory is adequate and no other explanations are needed. However, such a conclusion would be premature. The hegemonic war theory not only fails to provide a consistent answer as to whether a hegemonic or a rising power starts a war, but it is also inadequate in predicting when and under what conditions war will break out. That is why the theory has to be supplemented by an analysis of the domestic conditions of major powers.

Ideally, general wars, of which hegemonic wars are a subcategory, should be studied by using a comparative approach, which can be applied to study different types of wars, e.g., hegemonic and non-hegemonic ones, in terms of their causes and consequences. It may be, for example, that the role of domestic crises and their relationship to international political processes differ between hegemonic and nonhegemonic wars. The comparative approach should be built upon systematically selected case studies of different types of wars from which limited generalizations could be drawn. In the study of a limited number of general wars, such a method appears to hold more promise than somewhat mechanical statistical explorations. Another way of applying a comparative approach would be to contrast the prewar domestic processes and decisions in the hegemonic and rising powers with each other. In this chapter, such a comparison has been made only in a very limited way, and attention has primarily been paid to the challenging state, i.e., Germany, and its society. Historical evidence suggests that in all the major powers of Europe, a domestic crisis preceded the outbreak of world wars. In the hegemonic or near-hegemonic powers, England and the United States, such a crisis did not, however, directly lead to war. Their decisions to enter the world wars had clearly defensive motives, and the priority was to defend the prevailing Anglo-Saxon international order rather than to protect national territory. The strategic environment and the challenge of power transition affected the decisions of the British and U.S. governments to go to war in a more fundamental way than the domestic conditions. Domestic opinion was divided on the advisability of entering the war, although it was soon to accept the decision to that effect.

The decisions of Germany cannot, however, be grasped without considering the contemporary domestic circumstances. They were the necessary conditions for the outbreak of war, while the international structural explanations provide sufficient reasons for it. Before both world wars, the German economy was in crisis. The armaments programs had produced severe fiscal problems, which demanded the extraction of new taxes in a situation characterized by an underproduction of civilian goods in comparison to military goods. The implementation of such a policy threatened the social and political basis of the government, in particular, among the middle class. External expansion and aggression became a means of alleviating this dilemma by promising new resources and more freedom of operation. Without the domestic crises, the German aggressiveness that led to both world wars would probably have been much less decisive and less goal oriented.

At this juncture, the two world wars have to be distinguished from each other. For the first war, the domestic crisis in Germany was much more organic and internally explosive. Increasingly war appeared as the only way out of the domestic crisis. The autonomy of the military and the offensiveness of its doctrine tended to lock German policy onto an unalterable course. The cognitively closed political leadership refused to reflect upon this course in the light of new realities. The German case was the most obvious illustration of the fact that "the general prewar European domestic immobility was . . . the result of a tense impasse rather than tranquil stability, a condition inconducive to calm evaluation of international politics" (Farrar 1981, 99). The specific domestic situation in Germany was in search of war, which was provided by the prevailing state of the European balance of power. Germany's expansion for Lebensraum and its commitment to the great power status of Austria-Hungary gave plenty of opportunities for the breakdown of the international system. A considerable dose of miscalculation and paralysis in the German political leadership in July 1914 finally opened the floodgates of war. Farrar (1981, 194–196) claims that without the renunciation of one or more of the European powers of their status, the constellation of states was bound to plunge into war. Perhaps, but without the domestic tensions in Germany—and apparently also in Austria-Hungary and Russia—the disorganization of the system would have taken a much longer time and, more important, might have been managed in a peaceful manner.

In the case of World War II, a domestic crisis also pushed the country to external aggression. The management of this crisis called for new resources without which the discontent of the vital domestic groups would have been politically much more tangible. German expansion was locked, however, by Hitler's political visions rather than by military logic. In contradistinction to World War I, the German military from 1938 on was quite firmly under political control. The critical question was not *whether* Hitler was determined to go to war or not but *when*. An answer to this query can be obtained by comparing the state of the German economy and the country's armament programs with those undertaken by its adversaries. The combination of Germany's domestic economic problems and the rapid militarization of the "non-aggressive" group of countries led the Nazi leadership to conclude that 1939–1941 was the most propitious time to act. Somewhat ironically, domestic constraints on capabilities motivated Germany to start World War II.

World War I was a structural war, and World War II a mobilization war. In the latter type of war, the determination of the government to initiate hostilities is of greater importance. Deliberate decisions are made to utilize the existing opportunities in the external environment, but also to alleviate domestic pressures. In a structural war, decisions to go to war less explicitly reflect the impact of military strategies, domestic economic requirements, and the unstable nature of interstate relations. Wars of mobilization, or of opportunities, are wars of decisions. Structural wars are the outcome of structural variables about which decision makers can do little once the process toward war has begun. To avoid such wars, researchers have to contribute models of war-avoiding links between internal and external environments.

Notes

1. Michael Howard (1976) argues that "the wars of the nations" followed in the nineteenth century "the wars of revolutions" during the Napoleonic era and preceded "the wars of the technologists" in the two world wars. Ekkehart Krippendorff (1985, 300–328) comes to a related conclusion. The French revolution and the Napoleonic wars are seen as the turning point from the dynastic territorial state to the nation-state. The army was the central institution in the dynastic state; in the nation-state, the entire society was mobilized to support the war efforts and to render them legitimacy. Howard's categories of wars may not be interpreted to exclude each other. Despite an increasing technological character, warfare retained its nationalistic elements in both world wars; they were struggles between nation-states. An interesting query is whether nuclear weapons have eroded or strengthened the nation-state element of war. My impression is that military power has never in history been as centralized under state control as it is in the nuclear age. This point hints at an interesting secular trend from Howard's "wars of knights" and "wars of mercenaries," in which state control was limited, to the almost total state monopoly of mass destruction. Such a state monopoly of military force undermines the nation-state element by separating society from the control and legitimation of military

security. The growing popular rejection of nuclear and other weapons of mass destruction as a source of security testifies to this separation of state and society and to the ensuing crisis of legitimacy.

2. See Zinnes (1980, 336–344). A similar judgment has been made by Singer (1981, 11–12) who concludes that, with the exception of geographical position and economic-military strength, domestic factors are rather unimportant in accounting for the war proneness of nations.

3. See Bueno de Mesquita (1981). The essentially monadic nature of this theory has been briefly observed also by Wagner (1984): "There are far more than two possible outcomes to any war. And since the consequences of both fighting and not fighting depend upon what the potential enemy decides to do, a game-theoretic analysis would be necessary" (p. 423). Game theory is, of course, a way of formalizing, especially in its iterative mode, interactive decision situations.

4. Zinnes (1980, 344–351). She appears to accept, however, too easily the view that the growth of military spending is primarily owing to external pressures and interstate hostilities. In so doing, the autonomous domestic causes of arms buildup are neglected without sufficient justification.

5. In the historians' debate, doubts have been expressed as to whether the naval program really had such a pivotal role in the consolidation of *Sammlung* as Wehler and Berghahn, for example, argue. It has been pointed out that the naval policy and *Weltpolitik* released forces that undermined rather than strengthened industrial-agrarian cooperation. On this debate, see Berghahn 1979 and Eley 1982.

6. Interpretations of the economic and political roots of blitzkrieg differ in some crucial respects. Interpreters tend to agree, however, on its optimal nature in that the lightning strategy did not antagonize any significant segment of interests in Germany. This strategy promised a kind of war that would not break an economy already burdened by the rearmament program (see Kroener 1985).

References

Anderson, Stuart. 1981. *Race and Rapprochement: Anglo-Saxonism and Anglo-American Relations, 1895–1914.* Madison, N.J.: Fairleigh Dickinson University Press.

Berghahn, Volker R. 1971. *Der Tirpitz-Plan: Genesis und Verfall einer innenpolitischen Krisenstrategie unter Wilhelm II.* Düsseldorf: Droste Verlag.

———. 1973. *Rüstung und Machtpolitik: Zur Anatomie des "Kalten Krieges" vor 1914.* Düsseldorf: Droste Verlag.

———. 1976. "Naval Armaments and Social Crisis: Germany Before 1914." In Geoffrey Best and Andrew Wheatcroft, eds., *War Economy and the Military Mind,* pp. 61–88. London: Croom Helm.

———. 1979. "Politik und Gesellschaft im Wilhelminischen Deutschland." *Neue politische Litteratur* 24:2, pp. 164–195.

Bueno de Mesquita, Bruce. 1980. "Theories of International Conflict: An Analysis and an Appraisal." In Ted Robert Gurr, ed., *Handbook of Political Conflict*, pp. 361–399. New York: Free Press.

———. 1981. *The War Trap*. New Haven: Yale University Press.

Carr, William. 1972. *Arms, Autarky, and Aggression: A Study of German Foreign Policy 1933–1939*. New York: W. W. Norton.

Carroll, Berenice A. 1968. *Design for a Total War: Arms and Economics in the Third Reich*. Paris: Mouton.

Chan, Steve. 1984. "Mirror, Mirror on the Wall: Are the Freer Countries More Pacific?" *Journal of Conflict Resolution* 28:4, pp. 617–648.

Deist, Wilhelm. 1981. *The Wehrmacht and the German Rearmament*. Toronto: University of Toronto Press.

Doran, Charles F., and Wes Parsons. 1980. "War and the Cycle of Relative Power." *American Political Science Review* 74:4, pp. 947–965.

Doyle, Michael. 1986. "Liberalism and World Politics." *American Political Science Review* 80:4, pp. 1151–1169.

Eley, Geoff. 1980. *Reshaping the German Right: Radical Nationalism and Political Change After Bismarck*. New Haven: Yale University Press.

———. 1982. "Sammlungspolitik, Social Imperialism, and the Navy Law of 1898." In Geoff Eley, *From Unification to Nazism: Reinterpreting the German Past*, pp. 110–151. Boston, Mass.: Allen and Unwin.

Farrar, L. L., Jr. 1981. *Arrogance and Anxiety: The Ambivalance of German Power, 1848–1914*. Iowa City: University of Iowa Press.

Gasser, Adolf. 1973. "Der deutsche Hegemonialkrieg von 1914." In Imanuel Geiss and Bernd Jürgen Wendt, eds., *Deutschland in der Weltpolitik des 19. und 20. Jahrhunderts*, pp. 307–339. Düsseldorf: Bertelsmann Universitätsverlag.

Geyer, Michael. 1984. *Deutsche Rüstungspolitik 1860–1980*. Frankfurt am Main: Suhrkamp.

———. 1985. "The Dynamics of Military Revisionism in the Interwar Years: Military Politics Between Rearmament and Diplomacy." In Wilhelm Deist, ed., *The German Military in the Age of Total War*, pp. 100–151. Leamington Spa: Berg Publishers.

Gilpin, Robert. 1981. *War and Change in World Politics*. Cambridge: Cambridge University Press.

Gordon, Michael R. 1974. "Domestic Conflict and the Origins of the First World War: The British and the German Cases." *Journal of Modern History* 46:2, pp. 191–226.

Howard, Michael. 1976. *War in European History*. Oxford: Oxford University Press.

Kaiser, David E. 1980. *Economic Diplomacy and the Origins of the Second World War: Germany, Britain, France, and Eastern Europe, 1930–1939*. Princeton: Princeton University Press.

Kehr, Eckart. 1977. *Economic Interests, Militarism, and Foreign Policy*. Berkeley: University of California Press.

Kennedy, Paul. 1981. *The Realities Behind Diplomacy: Background Influences on British External Policy, 1865–1980*. Glasgow: Fontana.

_____ . 1982. *The Rise of the Anglo-German Antagonism, 1860–1914.* London: Allen and Unwin.

_____ . 1984. "The First World War and the International Power System." *International Security* 9:1, pp. 7–40.

Kerner, Manfred. 1981. *Staat, Krieg, und Krise: Die Varga-Diskussion und die Rolle des Zweiten Weltkrieges in der kapitalistischen Entwicklung.* Cologne: Pahl-Rugenstein.

Klein, Burton. 1948. "Germany's Preparation for War: A Re-examination." *American Economic Review* 28:1, pp. 56–77.

_____ . 1958. *Germany's Economic Preparations for War.* Cambridge, Mass.: Harvard University Press.

Kotowski, Christoph M. 1984. "Revolution." In Giovanni Sartori, ed., *Social Science Concepts: A Systematic Analysis,* pp. 403–450. Beverly Hills, Calif.: Sage Publications.

Krippendorff, Ekkehart. 1985. *Staat und Krieg: Die historische Logik politischen Unvernunft.* Frankfurt am Main: Suhrkamp.

Kroener, Bernhard R. 1985. "Squaring the Circle: Blitzkrieg Strategy and Manpower Shortage, 1939–1942." In Wilhelm Deist, ed., *The German Military in the Age of Total War,* pp. 282–303. Leamington Spa: Berg Publishers.

Lambi, Ivo Nikolai. 1984. *The Navy and German Power Politics, 1862–1914.* Boston, Mass.: Allen and Unwin.

Langhorne, Richard. 1981. *The Collapse of the Concert of Europe: International Politics, 1890–1914.* New York: St. Martin's Press.

Lebow, Richard Ned. 1981. *Between Peace and War: The Nature of International Crisis.* Baltimore: Johns Hopkins University Press.

Leng, Russell J., and Charles S. Gochman. 1982. "Dangerous Disputes: A Study of Conflict Behavior and War." *American Journal of Political Science* 26:4, pp. 664–687.

Levy, Jack S. 1983. "Misperception and the Causes of War: Theoretical Linkages and Analytical Problems." *World Politics* 36:1, pp. 76–99.

_____ . 1985. "Theories of General War." *World Politics* 37:3, pp. 344–374.

_____ . 1986. "Organizational Routines and the Causes of War." *International Studies Quarterly* 30:2, pp. 193–222.

Maoz, Zeev. 1983. "Resolve, Capabilities, and the Outcomes of Interstate Disputes, 1816–1976." *Journal of Conflict Resolution* 27:2, pp. 195–229.

Maier, Charles S. 1975. *Recasting Bourgeois Europe: Stabilization in France, Germany, and Italy in the Decade After World War I.* Princeton: Princeton University Press.

Mayer, Arno J. 1971. *Dynamics of Counterrevolution in Europe, 1870–1956: An Analytical Framework.* New York: Harper and Row.

_____ . 1981. *The Persistence of Old Regime: Europe to the Great War.* New York: Pantheon Books.

Midlarsky, Manus I. 1986. *The Disintegration of Political Systems: War and Revolution in Comparative Perspective.* Columbia: University of South Carolina Press.

Modelski, George. 1983. "Long Cycles of World Leadership." In William R. Thompson, ed., *Contending Approaches to World System Analysis,* pp. 115–139. Beverly Hills, Calif.: Sage Publications.

Modelski, George, and Patrick M. Morgan. 1985. "Understanding Global War." *Journal of Conflict Resolution* 29:3, pp. 391–418.

Most, Benjamin A., and Harvey Starr. 1983. "Conceptualizing 'War': Consequences for Theory and Research." *Journal of Conflict Resolution* 27:1, pp. 137–159.

Murray, Williamson. 1984. *The Change in the European Balance of Power, 1938–1939: The Path to Ruin.* Princeton: Princeton University Press.

North, Robert C., and M. Willard. 1983. "The Convergence Effect: Challenge to Parsimony." *International Organization* 37:3, pp. 339–358.

Osgood, Robert E., and Robert W. Tucker. 1967. *Force, Order, and Justice.* Baltimore: Johns Hopkins University Press.

Overy, R. J. 1982a. *The Nazi Economic Recovery 1932–1938.* London: Macmillan.

———. 1982b. "Hitler's War and the German Economy: A Reinterpretation." *Economic History Review* 35:2, pp. 272–291.

———. 1985. "Heavy Industry and the State in Nazi Germany: The Reichswerke Crisis." *European History Quarterly* 15:3, pp. 313–340.

Pearton, Maurice. 1982. *The Knowledgeable State: Diplomacy, War, and Technology Since 1830.* London: Burnett Books.

Petzina, Dietmar. 1977. *Die deutsche Wirtschaft in der Zwischenkriegszeit.* Wiesbaden: Franz Steiner Verlag.

Rasler, Karen A., and William R. Thompson. 1985. "War Making and State Making: Governmental Expenditures, Tax Revenues, and Global Wars." *American Political Science Review* 79:2, pp. 491–507.

Rosecrance, Richard. 1987. "Long Cycle Theory and International Relations." *International Organization* 41:2, pp. 283–301.

Rummel, Rudolph J. 1983. "Libertarianism and Violence." *Journal of Conflict Resolution* 27:1, pp. 27–71.

Singer, J. David. 1981. "Accounting for International War: The State of the Discipline." *Journal of Peace Research* 18:1, pp. 1–18.

Skocpol, Theda. 1979. *States and Social Revolutions: A Comparative Analysis of France, Russia, and China.* Cambridge: Cambridge University Press.

Smith, Woodruff D. 1986. *The Ideological Origins of Nazi Imperialism.* Oxford: Oxford University Press.

Steinberg, Jonathan. 1965. *Yesterday's Deterrent: Tirpitz and the Birth of the German Battle Fleet.* London: Macdonald.

Stone, Norman. 1983. *Europe Transformed, 1878–1919.* Glasgow: Fontana.

Thompson, William R., and Gary Zuk. 1986. "World Power and the Strategic Trap of Territorial Commitments." *International Studies Quarterly* 30:3, pp. 249–267.

Väyrynen, Raimo. 1983. "Economic Cycles, Power Transitions, Political Management, and Wars Between States." *International Studies Quarterly* 27:4, pp. 389–418.

Varga, Eugen. 1935. *The Great Crisis and Its Political Consequences: Economics and Politics 1928–1934.* London: Modern Books.

Vasquez, John A. 1986. "Capability, Types of War, Peace." *Western Political Quarterly* 39:2, pp. 313–327.

Wagner, R. Harrison. 1984. "War and Expected-Utility Theory." *World Politics* 36:3, pp. 407–423.

Wallerstein, Immanuel. 1984. *The Politics of the World-Economy: The States, the Movements, and the Civilizations.* Cambridge: Cambridge University Press.

Weede, Erich. 1984. "Democracy and War Involvement." *Journal of Conflict Resolution* 28:4, pp. 649–664.

Wehler, Hans-Ulrich. 1973. *Das deutsche Kaiserreich 1871–1918.* Göttingen: Vandehoeck & Ruprecht.

Ziebura, Gilbert. 1984. *Weltwirtschaft und Weltpolitik 1922/24–1931: Zwischen Rekonstruktion und Zusammenbruch.* Frankfurt am Main: Suhrkamp.

Zinnes, Dina A. 1980. "Why War? Evidence on the Outbreak of International Conflict." In Ted Robert Gurr, ed., *Handbook of Political Conflict,* pp. 331–360. New York: Free Press.

PART THREE

Research on Conflict Resolution

5

What Is the Use
of Conflict Theory?

Håkan Wiberg

The Problem

Since the inception of peace research about a generation ago, it has often been stressed that it does not intend to become just one academic discipline among others; the prevalent opinion in the peace research community is that peace research is distinguished by being (or having the ambition to be) transdisciplinary, value-oriented, and applied research. "Peace" and "conflict resolution" indicate the values to be served by generating findings that are applicable in engendering them. To what extent have these ambitions been fulfilled, judging from the state of the art today? To attempt to answer this question, we first have to look closer at the goals, the concepts, the tools, the puzzles, and the solutions. Given the space available, I will have to simplify and focus on the essentials, at the expense of finer shades and empirical detail, and the References at the end of the chapter are intended more to indicate where the reader can find the more encompassing arguments and studies than to support the argumentation presented here.

The Goals

At first, "peace" and "conflict resolution" appear to be rather consensual values. At least, ceteris paribus, everybody is for them, even if there is certainly no consensus in regarding them as supreme values that take priority over all others. The obvious goals are to preserve peace, to create peace, to facilitate conflict resolution, to develop early-warning indicators for dangerous forms of conflict, and to find nonviolent means of acting conflicts out.

Yet this picture of consensus does not survive a closer look at these value-loaded concepts. Different cultures and political orientations have rather different conceptualizations of peace (Macquarie 1973; Galtung 1981) and so have different peace researchers (IPRA 1970; Johnson 1976). Conflict can be conceptualized in very different ways, implying different and partly contradicting interpretations of what conflict resolution is to mean. Nor is there much consensus about what research priorities follow from the indicated practical goals: They look different depending on your cosmological, epistemological, and theoretical point of departure. In this respect, peace research does not differ from, e.g., sociology.

The Concepts

The essential disagreements have been about the concepts of peace, conflict and conflict resolution, and violence. Greatly simplified, the issues are the following.

Peace

One option is to define peace as the absence of war (or some wider class of violent, or even other, conflict behavior). This definition is often referred to as "negative peace," which in its turn is short for "negatively defined peace" (there is no value connotation in "negative" or "positive" in this context). If this definition is chosen, peace gets the same epistemological status as war: an empirical concept with rather little ambiguity. The price paid for this unambiguousness is getting a concept that is theoretically poor, fairly Eurocentric, and even so at variance with common parlance. Even Thomas Aquinas stated that *absentia belli* does not equate *pax* in the absence of *justitia* ("the absence of war does not equate peace in the absence of justice").

The second main option, that of positive peace, is defined as the *presence* of something, and peace is defined as the combination of positive peace and negative peace. There have been many different proposals as to the positive definiens: integration, justice, harmony, equity, freedom, etc., all of which call for further conceptualization. Even if we follow one single author over time, we can find a series of different proposals (Galtung 1964a, 1969, 1981, 1985). Most or all of the proposed concepts are normative, and several are theoretically rich.

Negative peace can be said to be a conceptual least-common denominator, but the term is clearly too small to express a consensual value orientation. For that, we must have some combination, and the continuing debate about exactly what combination enriches peace research theoretically.

Conflict and Conflict Resolution

The first conceptual difficulty concerning the concept of conflict stems from the fact that both in everyday and scholarly language, the term may be used to denote some kind of behavior, some types of attitudes, some state of incompatibility or contradiction between the goals or interests of actors or parties, or some combination of these. That problem can easily be solved by using different terms. The next problem is rather a matter of priorities: Whether to focus on conflict behavior, in particular the most harmful kinds, and look for removable causes or to focus on goal conflict and study how it can be resolved.

The third difficulty is much more serious: how to conceptualize conflict in the sense of incompatibility. The first delimitation can serve as an epistemologically neutral point of departure: There is a conflict between A and B if, and only if, there is no possible distribution of values that is acceptable to both. When we dig deeper, however, we find one of the most contentious issues in the peace research community (IPRA 1970), and we can identify two main options.

The first of these options consists of thinking of A and B as actors, implying among other things that they have conscious goals, in which case a conflict subsists if—and to the extent that—the satisfaction of A's goals precludes that of B's goals (whether logically, by virtue of scarcity, or because of causal linkages). Conflict resolution, then, consists of changing reality (by reducing scarcity or by changing the causal links), changing the demands of the actors (by compromise, horse-trading, persuasion, or sheer manipulation), or both so that a distribution of values is found that is subjectively acceptable to both of the actors and therefore can be agreed to. This resolution may be achieved by the actors themselves or by various kinds of intervention by third parties and conflict resolution mechanisms. With this option, the key concepts become clearly empirical (which does not mean easy—any historian, socialist, or psychologist can produce a long list of methodological problems in cutting through propaganda, bargaining tactics, and self-image defenses to assess what *are* the true goals of an actor). There is, however, ample room—and need—for theoretical analyses of bargaining and negotiation behavior, institutions for conflict resolution, etc.

The other main option takes as its point of departure the fact that there are *objective interests,* which are independent of the subjective states of mind of actors. It is their interrelation that determines the existence and degree of conflict, which is often seen as "built into the system." Conflict resolution, then, can only be achieved, if at all, by changing important features of reality, such as a social or international structure. This option comes in several different versions. In the mainstream version of the Marxist tradition (see, e.g., Mandel 1973), the point of departure is the labor theory of value (although some people question its theoretical value, e.g., Steedman 1978; Cohen 1978). From this theory is defined surplus value; class interests, which essentially concern control over surplus value; and classes, which are theoretically defined on the basis of class interests. The questions left for empirical research include, What forms of control over surplus value—and hence, what classes—do we find in what kinds of societies? Under what circumstances do classes ("in themselves") crystallize into social and political actors ("classes for themselves")? What form does the class struggle take under what circumstances, and who wins when?

"National interest" can be conceptualized in several different ways (Frankel 1970). In some of them, it refers to the goals of individual decision makers or results from a bargaining process between different decision makers. In others, however, national interest is construed as a very long-term entity that transcends governments and regimes, being determined, e.g., by geographical, strategic, or economic factors. Morgenthau (1967) assumes that states necessarily strive to maximize power; other scholars make weaker assumptions, e.g., in terms of national security (profoundly analyzed in Buzan 1983). Among the common ideas we find the notion that conflict, given anarchy, is built into the international system independent of individual perceptions and goals. Still other definitions of "interest" build on natural law, on basic needs, or on living conditions (Galtung 1971). In spite of a number of important differences (whether parties are taken for granted or defined from interests, whether the definition of interests is normative or—allegedly—nonnormative, etc.), the analyses of interest share the orientation that if you decline subjective definitions of goals, you have to have a *theory* to identify the movers of action. They also all imply that conflict (of the types they study) cannot be resolved by agreement; at best, it can be ameliorated, e.g., in terms of conflict behavior. Resolution calls for important changes in social reality: abolition of exploitation, world federation, redistribution of material conditions, etc.

Violence

As in the case of peace, the choice regarding violence is essentially between a narrow empirical concept and a wider theoretical one, referred to, respectively, as "direct violence" and "structural violence." The latter term was coined by Galtung (1969), and the essential idea is that structural violence exists to the extent that people die or suffer serious harm unnecessarily, as a consequence of distribution of resources rather than of overall scarcity. This idea obviously makes the concept theoretical, since its application calls for a comparison between, e.g., *actual* mortality and what it *would have been* under certain assumptions. At the same time, Galtung and Høivik (1971) have worked out an empirical methodology for measurement, and various empirical studies have been made (Høivik 1971, 1977; Köhler and Alcock 1976; Alcock and Köhler 1979). The concept has remained highly controversial, on political, philosophical, and empirical grounds (Gronow and Hilppö 1970; Derrienic 1972; Boulding 1977; Pontara 1978; Galtung 1987).

More could be said about conceptual options (I have omitted a number of positions that lie in between the respective ideal types), and, as a rule, the quest for a choice can be countered by asking, Why not both? This question leads to whole sets of important research issues, for example, How do conflicts of interests crystallize into goal conflicts and their parties into actors? and How are direct and structural violence and positive and negative peace related to each other?

The Tools

Another way of discerning different kinds of conflict theory is in terms of epistemological strategies and the intellectual tools that are used. In reality, we find most of the instruments from the toolbox of social science employed in some kind of research about conflict, so I shall discuss here only some main examples linked to the main intellectual strategies.

In yet another grand simplification, we may discern three main types of strategy of analysis in conflict theory (that do not exclude each other), focusing, respectively, on entities, structures, and situations. In the first approach, the causes of war and similar conflict behavior between parties (or of developments in conflict processes, like confrontation and escalation) are assumed to be *properties of entities* like the parties themselves, the dyads of conflicting parties, or the systems in which the parties are located. The strategy then consists of trying to identify such causes, discern the removable ones among them, and do further research into how these can be removed. A primary tool in this strategy is statistical (primary or secondary) analysis of data collected for the purpose. In very primitive versions, it is assumed that this analysis in itself will generate knowledge. In more sophisticated versions—from the classics (like Richardson 1960) to more modern, vast empirical projects (Singer 1979; Rummel 1975–1981)—the focus is on systematic testing of hypotheses, whether derived from the researcher's own theory or from other theories he or she wants to examine. A generation ago, this tool was rather new in international politics and to some extent seen as specific for peace research, but this newness is hardly the case any longer, witness the great number of such studies that have been carried out (main overviews in Vasquez 1976; Rummel 1979; Zinnes 1980).

Another main tool, or set of tools, is structural analysis. Here, the underlying imagery is not so much in terms of properties as causes as one of the very structure being one of conflict, the conflicts of interest built into it continuing to engender (potentials for) direct violence until the patterns of interaction that define the structure are changed so as to define a new one. There are several orientations that fall into this category: traditional Leninist theory of imperialism, the Latin American dependencia school (e.g., Frank 1978), and "world system" theory (Amin 1974; Wallerstein 1979). Typically, the interest lies more with analyzing the structures than with producing explanations of war, although there are exceptions (like Wallensteen 1973). Structural analysis tends to develop in an interplay between general social theory and case studies, but there have also been attempts at systematic quantitative testing (e.g., Gidengil 1978).

A third main tool has been produced by game theory. This strategy can be seen—in one sense—as an extreme version of the actor paradigm; in which it is generally assumed, inter alia, that events take place as (not necessarily intended) consequences of purposive action that is intended to reach certain goals under certain means-end assumptions. Game theory has forced much more rigorous formulations of the components of such explanations and has tended to concentrate more on the strategic structures of the situations in which decision makers find themselves than on the psychology of the decision makers.

Game theory proper is a branch of mathematics (for recent presentations, see Davis 1983; Zagare 1984). Two or more players are posited to make (parallel or sequential) decisions in a situation in which the consequences for each depends on the choices of all and are known to be known by all players, who also know that all players are rational in the sense that they try to arrive at consequences that rank as high as possible in their respective preference orders, which are also known to all. (Varieties of the theory make diversely strong assumptions on these demands.) The fundamental problems concern what (axiomatically defined) rational players will do in different kinds of games. In some games (e.g., two-person zero-sum), there is a unique solution; in others, the solution is a whole set of solutions; and in still others, it turns out to depend on exactly how we conceptualize "rationality." In games in which the solution is not unique, an interesting problem is what is a fair arbitration, given the strategic properties of the game and what they imply in terms of what the players have no reason to accept.

Game theory has been used as a tool, or as a point of departure, in several ways. It has contributed to the conceptual clarification of such key concepts as "rationality," "fairness," and "utility" (Rapoport 1960; Wiberg 1972; Elster 1979). By providing insights into the structures of decision situations, it has also stimulated a lot of theorizing with substantial content, when combined with substantial assumptions about empirically given actors. On the microlevel, this has been the point of departure of thousands of experiments designed to investigate how behavior (especially cooperative or conflictive behavior) is affected by personality, social background, situational setting, type of game, interaction, etc. (for overviews, see Wrightsman, O'Connor, and Baker 1972; Colman 1982). A special variation, with very interesting results, has consisted of having one genuine player play against a preprogrammed computer, or even two computers against each other (Axelrod 1983). On the macrolevel, there have been many attempts to apply theoretical game analysis to various kinds of decisions so as to model, e.g., arms races, deterrence policies, crisis behavior, or economic policies (Rapoport, ed. 1975; Shubik 1975; *World Politics* 1985; Ordeshook 1986; Brams 1975, 1985). In some cases, these attempts have involved the testing of predictive hypotheses, but the predominant mode of analysis is that of postdictive interpretations with their risks of circularity (balanced by other gains).

For other than epistemological purists, these three tools of analysis by no means exclude each other. What tool, or what combination of tools, to choose is primarily a matter of what kind of puzzle we want to solve.

The Puzzles

Scientific development usually means not only that one gets answers to some puzzles but also that the very puzzles are restructured and reformulated in response to theoretical insights and empirical findings. This situation is no less true for peace research. Let me start by demonstrating this fact for one of the main puzzles in early peace research: What are the causes of violence?—and the sought answer was a general theory of violence. Today, this ambition has largely been abandoned, seen as a parallel to looking for a general theory of fever.

There are several reasons for this abandonment, but let me limit myself to empirical argument. If there *were* some general causes of violence, transcending the level of aggregation, then one would expect positive correlations between the extent to which states suffer from, e.g., homicide, domestic conflict, and international conflict. In fact, there is no significant relationship between homicide and domestic conflict (Tilly 1981, 107), nor between homicide and war (Haas 1965), and Rummel (1979, 345) summarizes an extensive review of studies on the relationships between domestic and foreign conflict by concluding that they are independent processes. The overall correlations between indicators of these types of conflict are close to zero, and it is only when one breaks the universe of states down by, e.g., type of regime (Wilkenfeld 1973) that one finds correlations in the subcategories— and even then different indicators of domestic conflict correlate with different indicators of foreign conflict and with different time directions, depending on the type of regime. Zero correlations, of course, are not final (Mack 1975), but their importance is strengthened by Rummel's predicting statistical independence on the basis of a theoretical argument. To the extent that factor analyses can be used to decide theoretical questions, the original puzzle evolves into at least three different ones: one concerning international war, one concerning intrasocietal war, and one concerning more amorphous collective violence, referred to as "turmoil," "riots," etc. I omit the individual level here for the reason that causes of individual violence seem to cast fairly little light on the different kinds of collective violence. Analogizing across levels of aggregation appears to have little to warrant it in empirical terms, even when we look at the more successful examples. Galtung's structural theory of aggression (1964b) implies that states in rank disequilibrium should be more belligerent. This result is not found; the amount of rank discordance in the entire system does correlate with the amount of war in the system, but only when lagged ten to fifteen years (Wallace 1971), a finding that is rather difficult to interpret. The (social) psychology of decision makers is certainly relevant to collective violence—but that is about decisions to use collective violence, not about engaging in individual violence.

There are other ways in which the original puzzle has been transformed over time. The quest for "natural laws" was both translevel and transhistorical, and much doubt has been cast on the second ambition, too, as systematic research has developed (Tilly, Tilly, and Tilly 1975; Tilly 1981). The general trends has been away from the quest for natural laws and toward a "rational actor" analysis of social conflict. This type of analysis can be seen in such an exponent of the natural law–type frustration/aggression perspective as Gurr (1970), much of whose reported findings contain so many references to values and perceptions as to make them immediately interpretable in rational actor terms, and it is a main theme in Tilly's vast empirical studies of contentious behavior in several European states over the last few centuries.

The puzzle of war has also been decomposed in another way, in terms of phasing the conflict process and dividing it into one puzzle about what long-term factors make crises and confrontations more likely and another puzzle about what short-term factors underlie the escalation of some crises into wars and what factors support conflict resolution in others. In addition, a number of new puzzles have been added, or old ones have been modified, as the area of peace research has been conceptually enlarged by, e.g., "structural violence" and "positive peace." These puzzles have already been hinted at.

Solutions

In the heading of this section, "The" has been carefully omitted. It would be grossly immodest to claim that conflict theory has been able, so far, to achieve much more than clarifying some of the puzzles and providing some fragments of solutions. Here I will not try to piece these fragments together into any idealized picture but indicate their general drift in a few propositions, omitting a number of needed reservations and qualifications.

First, the systemic puzzle of war is largely unresolved. From a methodological point of view, this situation is not strange. We only have one international system nowadays, and systematic testing of hypotheses must therefore resort either to collecting systems over a vast area of space and time (which raises serious issues of comparability) or to cutting the modern system up into time slices (which raises statistical problems on independence of observations). Let us look at two particular pieces: culture and power structure. Sorokin (1937), after going through 2,500 years of wars and trying to relate them to his distinction between sensate and ideational cultures, concludes that this distinction does not account for much difference. There seems to be agreement that multipolar international systems are the most warlike ones, and unipolar, or near unipolar, systems the most peaceful, with bipolar ones inbetween (Melko 1973; Haas 1974; Thompson 1986). The picture gets more intriguing when we formulate the issue in terms of how close to perfect bipolarity the system is: Different authors using different indicators get different results (Zinnes 1980). These differences may be accounted for by Wallace (1973), who works with curvilinear regressions and finds a U-shape: most war at very high and very low levels of bipolarization. There is the possibility that it is not so much the characteristics of the international system that count as *change*.

Sorokin finds the most warlike periods to be those of transition from one dominant culture to another, and Bueno de Mesquita (1975) finds much higher correlations between war and changes in indicators of polarity than between war and the indicators themselves.

Second, war is a relation. Put that bluntly, the statement appears trite, but there is much research behind it. Most of this research is negative: Ever since Richardson (1960), the typical result of statistical analyses of how various properties of states relate to war (and hundreds of properties have been considered) has been "zero correlation." The main exceptions, where several studies have pointed to the same results, can be formulated in three sentences. Great powers are much more involved in war than others. The more boundaries a state has, the more wars it has. The more armed a state is in relation to its size, the more wars it gets involved in. Interestingly enough, all three of these properties are largely relational ones.

This host of nonfindings may depend on the wrong methods having been used, such as bivariate instead of multivariate analysis (Mack 1975). Zinnes (1980) argues that we may be better able to identify states that are heavily involved in wars by combining two kinds of variables: one that changes slowly (like amount of resources, level of development, governmental structure) and one that changes more quickly (unemployment, civil strife, suicide rates). Even here, however, the results are largely negative, and a better explanation of the non-findings might be that we have looked at the wrong level: the unit instead of the dyad.

This idea is also backed up by a number of positive findings (a systematic overview can be found in Rummel 1979). Let me give just two examples. The likelihood that a military confrontation between two states will escalate into war increases with the armament level of either, and increases particularly strongly if the confrontation has been preceded by an arms race (Wallace 1979). Wallensteen (1973), linking economic structure to war, finds a clear relationship between the extent to which a state dominates a region economically and the extent to which it gets into war with states in that region (usually themselves satellites of the first power).

Third, conflict is a process. This statement, too, is less trite than it appears; otherwise, the proportion of quantitative research that tests process models, rather than correlating conflict behavior with properties of the parties or (initial) relations between them, would have been much higher than it actually is.

On the microlevel, the net results of a great many game experiments strongly underline this point. Whatever correlations are found between the traits of a player and his or her game behavior, there is one variable that usually correlates much higher: What the other player did in the next-to-last move (Rapoport and Chammah 1965; Axelrod 1983). On the mesolevel, this fact is one of the main points to be derived from Tilly's studies of contentious behavior. In the process of conflict, groups learn how to organize to express their grievances, how to pick from existing repertories of behavior, and how to renew them or avoid parts of them. We do far better with models of rational—and flexible—actors than with causal models a la Durkheim. On the macrolevel, this point also appears to be a major trend of research results. Constellations of state and dyad variables may affect the likelihood that confrontations will end in war, but they do not determine that ending since so much depends on crisis interaction and the extent to which other features of it can balance those, like groupthink and error of attribution, that tend to reduce rationality.

One major conclusion is that conflict resolution is possible but difficult. It is possible because there tends to be rather little predetermination in conflict and crisis situations. It is difficult because the structures of decision situations are often such that it takes wisdom and creativity to arrive at cooperative solutions that benefit both parties.

Much game theory and other literature on bargaining and negotiations provide guidelines in this respect, and from this point of view conflict theory is already potentially useful, to some extent. The word "potentially" indicates a point stressed by Raiffa (1982) in his epilogue: Those theories are rarely operational, and they provide little guidance as to their implementation in concrete situations. This point should be added to the agenda of future puzzles to resolve.

References

Alcock, Norman, and Gernot Köhler. 1979. "Structural Violence at the World Level: Diachronic Findings." *Journal of Peace Research* 16:3, pp. 255–262.

Amin, Samin. 1974. *Accumulation on a World Scale: Critique of the Theory of Underdevelopment*. New York: Monthly Review Press.

Axelrod, Robert. 1983. *The Evolution of Cooperation*. New York: Basic Books.

Boulding, Kenneth. 1977. "Twelve Friendly Quarrels with Johan Galtung." *Journal of Peace Research* 14:1, pp. 75–86.

Brams, Steven. 1975. *Game Theory and Politics*. New York: Free Press.

———. 1985. *Superpower Games*. London: Yale University Press.

Bueno de Mesquita, Bruce. 1975. "Measuring Systemic Polarity." *Journal of Conflict Resolution* 19:2, pp. 187–216.

Burrell, Gibson, and Gareth Morgan. 1985. *Sociological Paradigms and Organizational Analysis*. Aldershot: Gower.

Buzan, Barry. 1983. *People, States, and Fear: The National Security Problem in International Relations*. Brighton: Wheatsheaf.

Cohen, G. A. 1978. *Karl Marx's Theory of History: A Defence.* London: Oxford University Press.

Colman, Andrew M. 1982. *Game Theory and Experimental Games: The Study of Strategic Interaction.* London: Pergamon.

Davis, Morton. 1983. *Game Theory: A Non-Technical Introduction.* New York: Basic Books.

Derrienic, Jean-Pierre. 1972. "Theory and Ideologies of Violence." *Journal of Peace Research* 9:4, pp. 361–374.

Elster, Jon. 1979. *Ulysses and the Sirens.* London: Oxford University Press.

Frank, Andre Gunder. 1978. *Dependent Accumulation and Underdevelopment.* London: Macmillan.

Frankel, Joseph. 1970. *National Interest.* London: Macmillan.

Galtung, Johan. 1964a. "An Editorial: What Is Peace Research?" *Journal of Peace Research* 1:1, pp. 1–4.

———. 1964b. "A Structural Theory of Aggression." *Journal of Peace Research* 1:2, pp. 95–119.

———. 1969. "Violence, Peace, and Peace Research." *Journal of Peace Research* 6:3, pp. 167–191.

———. 1971. "A Structural Theory of Imperialism." *Journal of Peace Research* 8:2, pp. 81–117.

———. 1981. "Social Cosmology and the Concept of Peace." *Journal of Peace Research* 18:2, pp. 183–200.

———. 1985. "Twenty-five Years of Peace Research: Ten Challenges and Some Responses." *Journal of Peace Research* 22:2, pp. 141–158.

———. 1987. "Only One Quarrel with Kenneth Boulding." *Journal of Peace Research* 24:2, pp. 199–204.

Galtung, Johan, and Tord Høivik. 1971. "Structural and Direct Violence: A Note on Operationalization." *Journal of Peace Research* 8:2, pp. 73–76.

Gidengil, Elizabeth. 1978. "Centres and Peripheries: An Empirical Test of Galtung's Theory of Imperialism." *Journal of Peace Research* 15:1, pp. 51–66.

Gronow, Jukka, and Jorma Hilppö. 1970. "Violence, Ethics, and Politics." *Journal of Peace Research* 7:4, pp. 311–320.

Gurr, Ted Robert. 1970. *Why Men Rebel.* Princeton: Princeton University Press.

Haas, Michael. 1965. "Societal Approaches to the Study of War." *Journal of Peace Research* 2:4, pp. 307–323.

———. 1974. *International Conflict.* Indianapolis, Ind.: Bobbs-Merrill.

Høivik, Tord. 1971. "Social Inequality." *Journal of Peace Research* 8:2, pp. 119–142.

———. 1977. "The Demography of Structural Violence." *Journal of Peace Research* 14:1, pp. 59–76.

IPRA, Studies in Peace Research. 1970. *Proceedings of the International Peace Research Association Third Conference.* Vol. 1, *Philosophy of Peace Research.* Assen: van Gorcum.

Johnson, L. 1976. *Conflicting Conceptions of Peace in Contemporary Peace Studies.* Beverly Hills, Calif.: Sage Publications.

Köhler, Gernot, and Norman Alcock. 1976. "An Empirical Table of Structural Violence." *Journal of Peace Research* 13:4, pp. 343–356.

Mack, Andrew. 1975. "Why Big Nations Lose Small Wars." *World Politics* 27:2, pp. 175–200.

Macquarie, J. 1973. *The Concept of Peace.* London: SCM Press.

Mandel, Ernest. 1974. *Introduction to Marxist Economic Theory.* New York: Monthly Review Press.

Melko, Matthew. 1973. *52 Peaceful Societies.* Oakville, Ont.: Canadian Peace Research Institute.

Morgenthau, Hans. 1967. *Politics Among Nations.* 4th ed. New York: Knopf.

Ordeshook, Peter C. 1986. *Game Theory and Political Theory: An Introduction.* London: Cambridge University Press.

Pontara, Giuliano. 1978. "The Concept of Violence." *Journal of Peace Research* 15:1, pp. 19–32.

Raiffa, Howard. 1982. *The Art and Science of Negotiation.* London: Harvard University Press.

Rapoport, Anatol. 1960. *Fights, Games, and Debates.* Ann Arbor: University of Michigan Press.

Rapoport, Anatol, ed. 1975. *Conflict in a Man-Made Environment.* Baltimore, Md.: Penguin.

Rapoport, Anatol, and Albert Chammah. 1965. *Prisoner's Dilemma: A Study in Conflict and Cooperation.* Ann Arbor: University of Michigan Press.

Richardson, Lewis Fry. 1960. *Statistics of Deadly Quarrels.* Chicago: Quadrangle Books.

Rummel, Rudolph J. 1975–1981. *Understanding Conflict and War.* Vol. 1, *The Dynamic Psychological Field* (1975). Vol. 2, *The Conflict Helix* (1976). Vol. 3, *Conflict in Perspective* (1977). Vol. 4, *War, Power, Peace* (1979). Vol. 5, *Just Peace* (1981). Beverly Hills, Calif.: Sage Publications.

Shubik, Martin. 1975. *Games for Society, Business, and War: Toward a Theory of Gaming.* New York: Elsevier.

Singer, J. David, 1979. *Correlates of War.* Vol. 1, *Research Origins and Rationale.* Vol. 2, *Testing Some Realpolitik Hypotheses.* Beverly Hills, Calif.: Sage Publications.

Sorokin, Pitirim A. 1937. *Social and Cultural Dynamics,* vol. 3. New York: American Book Company.

Steedman, Ian. 1978. *Marx After Sraffa.* London: New Left Books.

Thompson, William R. 1986. "Polarity, the Long Cycle, and Global Power Warfare." *Journal of Conflict Resolution* 30:4, pp. 587–615.

Tilly, Charles. 1981. *As Sociology Meets History.* New York: Academic Press.

Tilly, Charles; Louise Tilly; and Richard Tilly. 1975. *The Rebellious Century.* Cambridge, Mass.: Harvard University Press.

Vasquez, John A. 1976. "Statistical Findings in International Politics: A Data-Based Assessment." *International Studies Quarterly* 20:3, pp. 171–218.

Wallace, Michael. 1971. "Power, Status, and International War." *Journal of Peace Research* 8:1, pp. 23–36.

———. 1973. "Alliance, Polarization, Cross-Cutting, and International War." *Journal of Conflict Resolution* 17:4, pp. 575–604.

_____. 1979. "Arms Race and Escalation: Some New Evidence." *Journal of Conflict Resolution* 23:1, pp. 3–16.

Wallensteen, Peter. 1973. *Structure and War: On International Relations, 1920–1968.* Stockholm: Rabén & Sjögren.

Wallerstein, Immanuel. 1979. *The Capitalist World-Economy.* Cambridge: Cambridge University Press.

Wiberg. Håkan. 1972. "Rational and Non-Rational Models of Man." In Joachim Israel and Henri Tajfel, eds., *The Context of Social Psychology.* London: Academic Press.

Wilkenfeld, Jonathan, ed. 1973. *Conflict Behavior and Linkage Politics.* New York: McKay.

World Politics. 1985. Special issue, *Cooperation Under Anarchy.* Vol. 38, no. 1.

Wrightsman, Lawrence S.; John O'Connor; and Norma J. Baker, eds. 1972. *Cooperation and Competition: Readings on Mixed-Motive Games.* Belmont, Calif.: Brooks/Cole.

Zagare, Frank. 1984. *Game Theory.* Beverly Hills, Calif.: Sage Publications.

Zinnes, Dina A. 1980. "Why War? Evidence on the Outbreak of International Conflict." In Ted Robert Gurr, ed., *Handbook of Political Conflict,* pp. 331–360. New York: Free Press.

6

Understanding Conflict Resolution: A Framework

Peter Wallensteen

Concepts of Conflict

The concept of "conflict" continues to be an elusive one in spite of efforts by peace researchers and social scientists to clarify it. Conflict theory was central to the peace research of the 1950s and the early 1960s, but by the end of the 1960s, it was meeting with powerful opposition. It appeared that much of the theorizing assumed a symmetry between parties and overlooked basic asymmetries in the world system as well as within national units and social entities.[1] The influence of Marxist thinking during the 1970s failed to bring conflict theory forward, in spite of some efforts to relate, for instance, dependency theory to the outbreak of war and to the creation of autonomous societies.[2] In the 1980s, there have been efforts to renew conflict theory.

Conflict theory remains an important and potentially integrative element in peace research. The common preoccupation with the phenomena of conflict necessitates theoretical work on basic concepts of analysis so that different perspectives and different observations can be brought together. Much work still remains to be done, but an increasing number of insights have been gained concerning the relationship between arms races and the outbreak of war, the internal driving forces of arms races, the differences among centuries and systems in producing war, etc. Still, remarkably little has been achieved in the field of conflict resolution.[3]

We still urgently need to come to grips with the general theory of conflict and conflict resolution, and in this chapter I offer some suggestions for integrating symmetric and asymmetric perspectives. Focusing on the basic incompatibility of a given conflict can prove a fruitful point of departure as such a focus takes research in a different direction than if one focuses on the outer ramifications of a conflict, such as the actions and the attitudes of the parties involved.

Let me define conflict as a social situation in which a minimum of two parties strive at the same moment in time to acquire the same set of scarce resources. This definition means that conflict is a social phenomenon that involves a necessary condition, scarcity. In addition, there are three basic requirements if scarcity is to lead to a manifest conflict, one that poses a serious challenge to life and property: actors, issues, and actions.

Scarcity plays a peculiar role, being at the same time part of the issue of contention (the incompatibility) and a factor in the creation of social structures, i.e., an element in forming the actors. As we shall see, dealing with scarcity is a central element in conflict resolution processes.

Obviously there have to be organized actors (parties) for a conflict to become manifest and for action to be possible. On a basic level individuals are actors, but in peace research the interest is directed to collective entities (social groups and organizations) that are equipped with certain capabilities (organizational structure, access to weapons). The actor orientation in conflict analysis has been challenged, however, and the utility of also studying conflicts among processes has been emphasized.[4]

There has to be a minimum of one issue of contention (I prefer the label *incompatibilities*): at least two parties simultaneously striving to acquire the same scarce resources(s). However, such an issue does not have to be consciously perceived by the parties. Incompatibilities may be recognized by only one party, or by a nonparty, an observer; i.e., they may be latent.

Finally, there has to be action, i.e., conscious behavior on the part of the parties to achieve their goals. Actions are accompanied by attitudes, and sometimes the actions carried out by the parties fall into a "gray zone" of perceptions. Behavior is rarely as easily interpretable as is believed. For instance, actions perceived by one party as non-conflictual, or even mutually constructive, might, by an opponent, be thought of as hostile and destructive even in situations in which the parties agree on their opposite roles and what the incompatibility is about. In this respect, actions differ from the other elements in the definition of conflict. Even if one party denies that a given action is aimed at the opponent, the victimized party will find it difficult to share this view.

The gray-zone nature of some actions has to do with the fact that in most conflicts, there is also something the parties agree on (apart from agreeing on being in conflict with one another). For instance,

Figure 6.1. Concepts in conflict theory

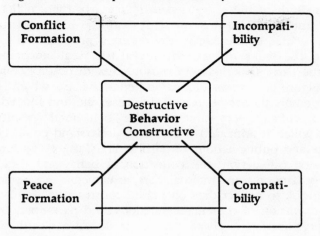

they might also be simultaneously striving for other goals that involve less scarce resources. Certain actions can bring out such "compatibilities" and thus reduce tension in a given conflict, eventually leading to a settlement.

The image of a threefold nature of conflict has long been used in conflict theory as a pedagogical way of illustrating its complexities. The conflict triangle, originally introduced by Johan Galtung but used by many others,[5] does not include actors or the formation of actors, and furthermore, it does not easily accommodate the reverse process, the peace-building aspect of the theory. Thus, it appears appropriate to complicate the issue further by incorporating these particular aspects (see Figure 6.1).

Figure 6.1 shows that peace thinking can focus on five different problems. First, the question of conflict formation results in analysis of the contradictions that are built into society: the organizing of actors, the influence of the actors, structural positions (topdog/underdog), the acquiring of (military) capabilities—i.e., analysis of actor preparation for action. This is the element that was most obviously lacking in the early attempts to establish conflict theory: The existence of actors was taken for granted.[6] As a matter of fact, a deeper understanding will be reached if the actor forming process is understood more completely. This element is particularly important since actors can be (and often are) formed to wage a particular conflict, that is, conflict is built into the actor forming process itself.

Second, that focus leads to analysis of incompatibilities, the goals stressed by the parties themselves (or as seen by an outside observer).

Often researchers have focused on questions of attitudes or formal statements. Both of these are necessary parts of the conflict, but the incompatibility itself requires an analysis of the history of the parties and, in particular, of the fate of the different propositions for conflict settlement. The latter analysis will reveal the "real" incompatibilities between the parties, as distinct from propagandistic pronouncements.[7]

Third, Figure 6.1. shows a focus on behavior itself, which is perhaps where the emphasis has been in peace research, and indeed, the first impetus to conflict theory came from the "behavioral revolution": The ease with which it appeared possible to understand conflict from the identifiable and public actions of parties. Thus, the 1960s saw a series of studies on interaction, the collection of behavioral data, and the amassing of data on wars, internal wars, armaments, etc. Some projects also undertook to collect data on more "constructive" behavior (such as trade, extension of diplomatic relations, and participation in international organizations). These studies produced a wealth of data, at least compared to the other elements of the conflict/peace process.[8]

Behavior has to be seen in terms of negative and positive transfers of value between parties. Negative actions, i.e., hostile and destructive actions between the parties, induce or maintain conflict. Positive actions, i.e., friendly and constructive actions between the conflicting parties, reduce conflict and lead to peace. As already noted, a perceptual problem is involved. Some, perhaps even most, actions are probably clearly understood in the same way by the parties (i.e., military actions), but some actions might be difficult to interpret. The extension of economic assistance from one party to another might be seen as a friendly gesture, but it might also be interpreted as a clever move aimed at subversion. One such case is the Marshall aid program, begun in 1947, and the ways in which it was officially perceived by the West and by the East. The contradictory interpretations of this particular program were colored by the overall perception of the incompatibilities among the parties.

An example of actions that are interpreted as positive by opposing sides in conflict would be the rescuing of innocent people in a disaster. A case in point is the agreement on a joint disaster-alert system between the United States and the USSR in the midst of strained relations between the two powers. The size of the gray zone of such interpretations might vary during a conflict, and in fact, the degree of agreement or disagreement of such interpretations of behavior is an indicator of the state of affairs of a given conflict. If both sides agree that actions are negative, the conflict is intensive; if there is agreement on a positive interpretation, the reverse is true; and if actions are interpreted in a contradictory way, the conflict is possibly in a volatile phase. The direction of movement, of course, can be determined only through an analysis of the previous phases of the conflict, and whether there is incompatibility or not is determined by a different set of analytical tools.

Fourth, the question of compatibilities, the existence of compatible goals between parties, needs to be analyzed. Surprisingly, little systematic analysis has been done in this field. It is perhaps typical that international law has produced analyses of procedural aspects (institutions for arbitration, mediation, etc.) rather than analyses of the substantial compatibilities.[9] The international negotiation machinery should be an important source of information. Furthermore, the situation inside units, where the consensus—at least theoretically—could be expected to be higher, requires more thorough analysis.

Finally, there is the question of peace formation. This aspect has often been treated on a vague theoretical level, in the form of proposals for a world government, regional organizations, or confederations. Often a quest for harmony lies behind such propositions. More concrete and realistic might be proposals that aim, for instance, at disarmament, which would also fall into this category: The actors may continue to exist, but they are not as "dangerous" when they are no longer armed. With the interest in the concept of "world order," this aspect has received renewed attention.[10]

Certainly there are a number of links among these different elements that can be studied. For instance, Which issues are the most likely to result in armed action? What is the connection between constructive action in one field (notably disarmament) and constructive action in another (reduction of tension over other incompatibilities)? and Which compatibilities are required for parties to be willing to reduce their armed capabilities?

Let me turn directly to the question of conflict resolution and to what Figure 6.1 can suggest in this regard. A number of different avenues open up. First, conflict resolution can mean the moving of the entire system of actors, issues, and actions away from a focus on incompatibility to a focus on compatibility. In this situation, the incompatibilities are still there, but the focus is changed in order to reduce the emphasis on conflict. Such a strategy of diversion of interest could involve, for instance, pointing out the many common interests that exist between the parties in the East-West conflict: ecological question, space exploration, poverty issues, etc. Mostly, such proposals do not deny the existence of conflict between the parties, but the hope is to make the incompatibilities, in the words of Galtung, "recede sufficiently into the background for the conflict to become non-salient."[11]

Second, the reduction of destructive action can be emphasized, such as by introducing third-party peacekeeping forces, erecting barriers between the parties, or stimulating the disengagement of military forces. In this category of action could also be included attempts to change the parties' perceptions of the conflict through education, normative considerations, or nonviolent actions (which build on rules restricting violent action).[12] The parties and their incompatibilities are left intact, but the conflict is pursued with other means: The conflict is transferred from a level of armed action to one of nonviolence. The incompatibilities, however, have not been removed.

The problem of these first two strategies is the same: They might enlarge the arena of conflict. In introducing new issues into the conflict in the hope of deflecting attention, they could bring about the reverse: a sharpening of attention and the discovery of more areas of conflict. Given that the basic incompatibility is general enough, not too much ingenuity would be required on either side to subsume the new elements into the old ones. However, there are so far no studies that would tell us what is the more likely outcome of such a strategy, or, under what conditions one of these strategies would result in a reduction rather than in a widening of contention. It appears, for instance, that the East-West conflict and the Arab-Israeli conflict have the potential of being "translatable" into almost any conceivable new arena. Other incompatibilities might be easier to deal with in this way, for instance, specific ethnic issues, and in such cases, these two strategies might be effective in containing conflict.

Third, conflict resolution could aim at transcending the incompatibilities as they are perceived by the parties themselves. This is a more restricted use of the concept of conflict resolution, and is the one preferred in this context, whereby conflict resolution means finding a solution to the basic incompatibility between the relevant parties in such a way that they (voluntarily) express their satisfaction with the outcome. This strategy does not necessarily or primarily involve an attempt to deflect attention or reduce the level of action.

This strategy, however does not exclude the first and second courses of action, and indeed, there might be important interaction. For instance, a cease-fire agreement is often seen as the first step toward the settlement of an incompatibility, and it could thus be part of a comprehensive strategy aimed at conflict resolution. The same is true for the idea of finding areas of mutual interest, again possibly broadening the area of action and inviting a change of attitude among the parties. With new interests being brought in, the political balance inside a given party might also change, giving more room of maneuver to those people who emphasize mutual interest. In the next section, an attempt is made to discuss systematically ways to transcend particular incompatibilities in order to indicate the range of possibilities that actually exist.

Fourth, there remain the problems of conflict formation and peace formation: the transformation of the parties and their mutual relationship. This strategy involves dissolving existing conflict formations and transforming them into peace formations. The central issue is the relationship between the actors, probably the most basic, hence the most difficult, issue of conflict analysis to grapple with. One must first tackle the problem of the existence of parties as parties. If it is true that parties have the supreme value of ensuring their own survival as a party, the solution of conflicts through the elimination of parties means the pursuit of conflict rather than the pursuit of peace. If any meaning is to be found for the elusive (but politically effective) concept of "national interest," it is the survival of the national entity as an entity of its own.[13] Few leaders appear ready to abandon their power in return for something that does not mean an increase of their own position, unless there is an orderly process to follow (with some chance of recovering their influence, for instance). Few units would easily accept their dismantling, whether they are political organizations, trade unions, or business enterprises. It sometimes appears that the essence of politics is the pursuit of organizational survival rather than more encompassing (not to mention compassionate) goals. Thus, any strategy to dissolve parties will be resolutely rejected by most parties in most situations.

More hope can be gained from observing the second problem, that the parties also strive for recognition, which is seen as a sign of the right to exist, preferably on an "equal" level. Recognition is an important value in itself as well as a means through which parties implement goals or live with their environment.

This question appears to be the subject of much of the discussion on dependence, the essence of which is often the unwillingness of a dominant party to listen to, appreciate, incorporate, or deal with the concerns of a dominated party. The underdog has to wage a conflict in order to establish itself as an equal—in a formal sense on a global scale and in a real sense on the local scene—in order to become accepted as a party and listened to. As such recognition means a change of power relationships, the topdog can be expected to resist and a struggle to follow.

A quick look at modern history shows that many existing states have engaged in such struggles for recognition, seeing themselves as rising from underdog positions: the American Revolution, which was directed against the British Empire, and the October Revolution, which was waged against an oppressive capitalist system, for instance. This pattern applies not only to states but also to trade unions, political parties, or even to business corporations. The present state of the world, as read by the parties, has emerged through struggle, sacrifice, and conflict. Much of this view is probably true, but so is the reverse: Many parties have not succeeded even though their sacrifices have been as great (or even greater) or their struggles more enduring. The parties of today, in other words, do not distinguish themselves from others because of their struggles but because of the fact that they won recognition and acceptance. Therefore, conflict formations actually can be dissolved through recognition and the real changes that such recognition involves, in order to end fighting but also perhaps before the fighting begins.

The third problem in dissolving conflict formations also involves dealing with the question of party formation itself. Often it appears that parties are the carriers of social conflict, which means that the mere forming of a party means the beginning of a conflict. Thus, the potential for societies to form new actors and new conflicts has to be part of the agenda of conflict resolution research. Conflict resolution studies cannot be content with just providing recipes for the handling of a continuous production of new conflicts. The formation of peaceful societies also has to be a part of the agenda. One starting point is the fact that different economic conditions generate different types of conflicts and different social structures generate different social issues. Conflicts in a slave society or a colonial state are different from those in capitalist and industrialist societies, for instance. Thus, the formation of conflict is linked to society as a whole. In a later section, I will consider some of these issues further and what they mean for the study of conflict resolution.

Transcending Incompatibilities

Incompatibilities are defined as situations in which two or more parties strive to acquire at the same moment in time the same scarce resource. Conflict resolution analysis focusing on incompatibilities tries to transcend the issue of contention between the parties. In this sense, the discussion is conservative. It "accepts" the parties, "allows" them to remain parties, and assumes mutual recognition. In this case, conflict resolution is for a particular set of conflicts, not all conflicts. Still, the discussion involves more than the mere freezing of a given (often militarily defined) status quo. A conflict is not settled by the mere fact that a cease-fire has been concluded and the weapons are silent. Transcending incompatibilities means changing the status quo, and it also gives the parties the joint experience of having overcome mutual contention to the mutual satisfaction of both sides.

From the definition, it follows that an incompatibility has three basic elements: mutually exclusive goals, scarce time, and scarce resources. All these elements are interconnected, as mutually exclusive goals involve either scarcity of time or resources (or both). The way the goals are presented by the parties influences the availability of time and resources. If the goals are formulated in an *absolute* way, a resolution might be more easily found, i.e., the parties strive to achieve a certain number rather than a certain share of the available resources. The numbers can be increased, or a compromise that gives a little to everybody can be found. If, however, the goals are put in a *relative* way, a resolution might be more difficult. If actor A wants 55 percent of all the available resources and actor B desires the same share, obviously an even split will not do; both parties want to have more than the other. In the first case, the parties can more easily change their goals because no principle prevents their doing so. In the latter case, such a principle ("more to A than to B") raises a barrier to a resolution of the conflict.

Thus, goals are changeable and so are many resources. Scarcity might not be total even though it often appears to be so. In this perspective, time and other resources are similar, as time can be regarded as a resource. Time lies ahead, in that sense it is without limits, but the lifetime of the parties limits their ability to consume this particular resource. As a result, incompatibilities involve two fundamental questions for conflict resolution: Assuming that the goals are constant, are the scarce goods variable? and Assuming that the scarce good is invariable, are the goals changeable in a way that promotes conflict resolution?

Scarce Resources

Scarce resources are often divided into material and nonmaterial ones, and the latter involves, for instance, time, sovereignty, or status. Furthermore, I have also indicated the importance of how goals are formulated. The most significant distinction, from the point of view of conflict resolution, is probably the goal formulation, that is, whether goals are defined in variable-sum terms (i.e., a certain amount) or in zero-sum terms (i.e., a particular order or priority). Let me illustrate this point by studying one nonmaterial and one material good: time and money.

If the goals of the parties are couched in absolute terms, the important question is whether the resources can be increased and/or divided. To increase available resources in a conflict involving money means that previously not included resources are brought into the picture, for instance, by loans or grants or by redefining the resources available. If the resources increase, both parties can simultaneously meet their goals. The conflict resolution task becomes one of inventing ways in which available resources can be made to increase. In fact, solving conflicts over economic issues seems to be one of the most common forms of conflict resolution, and it is carried out daily, whether via market mechanisms or in other ways. Concerning the nonmaterial resource, time is a constant only in the way it is perceived by the parties. For instance, the number of years available to the parties can be extended for a period not originally envisioned by them. This extension is parallel to the increases in money resources that are possible in conflicts over economic issues. Similarly, as time goes by and no solution is reached, much of the meaning of a conflict might disappear, because as an issue becomes old, it might become obsolete and irrelevant. Furthermore, since time can be divided, the time available can be shared among the parties.

The combining of resources, such as time and money, is a useful way to handle a particular incompatibility as this method can make it possible for the parties to find agreement without substantially changing their goals. Thus, actor A might have its demand, X units of resource R, met during the time period t_1, and actor B might get desired Y units of the same resource during the time period t_2. With the help of time, resources can be increased. In this way, the conflict is transcended, and there is no more conflict because the scarcity has disappeared.

Time and money are resources that can be both increased and divided, at least with respect to the perceptions of the parties. What about other resources that are not so easily seen in incremental terms but appear fixed, such as territory? Two parties contending for the same territory cannot be satisfied equally as the territory cannot easily be expanded. (Sometimes it can be increased, however, by claiming land from the sea or from the forest.) If the parties' attitudes to the territory are instrumental, i.e., to draw certain benefits from the territory, the conflict can be reformulated into one of joint exploitation and a fair sharing of the benefits/losses. If the attitudes are more expressive or symbolic, i.e., containing values that are dear to beliefs, the question might instead become one of preservation and access. In territorial disputes, in other words, the analysis becomes important: What is it really that the parties desire, and are their desires necessarily incompatible?

In many situations, a closer analysis shows that the disputed resource might not necessarily be the territory as such but the control of it. Thus, two states disputing a given piece of borderland are, in fact, concerned about control over that land rather than the area itself. Control, then, is the scarce resource really in dispute: The two parties believe they cannot have equal control at the same time. However, control, although not as nicely measurable as time or money, still is a variable resource. In fact, the lack of a clearly agreed way of defining "control" simplifies the search for compatible positions. There are different forms of control, such as control implied in concepts of sovereignty, administrative control, and popular rights. Thus, forms of divided control over a particular territory could be imagined: one party exercising control in terms of sovereignty, another one in terms of administration, and the inhabitants given a choice of citizenship or residential area.

Two factions competing for control of the same territory could divide the control by managing different bodies of the central authority (a closer scrutiny of the parties' positions might reveal that they actually desire to achieve very different things). This procedure is customary in parliamentary coalitions. Alternatively, the parties might agree to alternate control over time, something that is also a part of the parliamentary system through the regulation of time in office. Thus, it is not impossible; to increase and/or divide even so limited a value as territory: It might be the scarce resource of territorial control that is changed rather than the area itself. It is even possible to solve a conflict by having the parties agree to not exercise any control at all over a given area. Neutralization has been one solution in the post–World War II era, and the creation of an independent state as a buffer zone between rival major powers was a model in the nineteenth century.

Obviously, control is closely related to other values such as prestige and status. In a similar way, such resources can also be increased, for instance, by creating particular posts within an administrative hierarchy or by decentralizing government authority to create more de facto power to divide between the contenders.

The situation becomes more problematic when the goals are formulated in relative terms. Such is the case when actor A wants *more* than actor B, no matter how much A gets in absolute terms. Also, an agreement in which A as well as B in due time will each have its share might still leave the problem of who is going to receive its share first. The conflict is one of priority. Such conflicts can be based on prestige, with one party claiming superiority in one way or another (morally, on the basis of age, historically, legally, militarily, etc.), but they can also originate in fear—the agreement might not last so each party wants to secure its own share. A number of resolution attempts have foundered because of a stalemate over this type of issue: "We expect you to make the first move"; "If you do this, then we will carry out our part"; etc.

To be "first" involves the nonmaterial resource of time; to get "more" often involves material resources. In the latter case, the problem again is one of measurement. To have more depends on "more of what?" The measures might not be particularly clear to the parties, and consequently, formulas could be found to satisfy this demand without the opposing party even clearly experiencing a "loss." In fact, many conflicts that are based on a relative distribution of resources can be treated as conflicts of absolute distribution. Questions based on being first are more difficult to handle. When time is the disputed resource, it is obvious which party gets its share first; when control is disputed, it might be generally agreed that certain resources are more central than others—to control the capital, to control a legendary city, to be the president or the prime minister, etc. Such relative conflicts might be almost impossible to transcend unless one of the parties changes its goal.

In situations in which "first" means "not second," formulas can be worked out. For example, in diplomatic disputes, the parties can enter a room from different doors so that neither enters after the other. In situations in which "first" really means "before you, not parallel to you," neither an increase in nor a division of resources will do. Thus, such conflicts become important to study with respect to the variability of goals as the scarce good is no longer, by definition, variable.

Voluntary Change of Goals

Absolute as well as relative conflicts of the types just described can be transcended through a voluntary change of goals by one or more of the involved parties. It is important to stress the concept of *voluntary* change, i.e., a change that is not forced upon the parties. The use of arms between antagonists is intended to force a change upon the opponent (if not to eliminate the party altogether). Conflict resolution must, however, build on the principle of voluntary consent. It seems incompatible with a conflict resolution strategy to contribute to military pressure on one of the parties.

Changes in goals require that a previous position held by one or both parties is modified or abandoned. The changes can be unilateral or multilateral: In the former case, one party abandons its position in favor of coming closer to the opponent; in the latter case, both change (simultaneously or in consecutive order). However, no party can easily change its previous position as mental and physical energy have gone into formulating and defending it. A party needs a legitimate format for changing its position so that it can do so without jeopardizing its existence as a party or giving rise to an internal revolt.

There appear to be five basic ways of thinking that are used, individually or in combination, by parties to legitimize changes in position in public deliberations (and probably in internal ones as well):

- We have been pursuing the wrong (mixture of) goals.
- Our (most important) objectives have been achieved.
- The right procedure has now been applied.
- The objectives of the opponent have been frustrated.
- The other party has changed its goals (and so can we).

In the list, the reasons for changing the goals are described in terms of "right" or "wrong" in order to reinforce the point. In reality, parties will seldom explicitly agree that any drastic change has taken place. Mostly, changes will be announced openly and strongly only if there is a change in power inside the party (new leadership, a revolution) or if the parties jointly agree on a settlement (and then, the focus is on what was achieved rather than on what was not achieved and, in particular, on what the opponent did not accomplish).

A party might arrive at the conclusion that a "wrong" goal has been pursued by noting that the goal itself is not achievable and the party has simply departed from false theoretical or scientific principles. Changes in priorities are perhaps more likely to occur, for instance, the party or parties might eventually agree that mutual survival is preferable to continued danger and destruction: The costs of continuing an armed struggle might outweigh the benefits.

Goals might be dropped simply because a party realizes it has been asking too much; indeed, this seems to be the most common reason for reducing demands. At the outset, a party's demands will be highly general, as it might expect a rapid victory, but after a protracted struggle, some demands are abandoned, presumably in favor of the more essential ones. The opposite procedure is, of course, also possible: Instead of stubbornly sticking to only a very particular and narrowly defined demand, the party might actually make agreement possible by including additional goals.

The most typical reason is perhaps the claim that the "right mixture" has been achieved. Compromising and horse trading involve a give and take, and in their complex form, the package deal, they will involve so many different elements that it is impossible for the parties themselves (not to mention outsiders) to sort out who has won and who has lost. Thus, both parties might be able to say that the right mixture has been achieved—and they might very well be right if the agreement turns out to be durable.

A most interesting and innovative approach is the one suggested by Galtung in his work on institutionalized conflict resolution. By finding a procedure that is outside the contest, the parties can agree to change goals. In this case, the decision is the result of a procedure that has given a fair chance to each party. Although the outcome is not the desired one, the procedure is still the only acceptable one. Thus, a party can accept a defeat, even a significant one.[14] Examples of such procedures are for intranational conflicts, the democratic and legal systems; for international affairs, the UN Security Council (where the wording of the resolutions has to contain the "right mixture" in addition to the UN system's being acceptable to the parties); and arbitration. Such decisions might, of course, spark a new conflict and thus lead to a demand for new procedures, but such a result would involve other parties, which means that the first conflict has been resolved after all.

A separate problem concerns the timing of conflict resolution. What are the right moments for what types of conflict resolution? There have been some studies of this problem, and they suggest that a "ripening" process has to take place. Timing belongs to the important but nevertheless technical or procedural aspects of conflict resolution.[15]

Finally, it is important to consider what kind of solution is important for what kind of conflict. As the parties can disagree about who the parties are as well as about what they disagree on, different approaches might be required.[16]

Dissolving Conflict Formations

The settlement of existing incompatibilities rests on a mutual respect among the parties involved. The demands by one opposing side are taken by both sides to be acceptable demands, but not acceptable solutions to the problem, when the parties regard one another in a *symmetric* fasion. Much of the writing on conflict theory and conflict resolution has this as an explicit or implicit point of departure. However, the criticism of the early attempts to formulate conflict theory attacked this very assumption. The conflicts, it was argued, became intrinsically different if the parties approached one another in an *asymmetric* fashion. This argument refers to several different aspects of the relationship between the actors. Foremost among these seem to be the following:

1. asymmetric recognition: only one party is legitimate, the other(s) being defined as illegitimate

2. asymmetric principles of conflict and conflict resolution: one party is favored by existing rules over the other(s)
3. asymmetric participation in decision making: one party has (access to) more power than the other(s)

Together these asymmetries form fundamental aspects of topdog-underdog relations. Obviously, the distribution of power in the contemporary world tends to be highly skewed among states, within states, and between states and other types of actors. These factors taken together provide some of the reasons for the emergence of conflict and for conflict formation. Once asymmetries, or injustices, have been observed and described, an organization or organizations might be established, some of which might be prepared to wage armed conflict. Thus, the question of conflict resolution also has to involve the question of dissolving conflict formations.

The underlying principle for dissolving conflict formations often involves the idea of establishing symmetric relations between the parties. There are several conceivable ways in which such symmetry can be achieved: by awarding a similar status of recognition to the parties, through mutually agreed principles of conflict resolution, and through equal participation in decision-making. This principle also brings us back to the question of social structure.

Mutual Recognition

In a conflict in which the combatants do not regard one another as equal, positive interaction and negotiation will be difficult. If one side is defined as criminal by the other, contact is almost by definition excluded. If both sides have the same perception, obviously no one will be interested in working out a constructive relationship. In such a situation, recognition takes on not only a legal quality but also a moral one. If the other side is immoral, the one extending recognition runs the risk of being immoral as well. The problem is not one of academic or philosophical interest but of real consequence. For instance, Germany during the Nazi regime was seen as being both criminal and immoral, so the Allied decision to demand unconditional surrender was not only a realistic one but also a morally appealing one.[17] Also, dilemmas emerge on high levels, such as when "realities" force governments to extend recognition to regimes that are regarded as criminal.[18]

It appears that the interstate system is generally more equipped for handling this problem than the intrastate system, as most states agree on who the other states are—the moral question of regime quality remains unsolved, however. Given that most of the world's territory has been divided among states, the recognition of other states is fairly complete. International law, treaties, and conventions specify how relations are to operate.

However, the interstate system, in a world of increasing interdependence, faces new problems. It is no longer (say since 1947) common to ask for revisions of borders or to demand the elimination of entire states. Instead, the problem is which government to recognize within an already recognized territorial state. For a long period of time, the United States refused to recognize the regime in Beijing (1949–1978) or the one in Hungary (1956–1963). Similarly, the Soviet Union did not recognize West Germany until 1955. One solution has been to argue that the *legitimate* government is the representative of a given state, which means focusing on the process by which a given government has come into being. The rules of selection of a government within a given state become decisive. If, as is often true, governments have different ideas about what legitimate processes should be used, there is a fair chance that some governments will not be recognized by others. Such disagreements are at the heart of the disputes around who "really" represents China, Germany, Korea, Vietnam, and Kampuchea. This problem means, strictly speaking, that the internal affairs that determine what kind of a regime a given country has become an international issue. This situation is probably more true in the post–World War II period than it was before, and it indicates that the distinction between interstate and intrastate relations is becoming increasingly unclear.

The problems of recognition of parties in intrastate conflicts have several features. First, the methods of selecting governments are highly diverse. Second, such processes are often not particularly well adhered to. Third, there is, within most states, disagreement as to which parties are to be accepted as parties at all. When one party that is outlawed by some standards takes power, that fact obviously affects the intranational as well as the international pattern of recognition. Fourth, some evidence suggests that armed conflict is more common within states than among them, which means that intrastate problems have far-reaching consequences for the concept of conflict resolution in general. Fifth, a considerable number of intrastate conflicts concern the very existence and extension of given states, i.e., they have to do with the process of state formation. Consequently, the problem of recognition becomes even further complicated as recognition of certain actors could initiate similar challenges in other states.

How, then, are conflicts over recognition solved? Most such conflicts seem to find a "diplomatic" rather than a "real" solution as ways of living with conflicting representational demands are found. In a way, the day-to-day necessities force such nonsolutions on the parties: Economic transactions have to take place; human relations require some contact across highly sealed borders, directly or indirectly; etc. Such working arrangements, however, need a long time to be established, and foremost, they need to be built on some implicit recognition of the facts of life, i.e., that a given party does have de facto control over some territory and is administering it. Such recognition does not come easily. In the first phase of relations, it is more likely that each party waits for changes within the other. Only when such changes seem unlikely is recognition possible. Thus, it took more than twenty years to find a formula for intra-German relations, and formulas for Korea and China still have to be developed.[19] As could be expected, the outside world often is quicker to accept the realities, establishing de facto relations with both contenders.

The problem of recognition comes at an early stage, in particular when formalized negotiations are to be entered into. Indeed, informal contacts seem to be less uncommon among foes than is normally thought. There are several ways of establishing such links. For many years, the United States and the People's Republic of China negotiated through their respective embassies in Warsaw. The exchange of prisoners of war provides another channel of contact. However, any settlement involving the survival of both opposing parties will ultimately require some formal arrangement involving at least a minimum of formal recognition. Thus, the shape of the table for the Paris Peace talks during the Vietnam War became an issue: The seating was seen to reflect the actual constellation of parties on the battlefield, and since mutual recognition was lacking, a diplomatic solution had to be found.

To bring about recognition between two warring parties has sometimes been seen as a way to bring a war to a halt. Thus, four African states decided to recognize Biafra during the Nigerian War in the late 1960s, in the hope that this action would create a more symmetric relationship between the warring parties and thus make negotiations possible. Similarly, the PLO has managed to amass broad global support to force recognition of the PLO on Israel and thus make negotiations possible. Neither of these two attempts have been successful. Still, a party in conflict will be sensitive to the success of its opponent in gaining such recognition. The Federal Republic of Germany and the People's Republic of China objected to the recognition of "two Germanies" and "two Chinas" and actively tried to prevent the establishing of relations with the opponent. This policy was abandoned in the first case, in exchange for a general relaxation of tension, and has increasingly been circumvented in the second case, with most countries having de facto relations with Taiwan, particularly in the economic field. However, the refusal of recognition can prevent any actual settlement of a dispute for a considerable period of time. Indeed, to gain time might well be what is hoped for. Behind the refusal of recognition may lie the expectation that the conflict may eventually be won and a settlement avoided.

Obviously, the strategy of nonrecognition of any of the parties could be reverted to by the surrounding world. This approach would also result in a symmetrical relationship and provide possibilities of negotiation. The proclamation of neutrality by some states in wars between other states could be seen as a self-preserving action *and* as a declaration of nonrecognition of the aims and ambitions of any of the parties. From the perspective of the warring parties, neutrality will appear immoral; from the perspective of conflict resolution, it might be an important asset.

Mutually Agreed Upon Principles of Resolution

The following statement may seem like a truism, but nevertheless it cannot be repeated often enough: If there are available and reliable means for a nonviolent settlement of disputes, parties will most likely prefer those to military action. Thus, the absence of mechanisms of conflict resolution stimulates military action and, similarly, makes the settlement of armed conflict increasingly difficult. However, there is never a complete lack of such mechanisms, either in the interstate system or in intrastate relations. The problem is more difficult. The parties may perceive, more or less consonant with the verdict of an impartial observer, that the existing mechanisms are operating unfavorably and therefore are not reliable. This problem appears to apply to international law, which is believed to be too closely identified with European nineteenth-century politics and less relevant for today's problems of nuclear weapons and Third World demands for change. Similarly, in internal politics laws can be set up in such a way as to favor certain parties over others, even though the other parties might be accepted as parties in their own right. The history of rigged elections is a long one.

Symmetry can be created in two separate ways, however. First, all parties may participate in the formation of the rules as well as in the deliberations of the mechanism. This method largely applies to what takes place in the political process in international as well as in intranational relations. Second, none of the parties may participate in the making of rules and in deliberations. Instead, the rules gain legitimacy by tradition, divine authority, overall effectiveness, or their ability to give an equal and "fair" chance to each party. The last point might be most crucial. The PLO is using the resolutions of the UN General Assembly to support its position. Israel does not accept this stand, as it believes it has not had a fair chance of being heard by that particular organization. In a number of conflicts, parties have been reluctant to use the alternatives available as there might have been less than a fair chance of a decision in one's favor. The Falklands/ Malvinas conflict showed this situation clearly as there was an unwillingness to use the International Court of Justice. In asymmetric conflicts, the criterion of fairness might be decisive.

If there is a difference between international and intranational relations in terms of asymmetry, this field of research is probably an important one. Interstate relations have fewer such mechanisms, simply because, in their extreme, they would have to be more powerful than states. In intrastate relations, however, the systems of courts, parliaments, or elections can handle some disputes. The interstate system, in other words, requires more innovation; the intrastate system most likely requires a more equitable use of already existing systems.

Challenges to existing arrangements are important in asymmetric conflicts, and thus legitimate mechanisms of conflict resolution might be more difficult to establish. In fact, the interesting problem becomes, How to create new mechanisms? The historical record of conflict resolution suggests that a particular mechanism is useful for a period of time but sooner or later it requires replacement as the development of skills in circumvention reduces confidence in the mechanism. Thus, there might be a need for a continuous search for "better" or "more consensual" mechanisms. No arrangement is likely to be eternal. As an indication of this fact, very few political constitutions remain in their original form; instead, there are constant revisions, and indeed, most constitutions provide for such change.

For interstate relations, there is also the possibility of developing arrangements that are intentionally temporal in nature. Such mechanisms deal with particular issues or with conflicts arising from particular treaties or agreements. Thus, the resort to ad hoc measures, rather than to permanent institutions, would be one way of solving the asymmetries. This method might satisfy the parties that particular procedures are being applied. One example is the special arbitration to settle the economic issues of the hostage crisis between the United States and the Islamic Republic of Iran (a situation in which the parties did not have confidence in the established procedures and in which the Iranian side in particular questioned most of the existing mechanisms).

I do not mean to imply that such special arrangements, in due course of time, might result in a system of rules. Each such arrangement becomes a precedent that might be looked to when searching for a solution to other conflicts. Thus, the special arrangements will contribute to a reform of the presently existing rules, making them more consonant with the expectations of large audiences. In the long run, conflict resolution can lead to new ways of organizing the world.

Equal Participation

The problem of asymmetry is a problem of dominance. Decisions that are made without the actual involvement of all concerned parties will largely reflect only the interests of the participating parties. The rules of recognition and the rules of conflict resolution, for instance, are based on rules developed by the parties having the power to implement them. Conflicts challenging these particular rules may come from the parties that have no influence on the formation of the rules.

The question arises whether it is possible to construct a world order that would give a "fair" amount of influence to each party. Obviously the historical record is limited. Major global decisions have largely been in the hands of some few actors, mostly the major powers. The internal political scene may, theoretically, have an advantage over the interstate one, as it might be easier to identify concerned groups or to identify rules of participation. The democratic procedures directly address this particular problem. Empirically, such situations are found in only a few states. An interstate system that suggests an equality of parties (as in the UN General Assembly) is contravened by the concentrated distribution of power (as in the UN Security Council), but it also indicates a problem between nonstate actors and states, as many of the former (although not represented) might be much more significant than some of the latter (compare a multinational corporation with a small island state, for instance).

The most promising attempts to create equal participation have focused on actors that already are equal in influence and stature. The different concerts and leagues of major powers are examples of such attempts, as are efforts to establish regional organizations outside major-power influence (Nordic cooperation, for instance). All of these attempts build on the assumption that the involved parties are approximately equal and do not depend unilaterally on the others. This situation suggests that a degree of equal distribution of power among the participants is a necessary precondition, but it is also part of the continuing process. Attempts by one party (or a coalition of some) to enforce its will seem to frequently result in the disruption of the order rather than in actual control over it.

Consequently, the solution to the asymmetry problem might be sought in the creation of symmetry through more autonomy rather than the reverse. Only if parties can enter into cooperation via autonomous decisions will the order created be built on a solid foundation. An imposed order will last only as long as the party imposing it has the power to do so, no longer.

Equal participation might rest on the attainment of autonomy first, meaning, in many cases, withdrawal from an existing arrangement and rejoining it at a later stage but under new conditions. However, autonomy remains an elusive concept, and at some point it can be related more to recognition than to the establishment of equality between parties. In a world of inequalities, formal recognition can dissolve a conflict formation, but then the formal aspect is not simply symbolic but involves actual participation in decisions. The decisions, in turn, might not necessarily or immediately change the underlying inequalities, but they could, in the long perspective, mean a substantial shift in them. In this perspective, the entire UN negotiation machinery is of interest. That body means at least formal participation for all states, and thus, some impact is exerted on the final outcome. This outcome, to be sure, has been quite different from what the major states had anticipated or preferred. Still, those powers retain the possibility of successfully resisting the application of the outcome, as is shown by the position of the United States on Law of the Sea issues and the frequent use by the USSR of its veto in the Security Council.

Social Structures

The asymmetry problem cannot be dealt with only as a procedural issue as substantive issues are also involved. This fact brings us back to the notion of scarcity. Scarcity is a strong driving force; it is the ultimate determinator of the distinction between haves and have-nots. The fundamental issue in matters of equal distribution is the handling of scarcity. The definition of scarcity is partly culturally determined, and it is partly a matter of material needs. Access to economic goods determines the material well-being of individuals and of societies; access to less material needs, such as status and power, influence social standing. Therefore, in a fundamental sense, there is an inbuilt stratification in much of human activity. From the point of view of peace research, many types of stratification are probably of little interest. But some are, in particular those types of stratification that relate to the question of violence and war. It has been suggested that there are four clusters of values that are probably more likely than others to relate to violent conflict: issues of territory, military resources, ideology, and economics. In contrast, sports and music, for instance, involve considerable human effort and tension but rarely result in large-scale or global uses of violence.[20] The Marxist distinction of between antagonistic and nonantagonistic contradictions refers to this point.

Surprisingly little systematic peace research work has concerned the issue of what types of stratification are related to violence and war. The fact that major powers are more frequently at war than are most other actors is often taken for granted or is left unexplained. But this fact should probably be seen in the light of stratification: To come to the top requires considerable military resources and involvement in direct violence. To remain on top requires resources and military action. Decline will also be associated with warfare, however, so the interest in hegemonic war is thus of importance[21] as it relates to shifts and changes in society as a whole. The parties will change during the course of events and so will the incompatibilities and the actions. The conflict resolution aspect is whether these changes result in formations, or societies, that are less violent than the previous ones, or whether they simply invite a repetition of the old pattern (or worse, result in more conflict).

Conflict patterns change in other ways as well. The conflicts among feudal lords, kings, and subjects are no longer important, not because the lords and kings are now voting, but because they are no longer important actors determining the direction of society. This change means that society is, over time and through its own social and economic development, eliminating some types of conflict. These are not merely technological changes but profound social changes that lead to the replacement of one set of social incompatibilities by another. Such societal and structural changes have not received the attention of peace researchers, perhaps because the researchers have been using too short a time perspective. A deeper understanding of this issue requires information about conflict patterns that is accumulated in a way different from information about war patterns. It requires judgment about qualitative differences as well.

This area is a new and important challenge to peace research. It is important if we are to answer the fundamental question of where conflicts really come from. How are the actors formed that pursue conflict? What is the significance of scarcity for the generation of new actors? How have such transformations been handled in history? What examples are there of violent and nonviolent transformation?

Although conflict theory seems to assume a constant production of social conflicts, it must also acknowledge that there are variations over time and space in the occurrence of conflict. But the focus need not be on the generation of conflict but on the ways in which conflicts are handled and the forms that are produced to resolve them. This type of research might very well provide a catalog of the richness of human creativity.

Conclusion

Conflict theory and conflict resolution continue to be of central concern in peace research. The criticism of these concepts in the late 1960s led to an abandoning of any concerted effort in this area. Particularly, the question of symmetric and asymmetric relationships created problems within existing approaches. However, I am suggesting that such problems can be treated with some extension and elaboration of existing frameworks. By delineating two separate, but nevertheless interlinked, sets of problems, conflict theory can again emerge as a fruitful field for peace research efforts. It is suggested that there is, on the one hand, conflict material relating to the concept of incompatibility. This concept builds on a basic assumption of symmetry between the conflict parties. The issue in conflict resolution is the transcendence of such incompatibilities, and I have suggested a framework. On the other hand, there is also conflict material relating to the existence of the parties themselves and to their mutual relations. These are questions of conflict formation or party formation, and they relate to issues of recognition, principles of resolution, equality of participation, and the societal structure in which the parties are operating, in short, patterns of dominance. By dissolving conflict formations, such conflicts can also be resolved. The usefulness of these conceptions have to be tried in empirical study, but I believe that this particular framework might be useful in transcending the incompatibility between some early conflict theories and their critics.

Notes

The author is grateful for comments on this chapter by Miroslav Nincic, New York, and Kjell-Åke Nordquist, Uppsala.

1. Central works were, for instance, L. Coser, *The Functions of Social Conflict* (New York: Free Press, 1964); K. Boulding, *Conflict and Defense* (New York: Harper, 1962); A. Rapoport, *Fights, Games, and Debates* (Ann Arbor: University of Michigan Press, 1960); J. Galtung, "Pacifism from a Sociological Point of View," *Journal of Conflict Resolution* 3 (1959), pp. 67–84, and "A Structural Theory of Aggression, *Journal of Peace Research* 1 (1964), pp. 95–119. The most important criticism was raised by H. Schmid in "Politics and Peace Research," *Journal of Peace Research* 5 (1968), pp. 217–232.

2. Some of the impetus came from A. G. Frank, *Capitalism and Under-development in Latin America* (New York: Monthly Review Press, 1967), but many of the points were rapidly incorporated in peace research thinking, although the focus shifted from conflict theory to the conditions for autonomy; see, notably, J. Galtung, "A Structural Theory of Imperialism," *Journal of Peace Research* 8 (1971), pp. 81–117, and P. Wallensteen, *Structure and War: On International Relations, 1920–1968* (Stockholm: Rabén & Sjögren, 1973).

3. Important recent contributions to the question of arms races and the outbreak of war are M. D. Wallace, "Arms Races and Escalation," *Journal of Conflict Resolution* 23 (1979), pp. 3–16, and P. F. Diehl, "Arms Races and Escalation: A Closer Look," *Journal of Peace Research* 20 (1982), pp. 205–212. Concerning the internal driving forces of armaments, see M. Nincic, *The Arms Race: The Political Economy of Military Growth* (New York: Praeger, 1982), and regarding the question of conflict resolution, see I. W. Zartman, ed., *The Negotiation Process* (Beverly Hills, Calif.: Sage-Publications, 1978). The retreat from conflict theory is still visible, however, as in the abandoning of the concept of conflict resolution and the replacement of it with the vaguer concept of conflict management (see K. Boulding, "Future Directions in Conflict and Peace Studies," *Journal of Conflict Resolution* 22 [1978], p. 344).

4. U. Himmelstrand, "Formalised Historical Materialism as a Research Tool," *International Sociology* 1 (1986), pp. 113–135.

5. The conflict triangle was introduced by J. Galtung in "Conflict as a Way of Life," in H. Freeman, ed., *Progress in Mental Health* (London: Churchill, 1969); reproduced in J. Galtung, *Essays in Peace Research*, vol. 3, *Peace and Social Structure* (Copenhagen: Ejlers, 1978). It was later used by C. R. Mitchell in *The Structure of International Conflict* (New York: St. Martin's Press, 1981).

6. Fink, in reviewing the field, points out that many theorists have explicitly argued for the lower importance of the parties (see C. F. Fink, "Some Conceptual Difficulties in the Theory of Social Conflict," *Journal of Conflict Resolution* 12 [1968], p. 424). However, some of the earlier writers strongly emphasized classes as highly pertinent parties, notably, R. Dahrendorf, *Class and Class Conflict in Industrial Society* (Stanford: Stanford University Press, 1959).

7. The emphasis on incompatibility was pronounced not only in the work of Boulding but also in J. Burton, *Conflict and Communication* (New York: Free Press, 1969).

8. The Correlates of War project continues to be the most systematic and enduring endeavor in this field, providing invaluable data to the peace research community (see M. Small and J. D. Singer, *Resort to Arms: International and Civil Wars, 1816–1980* [Beverly Hills, Calif.: Sage Publications, 1982]).

9. An interesting early attempt is V. Aubert, "Competition and Consensus: Two Types of Conflict and Conflict Resolution," *Journal of Conflict Resolution* 7 (1963), pp. 26–42.

10. The work by the Institute for World Order remains the most pertinent, notably, R. Falk, *A Study of Future Worlds* (New York: Free Press, 1975).

11. J. Galtung, "Peacemaking: The Conflict Resolution Approach," in J. Galtung, *Essays in Peace Research*, vol. 2, *Peace, War, and Defense* (Copenhagen: Ejlers, 1976), p. 291.

12. The resolution of conflict under conditions of unarmed conflict behavior is treated suggestively in P. Wehr, *Conflict Regulation* (Boulder, Colo.: Westview Press, 1979), and in J. Steiner, "Non-violent Conflict Resolution in Democratic Systems: Switzerland," *Journal of Conflict Resolution* 8 (1969), pp. 295–304.

13. This is an important point of departure in P. Wallensteen, "Incompatibility, Confrontation, and War: Four Models and Three Historical Systems, 1816–1976," *Journal of Peace Research* 18 (1981), pp. 57–90. A similar point about organization is made in K. Boulding, "Organization and Conflict," *Journal of Conflict Resolution* 1 (1957), pp. 122–134.

14. With the help of the concept of metaconflict, this approach becomes understandable (see J. Galtung, "Institutionalized Conflict Resolution," *Journal of Peace Research* 2 [1965], pp. 356 f).

15. This concept was introduced by Zartman (see, for instance, S. Touval and W. I. Zartman, eds., *International Mediation in Theory and Practice* [Boulder, Colo.: Westview Press, 1985]).

16. To reach an agreement, a conflict might have to be crystallized so that the parties agree on what the issues are and who the parties are. At the same time, such a crystallized conflict might easily escalate to war (see K.-Å. Nordquist, *Conflict Crystallization* [Uppsala, Department of Peace and Conflict Research, forthcoming]).

17. The moral dilemma is addressed in M. Walzer, *Just and Unjust Wars* (New York: Basic Books, 1977), pp. 114–117, when discussing the demand for unconditional surrender and relating this demand to the Crusades. More limited views of the adversary seem to have been part of the "classic" notion of warfare.

18. A recent example is the United States' continued recognition of the Pol Pot regime in Kampuchea, thus allowing realpolitik considerations to override "humanpolitik" ones. The agony is expressed by Cyrus Vance when he portrays the U.S. position as "unpleasant" and the situation as "extremely distasteful" (C. Vance, *Hard Choices* [New York: Simon and Schuster, 1983], pp. 121–124).

19. Thus, Berlin is never mentioned in the Berlin accords of 1972 but is rather called "the relevant area" (personal communication).

20. Wallensteen, "Incompatibility, Confrontation and War," pp. 59–64.

21. This perspective is further elaborated by Raimo Väyrynen in Chapter 4.

7

International Regimes and Peaceful Conflict Regulation

Volker Rittberger

New Challenges to Peace Research

In recent years, peace researchers in Europe have again emphasized the analysis of containing the confrontational elements in the East-West conflict and of transforming conflict management in the direction of less offensive approaches. As a result, new books, articles, and pamphlets have emerged that initiate and sustain a "grand debate" about military strategy, the arms race and armaments dynamics, alternatives in security policy, etc. This renewed scholarly concern about the East-West conflict can hardly be surprising as the peace research community has been alarmed—like most people in Europe—by the rapid and grave deterioration of relations between the two superpowers that began in the late 1970s and accelerated during the first years of the Reagan administration. This very justifiable interest in examining critically prevailing strategic concepts and in devising potentially less self-destructive security policies notwithstanding, peace researchers should heed Dieter Senghaas's warning against a perspective on security and peace policy that reduces it to choices among strategic concepts and technological options (Senghaas 1986, 7 ff.).

By comparison, other topics of peace research have fared less well. Except for research on wars in the Third World, which has clearly expanded, North-South issues in general do not occupy center stage in the European peace research theater any longer. Similarly, European peace researchers have not shown much interest lately in reinvigorating the analysis of international cooperation. Existing cooperative mechanisms for conflict and crisis management have by and large been ignored. Most conspicuously, the process of European integration, i.e., the building of an "amalgamated security community" (Karl W. Deutsch) in Western Europe, is rarely, if ever, studied by peace researchers as an example of building a "peace structure" in the one world region that, historically, has stood out because of its tradition of warfare. By the same token, peace researchers do not seem to put much store in international, multilateral machinery for making collective choices— such as negotiations, conferences, organizations—as a method for advancing peace. In fact, these elements of associative peace strategies— whatever their effectiveness in various contexts—have been, at best, an occasional topic in the peace research literature (Czempiel 1986, 82 ff.; Opitz and Rittberger 1986).

I do not mean that peace researchers should refrain from getting involved in studying military-strategic aspects of security, examining the whole range of options already available in this field, and perhaps even putting forward other alternatives. Nevertheless, the debate about peace policy, building structures of peace, would lead one astray if it did not develop a broader horizon by giving a higher priority to the nonmilitary foundations of peace policy. As a part of reintroducing the politico-economic and institutional perspectives on peace policy, peace researchers should take a careful look at the literature on international regimes, which has grown substantially since the late 1970s and which represents an interesting new research focus among U.S. political scientists and economists. This literature claims to offer a new approach that promises to enlarge our knowledge about institutionalized cooperative responses to new collective situations impinging upon the security and welfare of states and their societies (Keohane 1984; Keohane and Nye 1977; Krasner, ed. 1983; Krasner 1985; Ruggie and Haas 1975; Wolf and Zürn 1986; Zürn 1987).

I am suggesting here that international organizations and regimes deserve serious consideration by peace researchers who do not equate "peace" with the "withering away" of the state (as, e.g., Krippendorff 1985) or some other miraculous event or process. Since the state is here to stay and the conditions of complex interdependence are likely to prevail for the foreseeable future, metastate mechanisms and institutions of policy coordination offer opportunities both for promoting and managing peaceful change and for working against it. I shall be interested here in analyzing the conditions that would seem to facilitate putting such metastate mechanisms and institutions to peaceful uses.

In order to illustrate the salience of institutionalized cooperation for building peace structures, it may be helpful to refer to George Modelski's research on alternating waves of innovations (Modelski 1981, 1982). He offers a model from which we can infer, normatively speaking, the functional necessity of creating equitable forms of cooperating in order to break out of the centuries-old cycles of global war and destruction.

This model (see Figure 7.1) is based on linking cycles of world hegemony defined by the prevailing distribution of overall power in the international system with long-term economic fluctuations defined by periods of growth and depression. According to this model, the history of the modern world system can be analyzed in cyclical terms, with each cycle passing through four typical phases.

1. The cyclical sequence begins with a *global war* caused by, and in turn causing, structural changes in the distribution of economic and political power in the international system. The end of this first phase is marked by the emergence of a hegemonic state (a "world power").

2. The economic and political expansion of this hegemonic *world power,* made possible by technical and social innovations, tends to shape the second phase of the overall cycle. At the same time, this phase also witnesses the spread of innovations and growth impulses from the hegemonic world power to other countries.

3. The third phase is characterized by tendencies of worldwide economic stagnation, if not depression. These developments deprive the hegemonic world power of the abundance of resources that enabled it to maintain "order" with noncoercive means. It is an era of *delegitimation* in which competitors for hegemonic status as well as disadvantaged states become increasingly reluctant to continue their acceptance of the "rules of the game."

4. In the final phase of the overall cycle, a further *deconcentration* of economic and political power in general and the relative status decline of the hegemonic world power in particular render the international system increasingly volatile. Technological-economic innovations that may occur in this phase tend to strengthen the challengers without diminishing the overall disparities that exist in the international system. At the end of this phase and, thus, of the overall cycle, a new global war sets the stage for the next act in the history of the modern world system.

Considering the physical limits to repeating this cycle after another global war today and assuming that the awareness of this condition is widespread among the world's policymaking elites, it is more than an abstract academic exercise if one opposes an alternative "peace cycle" to the traditional "war-cycle" history of the modern world system (see Figure 7.1).

Without relying on this model too schematically, it does serve to pinpoint the fact that the present international system needs a variety of institutionalized cooperation to mitigate the competition for power

Figure 7.1. CYCLES OF WORLD HEGEMONY

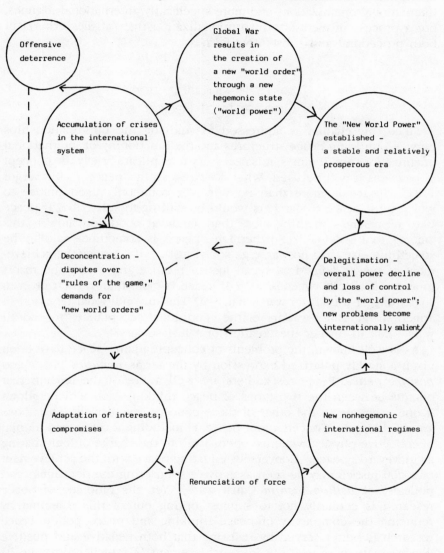

and wealth and the consequences deriving from the disparities in the distribution of these assets. Put differently, breaking out of the war cycle and entering into a peace cycle requires not only normative-institutional mechanisms of coordination and compensation, such as international organizations and more specifically, international regimes, but a process of metastate institutionalization that satisfies criteria of both procedural and substantive fairness.

Conflict Regulation and Concepts of Peace

Since this chapter is addressed to studying the interrelationships between building peace structures and the functioning of international organizations and regimes, it is necessary to explicate briefly the concept of peace as it will be used. What do we mean by "peace"? (Rittberger 1985). "Peace is more than no war!"—a commonly used phrase to which most peace researchers would be willing to subscribe. If peace is to represent something more than a no-war condition, how is this "more" to be defined? Furthermore, peace is sometimes said to be something else than no war, e.g., social justice; if so, does the achievement of peace defined as social justice require and justify the resort to arms (if all other means fail)? If peace is more than no war or even something else than no war, what is it? The unconditional negation of armed struggle and warfare or the conditional acceptance "to end all wars," i.e., to further the creation of a just society?

As is well known, the problems of conceptualizing peace have been given a starkly polarized expression by the terms *negative peace* and *positive peace*. Peace researchers are well aware of the tension that obtains between the two types of peace thinking, and which follows if one uses one or the other of these concepts exclusively. They pose an old dilemma: Conceiving of peace as including a categorical denial of collective physical violence opens itself to the charge of legitimating a "graveyard's peace." Conversely, equating peace with the achievement of social justice may be seen as actively sponsoring the doctrines (and policies) of *bellum justum* ("just war"). Yet, the rationale of peace research is certainly not to suggest opting out of this dilemma by reducing the complexity of peace thinking and peace policy. Peace research is better served by insisting that both negative and positive peace are twin values, the joint achievement of which represents its fundamental "prejudice."

However, the joint achievement of negative and positive peace remains an abstract postulate if the apparent incompatibilities between the two concepts cannot be reduced or overcome. This problem prompts us to look for a missing conceptual link that would connect both concepts. This connection can be established by introducing the concept of *peaceful conflict regulation.* This idea refers to a normative-institutional framework for making collective decisions in which participants' strategies are not subjected to any form of direct violence and in which decision rules apply to which rational actors would freely agree. Put differently, peaceful conflict regulation refers to making collective decisions based on procedural fairness.[1] Peaceful conflict regulation thus represents a link between negative and positive peace inasmuch as it facilitates reaching collective decisions about (positive) values such as liberty and justice without the use or threat of physical force and without an inbuilt bias discriminating arbitrarily among the various categories of actors.

To further clarify the meaning of peaceful conflict regulation, another conceptual distinction can be introduced, i.e., the notion of *effective conflict regulation.* This idea refers to any kind of authoritative collective decision making in an issue area following decision rules and procedures that do not satisfy standards of procedural fairness yet have been agreed to by the actors under pressure, but without being coerced. Put differently, these decision-making processes usually reveal strong inbuilt biases reflecting the power and wealth differentials among the participating states. The conceptual distinction between peaceful and (merely) effective conflict regulation appears necessary since it is conceivable that enlightened dictatorships in new, heterogeneous nations or hegemonic alliances between unequal, yet in certain respects close, partners may lead to at least some desirable outcomes as far as the achievement or distribution of positive values (security, welfare) is concerned. However, such results, being essentially imposed rather than negotiated or achieved by any other method of authentic consensus formation, fall short of fulfilling the prerequisites of peaceful conflict regulation.

The basic argument underlying these conceptual explications runs as follows. Negative peace achieved or maintained between countries (and within them) needs to be based on the reliable operation of peaceful conflict regulation between (and within) them lest it turns out to be a hollow peace. The durable absence of collective physical violence between and within nations (including the absence of organized repression by state agencies) will not be possible if people and nations lack recourse to mechanisms and institutions that regulate conflicts in any number of issue areas and that operate according to rules of procedural fairness.

Such rules and procedures of collective decision making will be considered legitimate, however, not only because, and to the extent to which, they foster negative peace and avoid "bias" or arbitrariness in the process of decision making. Their legitimacy will also hinge upon their capability to facilitate policy initiatives aiming at the allocation of values (satisfaction of human needs, protection of human rights, etc.) and to satisfy criteria of substantive fairness.[2] However, by their very nature, as consensus-based rules and procedures, these mechanisms and institutions of peaceful conflict regulation will, more often than not, produce outcomes that transcend the status quo conditions without ever satisfying the aspirations of effecting a radical departure from them. The price of peaceful conflict regulation almost invariably includes forgoing the option of revolutionary change while enhancing, though not guaranteeing, opportunities for furthering structural adaptations, which tend to reduce the preexisting inequities.

If the preceding conceptual explications and their underlying theoretical rationales are valid, then it may seem justified to conclude that the existence of a normative-institutional framework for peaceful conflict regulation constitutes an integral part of any peace structure, which is characterized, moreover, by a joint achievement of both negative and positive peace. Against the backdrop of this attempt to define the dependent variable of this chapter, its purpose can be stated more precisely: Do international organizations and regimes represent elements of a normative-institutional framework for peaceful conflict regulation and, if so, under what conditions?

International Regimes and Cooperation

Earlier, Modelski's model of alternating waves of innovation was introduced as a device to pinpoint the functional necessity of creating "fair international regimes." The next section will be devoted to discussing their feasibility. Here I take a close look at some prominent contributions to the recent scholarly debate on international regimes. Stephen Krasner refers to international regimes as a set of

> principles, norms, rules and decision-making procedures around which actor expectations converge. Principles are a coherent set of theoretical statements about how the world works. Norms specify general standards of behavior. Rules and decision-making procedures refer to specific prescriptions for behavior in clearly defined areas. For instance, a liberal international regime for trade is based on a set of neoclassical economic principles that demonstrate that global utility is maximized by the free

flow of goods. The basic norm of a liberal trading regime is that tariff and non-tariff barriers should be reduced and ultimately eliminated. Specific rules and decision-making procedures are spelled out in the General Agreement on Tariffs and Trade. [Krasner 1985, 4]

In addition to that definition, a detailed explication of the concept of an international regime provides the following elements to fill out the scope of its meaning (Wolf and Zürn 1986, 204 f.):

1. The definition of an international regime given above covers one issue area, but the concept does not exclude the existence of several regimes in different issue areas, which may interact with one another and which may be characterized by substantially the same principles and norms.

2. A normative-institutional arrangement to be recognized as an international regime needs to develop durability as well as a modicum of autonomy vis-à-vis the constellation of power and interest from which it originated. Put differently, international regimes presuppose that state actors (and perhaps politically relevant nonstate actors, too) are prepared to comply with their norms and rules while forgoing the option of achieving short-term gains at the expense of others; i.e., a habit of noncheating must prevail among the participants.

3. Effectiveness is another condition for an international regime to be fulfilled. Even though deviating behavior does not jeopardize per se the validity of norms and rules, the balance between observance and infraction must be such that deviations remain the exception and compliance the behavior pattern the participants can reliably expect from each other. Effectiveness may be enhanced if a particular regime facilitates the detection of "cheating."

4. International regimes originate in areas of international policy-making in which isolated (uncoordinated) decision making by state actors (behaving rationally by following current cost-benefit calculations) would yield suboptimal outcomes both individually and collectively. Thus, international regimes represent a normative-institutional framework that gives rise to behavior patterns which are different from what they would be if the "natural" constellations of power and interest remained unbounded.

International regimes and international organizations are not identical, yet they belong together as they overlap very frequently. Going back to Krasner's definition of an international regime, it can be seen that the elements "rules" and "decision-making procedures" are usually represented, in reality, by one or more international organizations with mandates pertaining to the issue area covered by a regime. Moreover, international organizations have often been a source for the creation or adaptation of international regimes; they can thus be called "regime-generating" or "regime-adapting policymaking systems" (Hauser 1986; Rittberger and Wolf 1985).

International regimes can come into existence by a myriad of methods (Faupel 1984). For instance, multilateral, global, or regional conferences have sponsored international regimes or have given an explicit foundation in international law to nascent, informal regimes. Such a move, in turn, has often led to the establishment of an international organization that specializes in collecting and disseminating pertinent information, supervising compliance with the regime's rules, extending technical assistance to one or another group of participants, and even examining, from time to time, the need for adapting a regime's legal basis (wholly or in part). As a consequence, there is no one-to-one relationship between international regimes and international organizations. Yet, if an area of international policymaking is covered by a regime, it is safe to assume that one or more international organizations are active in it. The reverse does not hold, however. There are few international organizations that perform necessary functions for more than one regime at a time—and some international organizations do not engage in any regime-related activity at all. Summing up, it can be stated that international regimes and international organizations represent elements of a normative-institutional framework for conflict management that stops short of using, or threatening to use, physical force. It remains to be seen whether or not they also represent components of an evolving peace structure among nations.

Rational decision-making models are the starting point of most academic work on international regimes. Aside from tackling conceptual problems, the debate on international regimes has mainly focused on the question of how regimes come into being. More precisely, this question has been phrased as follows: In which overall power configuration or issue-area–specific power configuration of the international system do international regimes emerge? A widespread answer has been given by the theory of hegemonic stability (Kindleberger 1973; Krasner 1976; Keohane 1980).

The theory is based on Mancur Olson's work on the production of "collective goods" (Olson 1965). Collective goods are defined by two characteristics. First, the consumption of a collective good implies no rivalry, i.e., if a collective good exists, the consumption of that good by actor A does not diminish the possibility of its consumption by actor B. Second, nobody can be excluded from the consumption of collective goods, i.e., if a collective good exists, everybody can consume it. These two characteristics imply that it appears rational for every sovereign actor to attempt to have a "free ride" and to have others pay for the costs of producing the collective goods in question.

As a consequence, it is argued, collective goods cannot be produced in an environment in which "anarchy" prevails. Therefore, collective goods can be produced only by a central authority or by extremely dominating actors. Proceeding from the assumption that international regimes in general provide collective goods (for a critique of this assumption see Russett 1985 and Snidal 1985), the theory of hegemonic stability suggests the following. In an international system that is characterized by anarchy, international regimes can be created only by a hegemonic power, *and* the stability and durability of international regimes presuppose that the hegemonic structure of the international system remains in place. Thus, this theory seems to exclude the possibility of creating "fair" international regimes, which, it has been said, are crucial to peaceful conflict regulation.

As several case studies have shown, the theory of hegemonic stability is capable of explaining the creation of international regimes, particularly in economic issue areas, yet it cannot account for the fact that existing international regimes do not dissolve if and when the power of the hegemonic state declines. To be sure, international regimes are likely to change if the relative power of the hegemonic state declines, yet this change does not necessarily imply a demise of the regime—a consequence to be expected on the basis of the theory of hegemonic stability. Confronted with this explanation gap, regime analysts have had to solve the puzzle of why existing international systems provide a normative-institutional framework for fostering and stabilizing cooperation in their respective issue areas despite the absence of an uncontested hegemonic power.

In order to solve this puzzle, Robert O. Keohane introduced the Coase theorem into the analysis of international regimes (Keohane 1984, 85 ff.). Coase argues that collective problems arising from the collective situation of "market failure" (generation of externalities such as pollution or nonproduction of collective goods such as defense) can be solved without relying on a central authority. Adapting this proposition to the level of the international system, it can be rephrased as follows: Collective goods can be produced without the existence of a world government or a hegemonic power.

To illustrate the Coase theorem and its counter-intuitive result, suppose that soot emitted by a paint factory is deposited by the wind onto clothing hanging outdoors in the yard of an old-fashioned laundry. Assume that the damage to the laundry is greater than the $20,000 it would cost the laundry to enclose its yard and install indoor drying equipment; so if no other alternative were available, it would be worthwhile for the laundry to take these actions. Assume also, however, that it would cost the paint factory only $10,000 to eliminate its emissions of air pollutants. Social welfare would clearly be enhanced by eliminating the pollution rather than by installing indoor drying equipment, but in the absence of either governmental enforcement or bargaining, the egotistic owner of the paint factory would have no incentive to spend anything to achieve this result.

It has frequently been argued that this sort of situation requires centralized governmental authority to provide the public good of clean air. Thus if the laundry had an enforceable legal right to demand compensation, the factory owner would have an incentive to invest $10,000 in pollution control devices to avoid a $20,000 court judgment. Coase argued, however, that the pollution would be cleaned up equally efficiently even if the laundry had no such recourse. If the law, or the existence of a decentralized self-help system, gave the factory a right to pollute, the laundry owner could simply pay the factory owner a sum greater than $10,000, but less than $20,000, to install anti-soot equipment. Both parties would agree to some such bargain, since both would benefit. [Keohane 1984, 85 f.]

Inspecting this example used to illustrate the argument more closely, it becomes obvious that the cooperation between the two actors will only be forthcoming if three prerequisites are fulfilled, which, however, are not met by an international system in a state of anarchy: One, there is sufficient communication among partners; two, there exists an authoritative system for establishing property rights and liability for action; and three, the transaction costs for the negotiations between the two firms are zero or at least very low.

Keohane argues that international regimes can contribute to the fulfillment of these three prerequisites for cooperation between sovereign actors coexisting in an environment without a central authority. Inverting the Coase theorem, Keohane argues that international regimes are created and maintained by states not because the above-mentioned three conditions are met *but* for their anticipated effects of establishing property rights and rules of liability, providing a sufficient two-way flow of information, and reducing transaction costs. The three prerequisites need some elaboration:

1. International regimes increase the exchange of information between the participants simply because they generate regularized interactions; moreover, they involve the creation of a network for specialized information gathering and exchange, as e.g., in the case of "confidence-building measures," according to the Conference on Security and Cooperation in Europe (CSCE) Final Act, or the adaptation

of an international organization charged with the generation of information, as for instance, in the case of International Atomic Energy Agency (IAEA) safeguards.

2. Interactions within an anarchic environment are characterized by the fact that there is no binding law, rather the opposite: Everyone acts according to his or her own determination of right or wrong. Obviously international regimes cannot create a legal framework comparable to national law. But they can provide a kind of "quasi law" in the form of mutually agreed upon "rules of the game," which allow for a certain measure of trust that the rules will generally be complied with and which contribute to the convergence of actor expectations. Put differently, international regimes provide a functional equivalent for an authoritative legal system, which we can call "quasi law," "rules of the game," or "codes of conduct."

3. International regimes decrease transaction costs by providing permanent transaction channels. This factor, too, increases the probability of cooperation.

In order to show that international regimes provide a normative-institutional framework for fostering and stabilizing cooperation in a given international issue area even after the relative power of the regime-sponsoring hegemonic state has declined, the game-theory model of prisoner's dilemma can also be used. This model deals with collective situations that produce suboptimal results, if actors follow their individual strategic rationality, and it points to cooperation as a rational optimization strategy. This model is used to demonstrate that issue areas regulated by international regimes have known collectively better outcomes than issue areas in which ad hoc cooperation, or no cooperation at all, has prevailed.[3]

"What makes it possible for cooperation to emerge is the fact that the players might meet again. This probability means that the choices made today not only determine the outcome of this move, but also can influence the later choices. The future can therefore cast a shadow back upon the present and thereby affect the current strategic situation" (Axelrod 1984, 12). The probability of future cooperation increases with the availability of a normative-institutional framework, which can provide for a certain durability and calculability of interactions in a given action space. The reason is that present and future have become interdependent for every actor looking rationally at his or her decision situation. In Axelrod's words, "the shadow of the future lengthens"; in this way, the costs of noncooperation are raised.

Cooperation under conditions of a prisoner's dilemma will obtain only if and when both players expect the other to cooperate. It follows that convergent expectations are a crucial prerequisite for cooperation in such a situation. Thus, the relevance of international regimes for cooperation rests on their capabilities to generate convergent expectations among participants by providing easily recognizable rules of the game, which are the more freely accepted the less biased they are, i.e., the less arbitrary discrimination among participants ("players") they involve.

The brief discussion of the Coase theorem shows the necessity of information in order to achieve optimal outcomes in collective situations of anarchy. With the help of the game-theory model of prisoner's dilemma, it can be demonstrated further that increased information tends to foster cooperation in such situations. First, the possibilities for cheating will be less, and therefore, the likelihood of attempting it, too. Second, misinterpretations of the other side's behavior will occur less frequently; thus, the probability of refusing to cooperate because of misperceptions will be lower. Third, metacommunication among participants about the constraints inherent in a situation of prisoner's dilemma will be facilitated, which, in turn, makes the participants sensitive to the pitfalls of "sovereign" cooperation.

To sum up these arguments in the briefest way possible, international regimes, once established, foster and stabilize international cooperation because of their functional utilities for sovereign states. One, international regimes improve the communication among the potential participants by decreasing the probability of cheating, by decreasing the probability of misperception and increasing mutual trust, and by providing a forum that allows for metacommunication about collective dilemmas. Two, international regimes provide rules of the game, which make expectations about the mutual behavior convergent and provide a functional equivalent for an authoritative legal system. Three, international regimes provide a framework for transactions that decrease their costs and increase the costs of noncooperation by "lengthening the shadow of the future."

It has been suggested that international regimes foster international cooperation by reducing constraints that are characteristic of interaction between sovereign actors. This reduction is accomplished by introducing a different set of constraints that follow from the characterization of international regimes as functional equivalents to central authority. This "realistic" perspective on international regimes takes the existence and continuation of the nation-state system for granted. However, it does not rule out the emergence of a functionally diversified normative-institutional superstructure constraining states to adopt cooperative approaches to international policymaking.

The argument presented so far requires two caveats. First, although it has been shown that international regimes can continue to exist in an issue area no longer dominated by a hegemonic power, this situation does not prove in and by itself that "fair" international regimes are possible. Put differently, even if international regimes, and international organizations as parts of them, do foster cooperation among nations, it does not follow that this cooperation is conducive to building peace structures. Cooperation leading in the opposite direction is by no means inconceivable and has been practiced by states time and again. Second, only at the level of theoretical reasoning has it been shown that international regimes and organizations foster cooperation among nations. It is not clear whether empirical evidence supports this theoretical proposition.

The next, and final, section will be devoted to examining, albeit briefly, the possibilities for international regimes and organizations to enhance both negative and positive peace. This examination will validate (or invalidate) the characterization of these regimes and organizations as normative-institutional frameworks for peaceful conflict regulation.

Conflict Regulation Through International Regimes

Negative Peace

The most striking innovation at the level of principles and norms for state conduct in this century has been the delegitimation of the *jus ad bellum* ("right to engage in war") and the demise of doctrines of *bellum justum* ("just war"). These developments have been furthered and given expression by the Charter of the United Nations and a host of other international legal instruments. Article 2, paragraph 4, of the charter reads: "All Members shall refrain in their international relations from the threat or use of force against the territorial integrity or political independence of any state, or in any other manner inconsistent with the Purposes of the United Nations."

However, it should not be overlooked that the UN Charter itself, as well as subsequent UN practice, provides for three exceptions to the general principle of prohibiting the threat or use of force in interstate relations. One exception, and the most sweeping in practice, involves the right of individual and collective self-defense (Art. 51). The enforcement measures under the charter's collective security provisions (chap. 7) make up the second lawful exception, second even though they have proved to be largely impracticable. Finally, armed struggle against colonial and apartheid rule in situations in which the colonial powers or apartheid rulers have consistently defied UN resolutions mandating peaceful change are considered a justifiable exception to the general principle of the nonuse of force. Yet it would amount to an overinterpretation of these exceptions if they were thought to indicate a resurgence of widely accepted doctrines of *bellum justum*. On the contrary—and the large number of local wars since 1945 notwithstanding—it appears that opposition to warfare and, thus, its delegitimation have been growing, particularly in countries that, traditionally, have been prone to armed conflict and in countries that display essential features of democratic rule (Garnham 1986).

It is undoubtedly true that the prohibition of the threat or use of force in interstate relations shares the fate of norms in general; i.e., that compliance by its addressees is not automatically assured. Moreover, enforcement mechanisms at the international level are relatively weak, if they exist at all. Yet, these factors do not preclude a recognition of the normative principle as valid. Still, we cannot assume the existence of a no-use-of-force regime in international affairs. At best, we may think of a nascent regime taking into account the propositions advanced in neorealists' writings about "complex interdependence," that military power has become inappropriate for dealing with issues that do not directly affect the status, the internal regime, or the territorial integrity of a country. In other words, the principle of nonuse of force already applies in most issue areas, with the exception of security matters.

Several international organizations and the United Nations, in particular, have been involved in collective efforts to prevent the outbreak of war or to put an end to hostilities through a variety of peacekeeping methods. In general, military and nonmilitary enforcement measures, approaches to the pacific settlement of disputes, and the use of peacemaking forces have not proved to be effective instruments for strengthening negative peace (Väyrynen 1985). In a recent quantitative study, Ernst Haas (1983) demonstrated the low rate of successful intervention by international organizations in international disputes, and he even concluded that the rate of success had actually declined since the end of the 1950s (Haas 1983, 204). Again, these findings must be put into perspective. They mean that in many issue areas, e.g., foreign investment, international disputes that arise and involve governments are no longer settled by the use of military force as was the case in the age of "gunboat diplomacy."

There remains the question of international security regimes that are less comprehensive than a no-use-of-force regime yet are capable of enhancing the likelihood of strengthening at least one aspect of negative peace, i.e., the prevention of nuclear war. At first sight, one is struck by the scarcity of international regimes in an issue area such as security, which seems to need them most. However, this fact can be explained, by and large, by the structural and behavioral constraints operating in this issue area: The conditions of a prisoner's dilemma are much more pronounced, and cooperation appears to carry high risks since a "wrong" move may put the very existence of an actor in jeopardy (Jervis 1983, 174).

Nevertheless, it would be inappropriate to dismiss the existence and importance of a number of security regimes with limited scope. The most significant of these is represented by the nonproliferation regime, which, so far at least, has helped to prevent the spread of nuclear weapons. The normative-institutional framework through which it operates consists of the IAEA, the Non-Proliferation Treaty (NPT), and the informal arrangements of the Suppliers' Club.

Another case coming under this heading may be called a "crisis management and prevention regime" based on the various "hotline" agreements: the declaration on Basic Principles of Relations Between the United States of America and the Union of Soviet Socialist Republics (1972), the Agreement on Prevention of Nuclear War (1973), and the provisions of Basket One of the CSCE Final Act (1975). Since this type of regime originated during the era of East-West détente, it may have weakened because of the crisis of détente.[4] As a third example of a restricted security regime, one might identify the denuclearization regime(s) of the global commons (areas not owned by specific states), albeit with considerable loopholes in the case of the oceans and outer space.

It should be noted that these limited security regimes have one characteristic in common: They are rooted, more or less, in the overall power structure of the international system in which the United States and the USSR control most of the relevant resources. Although these regimes can lay claim to a certain measure of effectiveness in enhancing negative peace, they exact a price, particularly from the nonnuclear participants, in terms of nonreciprocal losses of autonomy.

To sum up this section, it can be stated that the possibilities for international regimes and organizations to enhance negative peace are not easily ascertained. Obviously, a comprehensive global security regime does not exist. At the same time, the resort to arms has vanished from issue areas in which dispute settlement through the use of force was commonplace less than a century ago. International organizations have had limited success, at best, in preventing wars from actually breaking out, in ending ongoing hostilities, and in advancing the pacific settlement of disputes involving security matters. A small number of international security regimes that are limited in scope can be said to function more or less effectively, but although they contribute to international cooperation with regard to the prevention of nuclear war, their decision rules and procedures do not, in most cases, fulfill the prerequisites of peaceful conflict regulation.

Positive Peace

International organizations and regimes can be said to assist in enhancing positive peace to the extent to which they provide for peaceful conflict regulation. If they do, they represent the normative-institutional framework for an evolving peace structure. It bears repeating that peaceful conflict regulation refers to processes of collective decision making in which participants' strategies are not subjected to physical force and that follow decision rules and procedures to which rational actors would freely agree.

The scholarly debate in the United States about international regimes often takes the Bretton-Woods institutions as well as the General Agreement on Tariffs and Trade (GATT) as its reference cases to illustrate the stability- and welfare-generating potential of "liberal" international regimes supported by a hegemonic actor—in this instance, the United States. Since both the International Monetary Fund (IMF) and the World Bank apply starkly discriminatory decision procedures, they fall short, by definition, of being a framework for peaceful conflict regulation even though they may qualify as *effective* international policymaking systems. Adapting the "difference principle" of John Rawls's theory of justice (in the sense of substantive fairness) to the purposes of this section, one might say the following. International regimes and organizations that qualify as components of an evolving peace structure are those in which "social and economic inequalities are to be arranged so that they are . . . to the greatest benefit of the least advantaged" (Beitz 1979, 151). On all accounts, the inequalities built into the Bretton-Woods institutions and regimes do not disproportionately benefit developing countries. At least as far as the international monetary regime and the IMF are concerned, it is an open question whether developing countries derive any long-term benefit at all from participating in them. Thus, there is no convincing new evidence to suggest that the Bretton-Woods institutions and regimes have now become more of a part of an evolving peace structure than was the case in the early 1970s (Rittberger 1973).

As examples of international regimes and organizations approximating more closely the ideal of peaceful conflict regulation than the ones mentioned above one may cite the issue areas of civil aviation, transnational communication, and the uses of the ocean. The international civil aviation regime is based on the International Civil Aviation Organization (ICAO) and provides smaller developed as well as developing countries with a fair opportunity of getting access to the international air transport market. The origins of this regime go back to 1919 when, at the Paris Conference, the Aeronautical Commission elaborated a convention that recognized the unlimited sovereignty of states over the airspace above their territories. At the end of World War II, the ICAO was founded, and it provided a mechanism for the institutionalization of the state-centered civil aviation regime. The old civil aviation rules were reaffirmed by the Bermuda agreement in 1946. Even though some liberal provisions were included in the agreement (particularly with respect to transit rights),

> both the Chicago Convention and the Bermuda Agreement reaffirmed the basic principle that states had sovereign control over the airspace above their territories. At the beginning of the postwar period, the Third World thus encountered an international regime for civil aviation based on the authoritative allocation of resources. States negotiated routes directly, and had the final right of approval for fares. States had the right to designate private actors in the system. Moreover, the accepted norm for the Chicago-Bermuda regime implied that national airlines had the right to 50 percent of the passenger load generated within their home country. [Krasner 1985, 200 f.]

Thus, the civil aviation regime seems to provide procedural fairness. Moreover, it is hardly surprising that the distribution of material benefits in this issue area has turned out to be roughly equitable (Krasner 1985, 200 ff.).

In the issue area of transnational communication, no comprehensive international regime has yet come into existence. Instead, narrowly defined issue areas are dealt with separately in international policy-making. For instance, the flows of news, television programs, and transnational data are not regulated by any regime. Rather, these interactions are mostly controlled and coordinated by crude market and power mechanisms (Zürn 1987, 156 ff.), and the same applies to remote-sensing activities. Not surprisingly, the distributional outcomes in these nonregulated issue areas are highly inequitable. Yet, with respect to the use of direct-broadcast satellites and the distribution of satellite positions in the geostationary orbit, some emerging international regimes seem to come close to satisfying the criteria of peaceful conflict regulation: Both of these incipient regimes provide for procedural fairness in the decision-making process by using the framework of the International Telecommunication Union (ITU), in which the one-state, one-vote rule applies.

A measure of substantive fairness is achieved by restricting satellites put into the geostationary orbit to using only very high frequencies. Thus, the use of lower frequencies, particularly by developing countries, for earth-based communication is not infringed upon. Moreover, the ITU policymaking processes regarding the geostationary orbit have sought to prevent the establishment of a user regime on the basis of the first-come, first-served principle; instead, it has tended to make allowances for technological latecomers. In the field of direct-broadcasting satellites, the requirement of "prior consent" by potential receivers has been recognized. This requirement provides every country, and the technologically less advanced countries in particular, with the possibility of negotiating for participation in programming (Zürn 1987).

The issue area of ocean uses was to be regulated by a comprehensive international regime, but the regime of ocean uses agreed upon at UNCLOS III (UN Third Conference on the Law of the Sea) has not yet taken effect (Wolf 1981; Wolfrum 1984). If this regime does come into full existence, it can be stated that it would represent a bold step ahead in providing for more equitable uses of the global commons. One element of this would-be regime in particular—the international seabed regime—incorporates the requirements of peaceful conflict regulation to a very large extent. The seabed regime would approximate criteria of procedural fairness because its decisions would seek to prevent "automatic victory" for either developing or developed countries. Furthermore, the regime would seek to promote substantive fairness by distributing user fees charged for seabed mining operations to developing countries. However, both the international power distribution among the users of the oceans and the structure of the collective situation with regard to deep-sea mining may continue to render this would-be regime ineffectual for some time to come.

The preceding analysis suggests that the possibility of peaceful conflict regulation in international politics cannot be ruled out. It has been shown that international regimes, and international organizations insofar as they facilitate their institutionalization, can be conducive to building peace structures. Put differently, some of them fulfill the basic requirements of procedural and substantive fairness. The examples of the civil aviation regime, the regimes of direct-broadcasting-satellite application and of the geostationary orbit, and the ocean regime suggest that the creation of peace-building regimes is possible. To return to my starting point, peace researchers should invest greater efforts in ascertaining the conditions under which such international regimes emerge, persist, and expand, and they should help devise strategies to promote conditions that may be conducive to peace-building international regimes.

Notes

The author wishes to thank Michael Zürn for his valuable assistance in preparing this chapter.

1. By procedural fairness, I mean the application of certain rules to decision making about the allocation of values such as the rule of consistency or the rule of representativity. The purpose of these rules is to exclude "bias" arbitrariness in the decision-making process and, thus, to enhance the acceptance of both the process itself and its outcome (Bierbrauer 1982; Luhmann 1975).

2. Substantive fairness refers to rules for the equitable allocation of values. One conceptualization is provided by John Rawls through his "difference principle," which sets a single standard for evaluating allocative decisions. An alternative would consist of a multidimensional concept of substantive fairness (distributive justice), which takes an empirical approach toward ascertaining the criteria for evaluating allocation processes—such as the rule of proportionality, the rule of equality, or the rule of need (Bierbrauer 1982). It should be obvious that consensus about standards of distributive justice, or substantive fairness, is less easily achieved than consensus about rules of procedural fairness. However, procedural fairness sets the stage for decision-making processes in which all rules of substantive fairness will be considered, and which may thus enable the participants to reach fair compromises.

3. This outcome could also be demonstrated on the basis of other game-theory models (e.g., "dilemma of common aversions," Stein 1983). Indeed, the list of advantages of international regimes in overcoming collective dilemmas might be expanded by adding the results of all these possible analyses. However, doing so is not within the scope of this chapter. Game-theory models have also been used to explain the creation of international regimes by referring to the structure of collective situations (Oye 1985; Zürn 1987). This kind of explanation represents an alternative to the theory of hegemonic stability since it explains regime creation without referring to power constellations in an international issue area.

4. In a personal communication, Alexander L. George pointed out to me that the Nixon-Brezhnev agreements of the early 1970s have had little, if any, standing with the Reagan administration whereas President Carter had reaffirmed the U.S. commitment to the Basic Principles agreement during the Vienna meeting with Brezhnev in 1979. Neither the Geneva nor the Reykjavík summits produced any reference to the Basic Principles agreement.

References

Axelrod, Robert. 1984. *The Evolution of Cooperation*. New York: Basic Books.

Beitz, Charles. 1979. *Political Theory and International Relations*. Princeton: Princeton University Press.

Bierbrauer, Günter. 1982. "Gerechtigkeit und Fairness im Verfahren." In Erhard Blankenburg, Walther Gottwald, and Dieter Strempel, eds., *Alternativen in der Ziviljustiz*, pp. 317–327. Bonn: Bundesanzeiger.

Czempiel, Ernst-Otto. 1986. *Friedensstrategien: Systemwandel durch International Organisation, Demokratisierung, und Wirtschaft.* Paderborn: Ferdinand Schöningh.

Faupel, Klaus. 1984. "International Regime als Gegenstände für sozialwissenschaftliche Forschung." In *Jahrbuch der Universität Salzburg, 1981–1983*, pp. 94–105. Salzburg.

Garnham, David. 1986. "War-Proneness, War-Weariness, and Regime Type: 1816–1980." *Journal of Peace Research* 23:3, pp. 279–289.

Haas, Ernst B. 1983. "Regime Decay: Conflict Management and International Organizations." *International Organization* 37:2, pp. 189–256.

Hauser, Heinz-Michael. 1986. *Reform der Entwicklungsfinanzierung durch "Automatisierung"? Begründung, Ausgestaltung, und Umsetzung eines internationalen Reformkonzepts.* Baden-Baden: Nomos Verlagsgesellschaft.

Jervis, Robert. 1983. "Security Regimes." In Stephen D. Krasner, ed., *International Regimes*, pp. 173–194. Ithaca and London: Cornell University Press.

Keohane, Robert O. 1980. "The Theory of Hegemonic Stability and Changes in International Economic Regimes, 1967–1977." In Ole Holsti et al., eds., *Change in the International System*, pp. 131–162. Boulder, Colo.: Westview Press.

―――― . 1984. *After Hegemony: Cooperation and Discord in the World Political Economy.* Princeton: Princeton University Press.

Keohane, Robert O., and Joseph S. Nye, Jr. 1977. *Power and Interdependence: World Politics in Transition.* Boston: Little, Brown.

Kindleberger, Charles P. 1973. *The World in Depression, 1929–1939.* Berkeley: University of California Press.

Krasner, Stephen D. 1976. "State Power and the Structure of International Trade." *World Politics* 28:3, pp. 317–343.

―――― . 1985. *Structural Conflict: The Third World Against Global Liberalism.* Berkeley: University of California Press.

Krasner, Stephen D., ed. 1983. *International Regimes.* Ithaca and London: Cornell University Press.

Krippendorff, Ekkehart. 1985. *Staat und Krieg: Die historische Logik politischer Unvernunft.* Frankfurt am Main: Suhrkamp.

Luhmann, Niklas. 1975. *Legitimation durch Verfahren.* Neuwied: Luchterhand.

Modelski, George. 1981. "Long Cycles, Kondratieffs, and Alternating Innovations: Implications for U.S. Foreign Policy." In Charles W. Kegley and Pat McGowan, eds., *The Political Economy of Foreign Policy Behavior*, pp. 63–84. Beverly Hills, Calif.: Sage Publications.

―――― . 1982. "Long Cycles and the Strategy of U.S. International Economic Policy." In William P. Avery and David P. Rapkin, eds., *America in a Changing World Political Economy*, pp. 97–116. New York and London: Longman.

Olson, Mancur. 1965. *The Logic of Collective Action.* Cambridge: Harvard University Press.

Opitz, Peter J., and Volker Rittberger, eds. 1986. *VN—Forum der Welt.* Bonn. Bundeszentrale für politische Bildung.

Oye, Kenneth A. 1985. "Explaining Cooperation Under Anarchy: Hypotheses and Strategies." *World Politics* 38:1, pp. 1–24.

Rittberger, Volker. 1973. "International Organization and Violence—with Special Reference to the Performance of the UN System." *Journal of Peace Research* 10:3, pp. 217–226.

―――. 1985. "Ist Frieden möglich?" *Universitas* 40, pp. 1139–1149.

Rittberger, Volker, and Klaus Dieter Wolf. 1985. "Policy-Forschung und Internationale Beziehungen." In Hans-Hermann Hartwich, ed., *Policy-Forschung in der Bundesrepublik Deutschland,* pp. 204–211. Opladen: Westeutscher Verlag.

Ruggie, John Gerard, and Ernst B. Haas, eds. 1975. *International Responses to Technology.* Special Issue of *International Organization.* Vol. 29, no. 3.

Russett, Bruce. 1985. "The Mysterious Case of Vanishing Hegemony; or, Is Mark Twain Really Dead?" *International Organization* 39:2, pp. 207–231.

Senghaas, Dieter. 1986. *Die Zukunft Europas: Probleme der Friedensgestaltung.* Frankfurt am Main: Suhrkamp.

Snidal, Duncan. 1985. "The Limits of Hegemonic Stability." *International Organization* 39:4, pp. 579–614.

Stein, Arthur A. 1983. "Coordination and Collaboration: Regimes in an Anarchic World." In Stephen D. Krasner, ed., *International Regimes,* pp. 115–140. Ithaca and London: Cornell University Press.

Väyrynen, Raimo. 1985. "Is there a Role for the United Nations in Conflict Resolution?" *Journal of Peace Research* 22:3, pp. 189–196.

Wolf, Klaus Dieter. 1981. *Die Dritte Seerechtskonferenz der Vereinten Nationen: Beiträge zur Reform der internationalen Ordnung und Entwicklungstendenzen im Nord-Süd-Verhältnis.* Baden-Baden: Nomos Verlagsgesellschaft.

Wolf, Klaus Dieter, and Michael Zürn. 1986. "'International Regimes' und Theorien der Internationalen Politik." *Politische Vierteljahresschrift* 27:2, pp. 201–211.

Wolfrum, Rüdiger. 1984. *Die Internationalisierung staatsfreier Räume: Die Entwicklung einer internationalen Verwaltung für Antarktis, Weltraum, Hohe See, und Meeresboden.* Berlin: Springer Verlag.

Zürn, Michael. 1987. *Gerechte internationale Regime: Bedingungen und Restriktionen der Entstehung nicht-hegemonialer Internationaler Regime untersucht am Beispiel Weltkommunikationsordnung.* Frankfurt am Main: Haag & Herchen.

PART FOUR

Analysis of
Armament Economics

8

Armaments and Economic Performance

Göran Lindgren

Introduction

The relationship between armaments and economics has long intrigued peace researchers. Richardson sought to establish the connection between arms races and the outbreak of war, others have discussed the impact of the arms industry on defense decisions. Also, the economic impact of armaments has been given attention, particularly in the post-1945 period when armaments have become institutionalized in an unprecedented manner. The perspectives have varied. Sometimes studies have been done in order to avoid the ruin of companies or communities. Sometimes the question has been whether military resources can be used for civilian purposes. Either way, there is a need to know correctly the effects of armaments on an economy. As this need has been of considerable and growing attention, it is necessary to review the literature in this field. Peace research has consistently tried to raise and evaluate general theories, which often means the use of quantitative methods or methodologies comparing many cases. Thus, when here reviewing the state of the art in this field, I concentrate on studies with such a methodological outlook.

During the last few years, many studies have been published on the economic consequences of armaments. The United Nations has contributed to this development through commissioning studies for the Group of Governmental Experts on the Relationship Between Disarmament and Development; the final report of this expert group is based on forty reports from various countries (UN 1981, 171 ff.; Hovstadius and Wängborg 1981). The UN reports on the economic consequences of armaments (UN 1972, 1978, 1983a) have also been significant in stimulating research. According to some observers there is now clear evidence that the economic effects of diverting resources to military uses are overwhelmingly negative for industrialized economies (Huisken 1982, 13). A different tradition of thought, mostly Marxist influenced, argues that military expenditure (milex) still is necessary for the survival of capitalism (Baran and Sweezy 1968). Baran and Sweezy's theory is very germane but is not formulated in such a way that it can be tested without interpretation. The use of quantitative methods requires interpretation that can be done in different ways (e.g., Cypher 1974).

Pryor (1968) began the study of trade-offs within a national state budget or within a national economy. The question in the first case is which other parts of public expenditure will be reduced when milex is increased, and interest has often focused on expenditures for education and health. The second question concerns trade-offs within the entire national economy, not only the part that passes through the national state budget, and the results have not been conclusive. The effects on investment have been of central importance. A question frequently returned to is whether milex solves problems for countries in economic crises; here I will examine studies in Marxist as well as trade-off traditions.

Studies on the economic effects of military expenditure in developing countries often relate to the empirical macroeconomic studies made by Benoit (1973, 1978), in which he found a positive correlation between milex and economic growth. The critique is summarized in Kaldor (1978) and Ball (1983a). Most other studies on milex and developing countries have also been concentrated on the effects on economic growth. There are unfortunately not enough data for empirical research on these questions for planned economies, and there exist to my knowledge no empirical studies on their problems.

Research efforts have concentrated on five economic dimensions that are crucial for long-term development and structural change: investment, economic growth, employment, business cycles, and electoral cycles. All studies that concern just developing countries will be discussed only in the section on milex and economic growth since that connection is their primary focus. Inflation is an important problem, but the empirical investigations are so far few.

In this area—like many other areas of economics—studies have reached conflicting conclusions. The reasons differ, and there is, with existing data, no effective method for deciding which of them is correct (Blaug 1981, 261). For instance, most of the studies reviewed use statistical techniques, but the methods vary and they are not always clearly described. Most of the studies base their conclusions on association, but the covariation over time of two variables or the highly significant correlation coefficients between them gives only a hint of possible causal relations. A plausible theoretical link is needed to make the association really interesting.

The Appendix to this chapter summarizes the empirical studies in chronological order, giving information on year of publication, the page number for empirical evidence for the main conclusion, focus of attention, countries included in the empirical analysis, the period for the data and the main conclusion (in wording similar to the study but not verbatim). Let us now look at the research on the five relevant economic dimensions.

Military Expenditure and Investment

Investment is generally considered to be a crucial factor in economic growth and development. Future production is dependent on the available productive capacity, and reduced investments have therefore a more far-reaching effect than reduced consumption. There seems to be a broad consensus that investment and milex are substitutes in developed countries (Kennedy 1983, 198).

Ron Smith has repeatedly emphasized the effects of military spending on investments (Smith 1977, 1978, 1979, 1980a, 1980b; Smith and Smith 1983). In the first article his main finding is concerned with the relationship between military expenditure and investment: "The share of investment in GDP (I) was made a function of the share of military expenditure (M) and the rate of growth (G)" (Smith 1977, 72). Smith argues that to document the fact that military expenditure is used for stabilization, evidence of a positive state reaction function is required, "a state response to actual or expected increases in unemployment with increases in military expenditure." He finds no base for that in time-series evidence for the United States or Britain (Smith 1977, 68). Rather, he concludes that "high military expenditure leads to low investment, low growth and high unemployment." Since military expenditures involve substantial economic costs, they must be accounted for differently. Smith's suggestions include noneconomic reasons such as defense of the capitalist system, rivalry within the capitalist system, and an insurance against internal threats to the existing order (Smith 1977, 74).

Using data for fifteen countries and for the period 1960–1970, Smith finds a correlation of -0.73 (significant at 0.05) between milex and investment. To investigate this correlation further, he makes investment a function of military spending and the rate of growth and computes a following regression equation. The result is $R^2 = 0.546$, which means that 54.6 percent of the variation in investment is explained by milex and the growth rate. Smith comes to the conclusion that "all the results indicate, therefore, that the coefficient of M is not significantly different from −1" (Smith 1977, 73). Smith explains this finding as follows: Workers resist cuts in private consumption and public welfare. With given balance of payments and rate of utilization, the remainder of the output is divided between investment and military expenditure. Higher military expenditure leads to lower investment.

The negative correlation between milex and investment has been found also in other studies. Smith and other researchers have tested various countries and periods and found a robust relation (Russett 1969, 1970; Benoit 1973; Fontanel 1980; Rasler and Thompson 1984; Cappelen, Gleditsch, and Bjerkholt 1984). Chester (1978) failed to find it when investigating only private investment.

The conclusion from the reviewed studies is that the negative association between milex and investment is clearly established. The theoretical argument that is most plausible is that milex is regarded as nonconsumption and the boundary between consumption and nonconsumption is fairly stable (Smith 1979, 267). This conclusion corresponds with those of most studies, but the methods used are not totally appropriate. They all build on the statistical association of macroeconomic indicators; with other methods and disaggregated data, another picture might emerge.

Military Expenditure and Economic Growth

It is commonly assumed that higher investment leads to a higher growth rate (Evans 1969, 541; Adelman and Morris 1973, 76 ff.). Economic growth is here defined as increased GNP or GNP per capita. Those two measures are treated by many governments as goals per se, but it is important to bear in mind that they are measures of the material output of a nation and not measures of economic welfare. Economic development is something more than higher GNP.

There has long been a debate whether military expenditures promote economic growth or not. An early study by Benoit found a positive correlation, but he was not convinced that there was a causal link (Benoit 1973, 4). The debate has mainly concerned the effects of military spending in the Third World.

Benoit's results have been questioned by many. Some analysts have been unable to replicate his findings (Lim 1983), and it has been argued that Benoit's conclusions are not supported by his empirical evidence (Ball 1985, 291). Other studies for developing countries have found no positive association between higher milex and faster economic growth (Faini, Annez, and Taylor 1980; Nabe 1983; Biswas and Ram 1986; Maizels and Nissanke 1986), and negative influence on growth has been found by some (Deger and Smith 1983; Lim 1983; Lebovic and Ishaq 1987). A reasonable conclusion is that "there seems little doubt that, taken together, these studies negate the Benoit thesis" (Maizels and Nissanke 1986, 1127). The detailed critique that has been directed against Benoit's work and the results of more recent empirical studies suggest that there is no basis for assuming a general positive influence of milex on economic growth. Fredricksen and Looney (1983, 1985a; Looney and Fredriksen 1986) have reported that milex may promote growth in relatively resource-unconstrained countries. Since such countries are in the minority, these results do not change the general picture.

Several studies emphasize the differences among countries (for instance, Maizels and Nissanke 1986, 1137), and since the economic structure varies widely among developing countries, it seems unlikely that any strong general pattern will emerge. Biswas and Ram (1986, 362) argue that earlier results differ because of sample variations, specification choices, and different time periods. The inadequate quality of the economic data for developing countries makes it hard to believe that macroeconomic analysis can be sufficient to reveal a general pattern, even if such a pattern exists.

Nincic and Cusack suggest a connection between absolute changes in military expenditures and percentage changes in GNP per capita. Their hypothesis is based on the idea that "most people seem to think of and refer to fluctuations in GNP per capita in absolute terms. . . . If changes in percent growth or GNP per capita seemed to be empirically associated with changes in levels of military spending, a causal connection might well be established both in the public's and the politicians' eyes" (Nincic and Cusack 1979, 105). The authors observe a positive association between economic growth and increases in defense spending in the United States between 1948 and 1976, and they "believe that this association might generally be perceived as reflecting a causal link in the eyes of the relevant actors" (Nincic and Cusack 1979, 106).

Szymanski's interpretation of Baran and Sweezy leads him to the idea of a straightforward relationship in which a higher proportion of GNP used for military spending leads to higher growth per capita (Szymanski 1973a, 3). He divides his sample of eighteen countries into two groups after ranking them according to the percentage share

Table 8.1. Military expenditure and GNP growth per capita, GNP/cap growth %, and group means

Military Expenditure	1950-1968	1960-1968
High	3.5	3.7
Low	4.0	4.1

Source: From Szymanski 1973a, 7.

Table 8.2. Military expenditure and growth of GNP per capita for large and small countries, 1950-1968

Military expenditure	Large	Small
High	2.8	3.5
Low	6.1	3.2

Source: From Szymanski 1973a, 8.

Note: Average annual percentage growth for 18 industrialized countries

of the GNP that is used for military expenditure. The result is found in Table 8.1. He concludes that "thus, in a very basic sense, military spending, instead of leading to economic growth, actually appears to be a cause of at least relative stagnation" (Szymanski 1973a, 6). What he has shown is that the countries that use a smaller share of the GNP for military ends have a slightly higher rate of growth. For the longer timespan, there are three countries with a growth of 5 percent or more. Two of them, Israel and West Germany, are in the group of high military expenditure, and one, Japan, is in the other group. The basis for Szymanski's conclusion is thus rather weak.

Szymanski further divides the countries into four groups and then places the largest countries (according to GNP size) in one group and twelve smaller ones in another group (see Table 8.2). Szymanski interprets the results shown in the table as "compatible with the thesis that military research and development results in a distortion of the economy which hinders economic growth. Those among the biggest developed countries that develop military technology are growing more slowly than those that are not leading developers" (Szymanski 1973a, 7). The idea is that military development and research hinders economic growth but that high military expenditure without domestic military development and research promotes economic growth. To investigate the idea, one ought to study how large a part of the military expenditure is used for R&D. Szymanski does not do that. Another fact that contradicts this idea is that countries do not get already developed weapons for free. On the contrary, the rising costs of R&D have had the consequence that the export of weapons is playing an increasingly important role in the budget for weapons. Long production series are needed to make research, development, and production of weapons systems economically feasible.

Other studies on the relations between milex and economic growth differ in their results. Most researchers, like Szymanski, have found that milex hinders economic growth (see Lee 1973). Some have concluded that the negative effect on growth is owing to reduced investments (Benoit 1973; Smith 1977, 1978; Fontanel 1980; Smith and Georgiou 1983; Cappelen, Gleditsch, and Bjerkholt 1984), and it has also been argued that milex competes for resources that are used for the production of export goods and thereby hampers export-led growth (Rotschild 1973).

One important factor that is not always considered in the research design is that one ought to expect substantive differences depending on whether there is excess capacity or fully utilized resources in the economy. All theory should lead one to find milex stimulating inadequate demand when there is idle production capacity, and as an effect, economic growth should result. This idea is supported by Brown and Kelleher (1971), who found that milex is less reducing on most GNP components in a situation with excess capacity. There are many dangers in looking too crudely at milex. If aggregate demand is viewed as "some homogenous fluid" (Smith 1979, 264), one cannot take sectoral differences into account. Other studies as well have been unable to find any association between higher milex and economic growth (Nardinelli and Ackerman 1976; Faini, Annez, and Taylor 1980; DeGrasse 1983).

Among the few studies that have found a positive relationship is one conducted by Eric Chester, who introduced population growth rate and the change in the workforce in agriculture and then found no clear evidence of a negative relationship between milex and growth (Chester 1978, 295). His model specification has been challenged by Smith, who maintains that even if the estimations are imprecise, the balance of the evidence seems to be that milex reduces growth (Smith 1978, 304).

Another proponent of positive relationships between milex and economic growth has an unusual idea. Weede (1983, 1986) investigates the hypothesis that higher military participation ratios (measured as military personnel actually on duty per 1,000 population of working age; Taylor and Hudson 1972, 20, 38) are associated with higher economic growth rates. He finds his "indirect evidence looks cumulative and consistent" in supporting his hypothesis (Weede 1983, 18). The explanation offered is that "discipline or the habit of obeying orders are about as useful as abilities or skill in promoting economic growth" (Weede 1983, 13). However, this explanation would seem to apply better to developing countries than to industrialized countries. His data for ninety-five countries with different economic structure analyzed with regression techniques do lend some support to his hypothesis, but they also clearly show that "the military participation rate is not the key to explaining economic growth" (Weede 1983, 16).

The results of the studies on economic growth are not as uniform as those on investment. Nevertheless, the overwhelming conclusion seems to be that higher milex is not associated with economic growth. More research is needed, especially research that takes different phases in the business cycle into account.

Military Expenditure and Employment

A common argument against disarmament is that it will lead to unemployment, but the existing studies do not support this argument. There is reason to believe that other government expenditures will create more jobs with the same amount of government expenditure— on the national level but not always on the regional or local level as there are no automatic mechanisms to replace disappearing military-related employment with civilian employment in the same city or region.

Military expenditures create employment not only in the armaments industry but also more directly by employing people in the armed and the paramilitary forces. One estimate of the numbers involved on a global basis gives the following result (Sivard, cited in Lindroos 1980, 14): armaments industry, 25–30 million persons (41–45 percent); armed forces, 23 million (35–38 percent); and paramilitary forces, 13 million (20–21 percent). The basic question is whether these figures represent more or less employment than would be expected from the resources used on milex. Obviously, milex can create employment if the alternative is no other public or private spending, but the relevant comparison is how much employment can be generated with other uses of the same amount of resources. There have been some attempts to answer this question, but let me first consider the macroeconomic evidence.

Smith suggests that the share of military expenditure in output affects the unemployment rate. His hypothesis is that "nations with

high levels of military expenditure should have higher levels of util-
isation and lower levels of unemployment than states with low military
expenditure" (Smith 1977, 66). When he computed the correlation
between these two variables for cross-sectional data from eight countries
in 1973, he got a correlation coefficient of +0.79. Since the coefficient
should have been negative to support his hypothesis, he concludes
that many states must have found alternatives to military spending for
maintaining employment (Smith 1977, 67). On the other hand, Chester
(1978, 295) found no convincing evidence of a direct link between
milex and unemployment, and Smith later found the same (Smith 1978,
302).

The interpretation of these results is not obvious. Data from more
than one country are less reliable than data from only one country,
since data on unemployment are not standardized for intercountry
comparisons. This fact suggests that cross-sectional approaches are
inadequate for answering this question.

Szymanski has three hypotheses directly relating to unemployment.
The first one is that "the greater the ratio of military spending to GNP,
. . . the less the rate of unemployment" (Szymanski 1973a, 3). This
is almost exactly the same hypothesis as above—the only difference
is that Szymanski relates GNP instead of GDP as Smith does. The
former divides the countries into different subgroups according to high/
low milex; size of the economy, big/small (GNP); wealth per capita,
rich/not so rich; and level of nonmilex, high/low. The results can be
seen in Table 8.3. Of the seven categories, five show lower rates of
unemployment for the group with higher military expenditures. Szymanski concludes that "[i]n general, as expected, the level of military
spending is negatively correlated (with some significant exceptions)
with unemployment" (Szymanski 1973a, 9).

Szymanski also found that "the higher the level of total government
spending, the lower the level of unemployment" (Szymanski 1973a,
10). He then makes a rather questionable comparison between the
employment effects of different state expenditures: "It should be noted,
however, that while nonmilitary expenditure reduces unemployment,
its effect in this regard is not as pronounced as that of military
expenditure. This is no doubt because military spending, whether on
salaries or hardware, necessarily results in more jobs per unit of
expenditure than does much of nonmilitary expenditure, which is
largely for welfare-type expenses, which produces fewer jobs" (Szymanski 1973a, 10). The last sentence contradicts a number of other
studies (Lindroos 1980, 116 f.; Albrecht 1978, 25 f.; DeGrasse 1983, 12
f.). Why welfare-type expenditure necessarily should result in fewer
jobs is not explained and seems to be an ill-founded assumption.

Table 8.3. Percent unemployed, military expenditure, and three other variables

	Military Expenditure	
	High	Low
Rich	2.4	3.0
Poor	1.9	2.4
Big	3.1	1.8
Small	1.7	3.1
High nonmilitary expenditure	1.5	2.1
Low nonmilitary expenditure	3.0	2.2
All countries	1.9	2.9

Source: Szymanski 1973a, 7-9.

Like Chester (1978) and Smith (1978), DeGrasse (1983) also found no association between milex and unemployment. As for economic growth, it seems important to distinguish among different phases in the business cycle. In an economy with excess capacity, increased milex can create jobs without crowding out other types of employment even if milex creates fewer jobs than the same amount of public expenditure would in another sector. Fontanel (1980, 65) argues that in the long run, milex reduces the potential for activities that are more essential to economic growth, favors stricter control of workers, and stimulates new possibilities for the growth of nonwage income. The relationship between milex and employment seems to be too complex to capture by correlation or regression methods.

There have been attempts to look at more disaggregated data for employment, studies that have mainly concerned the United States. Blank and Rotschild found that milex generated employment but more so for men, engineers, and highly paid employees than for other categories (Blank and Rotschild 1985, 693). U.S. spending on military personnel—a decreasing part of defense spending—gave jobs to groups with high unemployment, e.g., young people and blacks. Their conclusion was that conversion will be progressively less problematic since it will affect fewer people and those affected will have less trouble finding new jobs because of their skills.

Military Expenditure
and Business Cycles

Smith suggests that "military expenditure is required not so much to maintain full employment as to stabilise the system" (Smith 1977, 67). As a measure, Smith uses the standard deviation of the growth rate, but this measure is slightly inappropriate since one could argue that economic fluctuations that affect decision makers are more accurately observed in changes in inflation and employment. Smith finds a correlation of −0.26 between the share of military expenditure in output and the standard deviation of the growth rate for the period 1960–1970. Since this figure is not very convincing for the given hypothesis, he points out that there can be another chain of causation. As growth, stability, and military spending are significantly correlated, states with high military expenditure tend to have a low growth rate and therefore lower fluctuations (Smith 1977, 67).

The main reason why high military spending would be stabilizing is that military procurements involve long-term planning and predictability. The other main chain of reasoning assumes that the possible manipulation of milex will give opportunities for stabilizing the economy. Cypher writes, "Without [a large military] sector, which is easily expanded as well as contracted, advocates of fiscal manipulation would be left with a small and relatively rigid Federal Budget" (Cypher 1974, 4). This statement is the core of the underconsumptionist theory, according to which military expenditure can compensate for the lack of demand. Cypher and Krell describe this as a countercyclical policy, and the term *electoral cycle* corresponds to a similar line of reasoning. Countercyclical policy is the independent variable in one of Cypher's hypotheses and in one of Krell's. Cypher wants to analyze how military expenditure has been used as "an instrument of capitalist planning in order to moderate (and sometimes reverse) both cyclical tendencies as well as tendencies toward secular stagnation" (Cypher 1974, 1).

Krell sets up two conditions. First, "If military spending is driven by a desire to keep up aggregate demand and to stabilize fluctuations in the business cycle, then military spending should figure prominently among the instruments of fiscal policy and it should actually be used in such a fashion, either within the 'political' business cycle (in order to help Presidential election campaigns) or countercyclically." Second, 'If domestic economic interests and/or considerations are the driving forces behind U.S. military spending, then by implication foreign policy and strategic considerations are not, and ought to subordinate to these

Table 8.4. Growth of military expenditure and GNP
by fiscal year (in percent)

	Growth of Military Expenditure	Real GNP Growth
1948	-11.1	4.6
1949	7.6	0.0
1950	4.7	8.5
1951	123.3	9.6
1952	17.2	2.4
1953	-17.4	6.9
1954	-30.3	-3.4
1955	7.6	8.3
1956	19.9	2.4
1957	2.6	1.8
1958	8.1	-2.9
1959	3.7	4.2
1960	-3.4	2.2
1961	6.6	0.7
1962	1.4	7.1
1963	14.1	3.5
1964	4.7	6.0
1965	0.0	5.5
1966	11.2	7.4
1967	20.7	3.6
1968	5.1	5.0
1969	3.0	2.7
1970	-1.6	0.4
1971	1.1	2.2
1972	5.5	6.3

Source: Cypher 1974, 5.

economic interests and considerations" (Krell 1981, 223). These two
conditions are not easily translated into testable hypotheses.

The study of military spending as a countercyclical instrument
preferably calls for quantitative data on the budget, as well as qualitative
data on the decisions. Cypher reaches his conclusions purely on the
basis of data concerning the annual growth of military expenditure
and the annual real growth of GNP for the period 1948–1972 (see
Table 8.4). Cypher concludes that "one can see that in the postwar
recessions of fiscal years 1949, 1958, and 1961, military expenditures
were used as counter-cyclical devices in order to end these recessions"

Table 8.5. Causes and effects in U.S. military expenditures

	Cause		Effect
	Fiscal Policy	Foreign/Defense Policy	
Cuts	(1952) 1957 (1969) 1976?	1945-1948 1952-1954 1964 1969-1975	Aggravating downturns: 1952-1954 1957 1969-1970
Increases	1972 1975	1949 1950-1952 1958 1961-1963 1965-1968 1980-	Countercyclically in a recession: 1949 1958 1961 1980-1981

Source: Krell 1981, 236.

(Cypher 1974, 6). This conclusion seems rather questionable. When Cypher is a little more specific, he argues that "military expenditures by being left at a level 51 percent greater than in 1950, acted as a counter-cyclical stabilizing device" (Cypher 1974, 6). The difference between "were used as" and "acted as" is important. In the first case, military spending is used as an instrument for economic policy, but in the second case, it has a stabilizing effect that is not necessarily intended. To demonstrate that military expenditures are used as an *intended* instrument for economic policy requires more evidence.

If military spending is actually used as a countercyclical instrument, "then military spending should figure prominently among the instruments of fiscal policy" (Krell 1981, 223). To show that military expenditures are considered as such an instrument is not easy. Nincic and Cusack refer to what they call "some anecdotal evidence" from Richard Nixon, when he recalled a situation in which military spending was recommended (but not actually used) for increasing total demand (Nincic and Cusack 1979, 106). Krell on the other hand thinks that "the shuffling back and forth of a few very low percentage points of the defense budget in line with the general direction of fiscal policy certainly cannot be considered equivalent to 'economic factors driving U.S. military expenditures' " (Krell 1981, 237). The grounds for this statement are summarized in Table 8.5.

Krell bases his analysis on qualitative data as well as on "a textual analysis of the Economic Reports of the President" (Krell 1981, 223); thus, his conclusion seems to be more firmly based than that of Nincic and Cusack, which is mainly based on statistical analysis. Krell's conclusion is that military expenditure is only one of many possible instruments for fiscal or economic policy and that its relative weight has declined (Krell 1981, 236).

Other studies on the use of milex as an economic instrument give support to the idea for the U.S. setting. Griffin et al. found that military expenditures "do appear to be employed as a counter-cyclical fiscal instrument by the state, and their use seems to be affected predominantly by economic fluctuations and trends in politically and economically dominant sectors of labour and capital" (Griffin, Wallace, and Devine 1982, 8). Smith and Georgiou (1983, 11) found some evidence that U.S. milex is used as an economic regulator, but there is no evidence to suggest that milex is used as an economic regulator in other countries.

Military Expenditure and Electoral Cycles

The discussion about the use of military spending as a countercyclical device leads naturally to the question of whether there is an electoral cycle. Nincic and Cusack have addressed this problem most systematically. They pose and try to answer four questions: "(1) Does economic performance influence electoral outcomes for incumbent political authorities? (2) If so, do incumbents attempt to manipulate the economy for their electoral ends? (3) Do military expenditures affect economic performance? (4) Is there reason to believe that military spending might, at least partially, be used by incumbents for political-electoral purposes?" (Nincic and Cusack 1979, 104). Summarizing two studies, they conclude that "it would appear, that, at least in the US context, economic performance has an important influence on electoral outcomes for incumbent politicians" (Nincic and Cusack 1979, 104). They also find evidence of a political business cycle that is the result of attempts to make improvements in the national macroeconomic performance coincide with the electoral cycle.

After affirmative answers to the first two questions, they quote Cypher's study on the third question. On the fourth question, concerning political ends, Nincic and Cusack suggest that before elections, governments will promote growth and full employment by expansionary economic policy and after elections, they will try to curb inflation by a more restrictive policy (Nincic and Cusack 1979, 107). Putting all their hypotheses together, they get a predictive model for changes in U.S. military spending. When they confront this model with data for the period 1948–1976, they are able to account for over 70 percent of the variance. This result is hardly surprising since the model uses many variables and more variables tend to increase R^2.

Krell uses another method to examine whether there is an electoral cycle and finds the evidence for an electoral defense cycle dubious (Krell 1981, 227). The basis for this dubiousness is mainly a chart showing military expenditures, fiscal policy, and the business cycle for the years 1945–1979. In this chart, presidential election years are also shown. Krell's conclusion is that "there is some evidence of an electoral defense cycle. The evidence is not very strong . . . it is contradictory, and in *both* [my emphasis] directions" (Krell 1981, 236).

Since Nincic and Cusack use data for the period 1948–1976 and Krell uses data for 1945–1979, and both studies focus on the United States, the difference in the results needs some explanation. The most obvious reason is that the studies use different methods. The question then is which method is most appropriate. Krell's study, which is the more recent one, cites both Nincic and Cusack and other authors with different findings. Krell argues that "it is very difficult to trace the economic influences of military expenditures with correlational methods, autocorrelation may be a serious problem, as well as the disaggregation of the independent from the dependent variables" (Krell 1981, 222). The problem of autocorrelation is not a problem for Nincic and Cusack since their statistical methods include ways of testing that (Nincic and Cusack 1979, 108 f.).

An important aspect of the difference between military expenditure and other public expenditure in the United States is given by Nincic. He suggests that high defense expenditure is the only federal expenditure that is compatible with a preference for a small overall federal budget (Nincic 1982, 40 f.).

The conclusion from the two investigations is not unanimous. Krell did not find strong evidence of an electoral defense cycle. Nincic and Cusack, on the other hand, found that "it is thus possible to explain the dual domestic function of military spending as a means of: (a) stimulating the economy in anticipation of electoral benefits, and (b) compensating for shortfalls in private consumption and investment" (Nincic and Cusack 1979, 112).

Both of these two solid studies by Krell and Nincic and Cusack try to answer the same question and use data from the same country and period, but they come to widely different conclusions. This situation is an indication that the methods used need further elaboration if we are ever to reach the point at which we can state at least a preliminary common conclusion.

Some other studies also touch on this question. Ostrom (1977) investigated an arms race model versus an organizational model and found neither acceptable. In a later study, he found better performance for a model that combined arms races and domestic influences (Ostrom 1978). Cusack and Ward (1981, 460) studied economic considerations that did extremely well in explaining changes in U.S. milex.

The conclusion of all this discussion is not very clear. Time-series studies on national aggregates without consideration of sectoral differences and different contents of milex seem to be insufficient. The data needed for an analysis that could take these differences into account are unfortunately not easily available. There are more "armchair theorists who conduct statistical exercises" than people "trying to provide a reasonable statistical structure" (Blackaby and Ohlson 1982, 291). This situation is not surprising since the latter task demands institutional backing and the result is less easily published. If more countries provided information on their military budgets, all research in this field would be much better off.

Conclusion

In order to fully assess the economic consequences of military spending, we would require considerably more research than has been carried out so far. Regarding less developed countries, the focus has almost entirely been on economic growth. There is no general agreement, but the evidence seems to indicate that milex is not favorable for economic growth in developing countries—possibly it is detrimental. Most investigations deal with industrialized market economies, and let me review the effects of milex in those economies on the five economic dimensions selected for discussion. It is clear from the studies examined that investment suffers from higher military expenditures, and this effect is serious because it undermines future production capacity. The effects on economic growth are more complex. Reduced investments have an effect on economic growth, but other linkages are not clearly demonstrated. The relationship between employment and military spending seems to be more complex than the methods and data used so far can handle. Whether or not military expenditure can be used as a countercyclical or an electoral instrument is not clear as there are contradictory conclusions.

The first and main problem with the reviewed studies is that the data used are too general because of the high level of aggregation, the phases in the business cycles, and the question of cross-sectional versus time-series data. Of course, knowledge about the economic impact of milex can be drawn from macroeconomic data, but really interesting discoveries can probably be made only with disaggregated data. The defense industry has different characteristics in different countries and regions. Exactly *how* milex is composed is very important for the impact of higher milex. If rising milex consists of procurement of more military aircraft that are mainly imported, the situation would be quite different than if it consists of a prolonged general conscription. The availability of human resources and excess capacity in different sectors are obviously also important.

Second, if the consequences of military expenditure were investigated with regard to the business cycles, much would be gained. In a situation with insufficient aggregate demand and idle resources, milex can add the extra demand that is needed to get the economy going. On the other hand, milex can result in even more pressure for rising inflation and bottleneck problems in an economy with fully utilized resources. This result can be even more pronounced in a sector where military procurement constitutes a substantial part of the production. Many of these effects are not unique for milex; they are more or less the same for any kind of public expenditure. A central focus in research should thus be to what extent milex is different from any other public expenditure.

Third, can one expect to learn anything useful by making cross-sectional studies of, for instance, Norway and the United States? Something, but not very much. There are many similarities among industrialized market economies, but since their industrial capacities have developed according to different patterns and their military procurement and manpower are differently organized, it seems dubious that cross-sectional study is the best research design. The economic scene is too complex to be reduced to one single figure for GNP or some other national aggregate. If the effect of milex is heavily influenced by some specific institutional arrangement in one country, it seems that even very complicated econometric models will not help us if we insist on using some national aggregate as our measure.

The arguments presented here lead to the conclusion that analysis on a more disaggregated level is urgently needed.

Table 8.A. Empirical studies on the economic consequences of military expenditure in chronological order

Author Year	Page No.	Focus	Countries	Time period	Main conclusion
Pryor 1968	124	Trade-offs	1 OECD + 3 centrally planned economies	1956-1962	No standard pattern for trade-offs
Russett 1969 1970	424 168	Trade-offs in GNP	US, Can, UK Fra	1938-1967	Consumer pays most, investment hard hit
Brown and Kelleher 1971	408	Milex on GNP, consumption and investment	US	1947-1970	Milex depresses most GNP components but less during excess capacity or with increasing money supply
Hollenhurst and Ault 1971	761	Comment Russett 1969	US	1939-1968	Trade-offs have shifted substantially over the period
Benoit 1973	119	Milex and economic growth in LDCs	44 LDC	1950-1967	No decisive demonstration that defense promotes growth
Benoit 1973	147	Appendix on milex and econ. growth in OECD	19 OECD	1950-1965	Probably negative growth effect in developed countries because of inverse correlation between milex and investment
Lee 1973	72, 90	Trade-offs, milex on economic growth	US	1946-1972	Trade-off between milex and social welfare; milex is detrimental for economic growth
Lieberson 1973	68	Milex and corporate income	US	1916-1965	Corporate income is not deeply dependent on milex

Author/Year		Topic	Sample	Period	Finding
Rotschild 1973	810 f	Milex and economic growth	14 OECD	1956-1970	Milex may reduce export and thereby hamper export-led growth
Szymanski 1973a	7 ff	Milex and stagnation	17 OECD +Israel	1950-1968	Milex reduces unemployment but hinders economic growth
Cypher 1974	5	Milex on economic cycles and stagnation	US	1947-1972	Milex used counter-cyclically
Caputo 1975	438	Trade-offs	Australia, Sweden, UK, US	1950-1970	The assumption of an explicit trade-off between milex and welfare should be re-examined
Nardinelli and Ackerman 1976	14 f	Milex and economic growth	US	1905-1973	Effect of defense on GNP is clearly negative
Dabelko and McCormick 1977	149 ff	Trade-offs educ/health	76 (OECD + LDC + centrally planned economies)	1950-1972	Personalist regimes have highest opportunity costs
Ostrom 1977	259	Arms race vs. organizational politics model	US	1954-1973	Neither model is accepted as adequate forecasting tool
Smith 1977	71 f	Trade-offs, milex on economic cycles and stagnation	15 OECD	1960-1970	Trade-off between milex and investment
Chester 1978	294 ff	Comment Smith 1977 trade-offs	15 OECD	1960-1973	Milex leads not to unemployment, slow growth or replacement investment
Hartley and McLean 1978	292	Comment Smith 1977	UK	1948-1973	Defense expenditures affect voters

Table 8.A. (cont.)

Hill 1978	49	Determinants of milex	109 (OECD + LDC + centrally planned economies)	1965	No single explanation for all nations
Ostrom 1978	953	Combination of arms race and domestic models	US	1954-1976	A synthesis of competing models into a reactive linkage model performs better than previous models
Smith 1978; Smith and Smith 1980	303 f; 52	Comment Chester, Hartley and McLean 1978	15 OECD	1960-1970	Negative effect of milex on investment greater than positive effect on R&D, net effect on growth negative
Nincic and Cusack 1979	108 f	Milex on economic cycles	US	1948-1976	Milex variations arise from political considerations
Peroff and Podolak-Warren 1979	31	Trade-off between milex and health	US	1929-1974	Trade-off between federal health and defense appropriation requests and even greater between total health and defense expenditure
Smith 1979	271 f	Milex and investment	14 NATO	1947-1973	Milex and investment have been close substitutes
Faini et al. 1980, 1984	8, 493	Milex and economic growth	69(OECD+LDC)	1952-1970	No evidence for greater milex associated with higher growth rates
Fontanel 1980	62	Milex and economic growth	France, Morocco	1958-1979	Milex has strong negative effect on investment in France
Smith 1980b	26, 30	Milex and investment	14 OECD	1954-1973	Milex and investment have robust negative association
Cusack 1981	8 ff, 15	Trade-offs in GNP	32 (OECD+LDC)	1960-1977	Higher milex reduces private consumption, lower milex promotes investment

Author/Year		Topic	Countries	Years	Findings
Cusack and Ward 1981	455	Arms race vs. domestic environment	US, USSR, China	1949-1978	U.S. milex may be best explained by the political economic cycles
Krell 1981	228 f, 236	Milex on economic cycles	US	1945-1979	Milex changes explained by foreign policy
Griffin et al. 1982	11	Milex on economic cycles	US	1949-1976	Milex employed as countercyclical fiscal instrument
Russett 1982	772, 775 f	Trade-offs milex and health and education	US	1941-1979	Absence of relationship between milex and federal social spending before Reagan
Deger and Smith 1983	345 f	Milex on economic growth in LDCs	50 LDCs	1965-1973	Milex has negative effect on economic growth
DeGrasse 1983	210 ff	Milex and economic growth	17 OECD	1960-1980	Nations with a larger military burden tended to invest less; weak evidence for higher milex correlation with real economic growth
Domke et al. 1983	34	Trade-offs	US, UK, FRG, France	1947-1978	No trade-offs in peace time; internat. factors determine most US milex
Fredriksen and Looney 1983	639	Milex on economic growth in LDCs	37 LDCs	1960-1973	Milex may increase economic growth in relatively resource-unconstrained countries but not in resource-constrained countries
Leontief and Duchin 1983	80 ff	Input-output analysis for scenarios	15 regions	1967-1978	Virtually all countries can increase total output and per capita consumption with reduced milex
Lim 1983	380 f	Milex and economic growth in LDCs	54 LDCs	1965-1973	Milex detrimental to ec. growth; Benoit's results not replicated

Table 8.A. (cont.)

Nabe 1983	585	Milex and development in Africa	26 African countries	1967-1976	Economic growth is not positively affected by milex
Smith and Georgiou 1983	9,12	Milex and investment	US, UK, FRG	1954-1979	Negative relationship between milex and investment; some support U.S. milex as regulator
Weede 1983	15	Military participation ratio and economic growth	95 (OECD+LDC)	1960-1977	Positive impact of military participation ratios on economic growth
Cappelen et al. 1984	370	Milex and economic growth	17 OECD	1960-1981	Milex has positive effect on output of manufactured goods and negative effect on investment; net effect on GDP is negative
Chan 1984	7,14	Milex and economic growth	24 OECD	1961-1980	Higher per capita levels of milex related to slower growth; increasing milex related to faster growth
Dunne and Smith 1984	304	Simulation of reduced UK milex	UK	1983-1987	Reduced milex will lead to net growth in employment
Rasler and Thompson 1984	15 f	Milex on investment and economic growth	UK, US, Japan France, FRG	1831-1980	Systemic leadership is payed for by lower investment
Starr et al. 1984	117	Milex and inflation	US, UK, France, FRG	1956-1979	Mutual relation milex/inflation in France and FRG but not for US and UK
Woodbury and Zuk 1984 Zuk and Woodbury 1986	13 ff 459 ff	Milex and electoral cycles; US-USSR relations	US	1947-1984	No obvious connection between national elections and milex

Author/Year		Focus	Countries	Years	Findings
Blank and Rotschild 1985	691	Milex and employment	US	1963-1984	Milex generates demand for highly paid workers in private firms and low-paid government workers
Fredriksen and Looney 1985a	209	Milex on economic growth in LDCs	95 LDCs	1965-1973	Milex can promote economic growth in many developing countries
Keman 1985	30	Trade-off welfare/warfare	17 OECD	1962-1982	Both welfare and milex increased before 1973; after 1973 milex replaced welfare expenditure
Biswas and Ram 1986	369	Milex on economic growth in LDCs	58 LDCs	1960-1977	Milex neither helps nor hurts economic growth significantly
Dixon and Moon 1986	674	Milex, military participation and control on basic needs	116 (OECD, LDC, centrally planned economies)	1960-1978	Milex has little impact on welfare measured by Physical Quality of Life Index
Looney and Fredriksen 1986	334	Milex on economic growth in LDCs	61 LDCS	1970-1982	Milex is not the burden to foreign exchange abundant countries as it is to constrained countries
Maizels and Nissanke 1986	1134 ff	Determinants of milex in LDCs	83 LDCs	1973-1980	Central government share of GDP single most important explanatory variable; different factors in various countries
Weede 1986	304 ff	One of four focus is military participation ratios and economic growth	32 LDCs	1970-1979	Higher military participation ratios associated with faster economic growth
Lebovic and Ishaq 1987	122 ff	Milex on economic growth in the Middle East	19 (LDC+Israel)	1973-1982	Milex has suppressed economic growth

References

As a part of the research for this chapter, an extensive computerized bibliography on the economics of armaments has been assembled. It can be obtained from the author (Department of Peace and Conflict Research, Uppsala University, Östra Ågatan 53, S-753 22 Uppsala, Sweden). An earlier version of this essay appeared in the *Journal of Peace Research* 21:4 (1984), pp. 375–387. I am grateful for valuable comments from Peter Wallensteen, Miroslav Nincic, Nils Petter Gleditsch, and Ragnhild Lundström.

Adelman, Irma, and Cynthia Taft Morris. 1973. *Economic Growth and Social Equity in Developing Countries.* Stanford: Stanford University Press.

Albrecht, Ulrich. 1978. "Researching Conversion: A Review of the State of the Art." In Peter Wallensteen, ed., *Experiences in Disarmament,* pp. 11–43. Uppsala: Department of Peace and Conflict Research, Uppsala University.

Ball, Nicole. 1983a. "Defense and Development: A Critique of the Benoit Study." *Economic Development and Cultural Change* 31:3 (April), pp. 507–524. A shorter version appears in Helena Tuomi and Raimo Väyrynen, eds., *Militarization and Arms Production,* pp. 39–56. London and Canberra: Croom Helm, 1982.

———. 1983b. "Military Expenditure, Economic Growth, and Socio-Economic Development in the Third World." *Nordic Journal of Latin American Studies* 22:1-2, pp. 5–20.

———. 1985. "Defense Expenditures and Economic Growth: A Comment." *Armed Forces and Society* 11:2 (Winter), pp. 291–297.

Baran, Paul, and Paul Sweezy. 1968. *Monopoly Capital.* Harmondsworth, Eng.: Penguin.

Benoit, Emile. 1973. *Defense and Economic Growth in Developing Countries.* Lexington, Mass.: Lexington Books.

———. 1978. "Growth and Defense in Developing Countries." *Economic Development and Cultural Change* 26:2 (January), pp. 271–280.

Biswas, Basudeb, and Rati Ram. 1986. "Military Expenditures and Economic Growth in Less Developed Countries: An Augmented Model and Further Evidence." *Economic Development and Cultural Change* 34:2 (January), pp. 361–372.

Blackaby, Frank, and Thomas Ohlson. 1982. "Military Expenditure and Arms Trade: Problems of Data." *Bulletin of Peace Proposals* 13:4, pp. 291–308.

Blank, Rebecca, and Emma Rotschild. 1985. "The Effect of United States Defence Spending on Employment and Output." *International Labour Review* 124:6 (November-December), pp. 677–697.

Blaug, Mark. 1981. *The Methodology of Economics.* Cambridge: Cambridge University Press.

Brouthers, Lance. 1984. "Comment on Russett." *American Political Science Review* 78:1 (March), pp. 202–204.

Brown, Kenneth M., and Michael J. Kelleher. 1971. "The Impact of Military Expenditures upon the U.S. Economy." *Econometrica* 39:4 (July), p. 408 (abstract).

Cappelen, Ådne; Olav Bjerkholt; and Nils Petter Gleditsch. 1982. *Global Conversion from Arms to Development Aid: Macroeconomic Effects in Norway.* PRIO publication S-9/82. Oslo: PRIO.

Cappelen, Ådne; Nils Petter Gleditsch; and Olav Bjerkholt. 1984. "Military Spending and Economic Growth in the OECD Countries." *Journal of Peace Research* 21:4, pp. 361–373.

Caputo, David A. 1975. "New Perspectives on the Public Policy Implications of Defense and Welfare Expenditures in Four Modern Democracies: 1950–1970." *Policy Sciences* 6, pp. 423–446.

Chan, Steve. 1984. "Defense Spending and Economic Performance: Correlates Among the OECD Countries." Paper delivered at the annual meeting of the International Studies Association, Atlanta, Georgia.

———. 1985. "The Impact of Defense Spending on Economic Performance: A Survey of Evidence and Problems." *Orbis* 29:3 (Summer), pp. 403–434.

Chester, Eric. 1978. "Military Spending and Capitalist Stability." *Cambridge Journal of Economics* 2:3, pp. 293–298.

Cusack, Thomas R. 1981. *The Economic Burden of Defense: A Comparative Study.* IIVG/dp 81-118. Berlin: International Institute for Comparative Social Research. Wissenschaftszentrum Berlin.

Cusack, Thomas R., and Michael Don Ward. 1981. "Military Spending in the United States, Soviet Union, and the People's Republic of China." *Journal of Conflict Resolution* 25:3 (September), pp. 429–469.

Cypher, James. 1974. "Capitalist Planning and Military Expenditures." *Review of Radical Political Economy,* pp. 1–19.

Dabelko, David, and James M. McCormick. 1977. "Opportunity Costs of Defence: Some Cross-National Evidence." *Journal of Peace Research* 14:2, pp. 145–154.

Deger, Saadet, and Ron Smith. 1983. "Military Expenditure and Growth in Less Developed Countries." *Journal of Conflict Resolution* 27:2 (June), pp. 335–353.

DeGrasse, Robert W., Jr. 1983. *Military Expansion Economic Decline: The Impact of Military Spending on U.S. Economic Performance.* New York: Council on Economic Priorities/Sharpe.

———. 1984. "The Military: Shortchanging the Economy." *Bulletin of the Atomic Scientists* 40:5, pp. 37–40.

Dixon, William J. and Bruce E. Moon. 1986. "The Military Burden and Basic Human Needs." *Journal of Conflict Resolution* 30:4 (December), pp. 660–684.

Domke, William K.; Richard C. Eichenberg; and Catherine M. Kelleher. 1983. "The Illusion of Choice: Defense and Welfare in Advanced Industrial Democracies, 1948–1978." *American Political Science Review,* 77:1 (March), pp. 19–35.

Dunne, J., and R. P. Smith. 1984. "The Economic Consequences of Reduced UK Military Expenditure." *Cambridge Journal of Economics* 8:3, pp. 297–310.

Evans, Michael K. 1969. *Macroeconomic Activity.* New York: Harper and Row.

Faini, Riccardo; Patricia Annez; and Lance Taylor. 1980. "Defense Spending, Economic Structure, and Growth: Evidence Among Countries and Over Time." Report to UN Group of Governmental Experts on the Relationship Between Disarmament and Development. Shorter version in *Economic Development and Cultural Change* 32:3 (April 1984), pp. 487–498.

Fontanel, Jacques. 1980. "Formalized Studies and Econometric Analyses of the Relationship Between Military Expenditure and Economic Development." Paper prepared for UN Group of Governmental Experts on the Relationship Between Disarmament and Development.

―――. 1984. *L'économie des armes.* Paris: Editions La Decouverte.

Fredriksen, P. C., and Robert E. Looney. 1983. "Defense Expenditures and Economic Growth in Developing Countries." *Armed Forces and Society* 9:4 (Summer), pp. 633–645.

―――. 1985a. "Another Look at the Defense Spending and Development Hypothesis." *Defense Analysis* 1:3, pp. 205–210.

―――. 1985b. "Defense Expenditures and Economic Growth in Developing Countries: A Reply." *Armed Forces and Society* 11:2 (Winter), pp. 298–301.

Friedman, Samuel R. 1974. "An Alternative Model to Szymanski's." *American Journal of Sociology* 79:6 (May), pp. 1459–1462.

Griffin, L. J.; M. Wallace; and J. Devine. 1982. "The Political Economy of Military Spending: Evidence from the United States." *Cambridge Journal of Economics* 6:1, pp. 1–14.

Hartley, Keith, and Pat McLean. 1978. "Military Expenditure and Capitalism: A Comment." *Cambridge Journal of Economics* 2:3, pp. 287–292.

Hill, Kim Quaile. 1978. "Domestic Politics, International Linkages, and Military Expenditures." *Studies in Comparative International Development* 13:1 (Spring), pp. 38–59.

Hollenhurst, Jerry, and Gary Ault, 1971. "An Alternative Answer To: Who Pays for Defense?" *American Political Science Review* 65:3 (September), pp. 760–763.

Hovstadius, Bo, and Manne Wängborg. 1981. "The United Nations Study of Disarmament and Development: An Overview." *Journal of Peace Research* 18:2, pp. 209–217.

Huisken, Ron. 1982. "Armaments and Development." In Helena Tuomi and Raimo Väyrynen, eds., *Militarization and Arms Production,* pp. 3–25. London and Canberra: Croom Helm.

Johnson, Harry G. 1975. "Egregious Economics as Pacifist Propaganda." *Armed Forces and Society* 1:4 (August), pp. 498–504.

Kaldor, Mary. 1978. "The Military in Third World Development." In R. Jolly, ed., *Disarmament and World Development,* pp. 57–82. Oxford: Pergamon Press.

―――. 1981. *The Baroque Arsenal.* New York: Hill and Wang.

Keman, Hans. 1985. "Economic Decline, Cold War Structure, and the Trade-Off Between Welfare and Warfare in 17 Capitalist Democracies." *Current Research on Peace and Violence* 8:1, pp. 24–36.

Kennedy, Gavin 1975. *The Economics of Defence.* London: Faber and Faber.
———. 1983. *Defense Economics.* London: Duckworth.
Krell, Gert. 1981. "Capitalism and Armaments: Business Cycles and Defense Spending in the United States 1945–1979." *Journal of Peace Research* 18:3, pp. 221–240.
Lebovic, James H., and Ashfaq Ishaq. 1987. "Military Burden, Security Needs, and Economic Growth in the Middle East." *Journal of Conflict Resolution* 31:1 (March), pp. 106–138.
Lee, Jong Ryol. 1973. "Changing National Priorities of the United States." In Bruce M. Russett and Alfred Stepan, eds., *Military Force and American Society,* pp. 61–105. New York: Harper and Row.
Leontief, Wassily, and Faye Duchin. 1983. *Military Spending: Facts and Figures, Worldwide Implications, and Future Outlook.* New York: Oxford University Press.
Lieberson, Stanley. 1973. "An Empirical Study of Military Industrial Linkages." In Steven J. Rosen, ed., *Testing the Theory of the Military-Industrial Complex,* pp. 61–83. Lexington, Mass.: Lexington Books.
Lim, D. 1983. "Another Look at Growth and Defense in Less Developed Countries." *Economic Development and Cultural Change* 31:2 (January), pp. 377–384.
Lindroos, Reijo. 1980. *Disarmament and Employment.* Tampere, Fin.: Tampereen Pikakopio.
Looney, Robert E., and P. C. Fredriksen. 1986. "Defense Expenditures, External Public Debt, and Growth in Developing Countries." *Journal of Peace Research* 23:4, pp. 329–338.
Maizels, Alfred, and Machiko K. Nissanke. 1986. "The Determinants of Military Expenditures in Developing Countries." *World Development* 14:9, pp. 1125–1140.
Mosley, Hugh G. 1985. *The Arms Race: Social and Economic Consequences.* Lexington, Mass.: Lexington Books.
Nabe, Oumar. 1983. "Military Expenditures and Industrialization in Africa." *Journal of Economic Issues* 17:2 (June), pp. 575–587.
Nardinelli, Clark, and Gary B. Ackerman. 1976. "Defense Expenditures and the Survival of American Capitalism." *Armed Forces and Society* 3:1 (November), pp. 13–16.
Nincic, Miroslav. 1982. *The Arms Race: The Political Economy of Military Growth.* New York: Praeger.
Nincic, Miroslav, and Thomas R. Cusack. 1979. "The Political Economy of US Military Spending." *Journal of Peace Research* 16:2, pp. 101–115.
Ostrom, Charles W., Jr. 1977. "Evaluating Alternative Foreign Policy Decision-making Models." *Journal of Conflict Resolution* 21:2 (June), pp. 235–266.
———. 1978. "A Reactive Linkage Model of the U.S. Defense Expenditure Policy-making Process." *American Political Science Review* 22:3 (September), pp. 941–957.
Peroff, Kathleen, and Margaret Podolak-Warren. 1979. "Does Spending for Defense Cut Spending on Health?" *British Journal of Political Science* 9:1 (January), pp. 21–39.

Pryor, Frederic L. 1968. *Public Expenditures in Communist and Capitalist Nations.* Homewood, Ill.: Irwin.

Rasler, Karen A., and William R. Thompson. 1984. "Longitudinal Change in Defense Burdens, Capital Formation, and Economic Growth." Paper delivered at the annual meeting of the International Studies Association. Atlanta, Georgia.

Reich, Michael. 1972. "Does the U.S. Economy Require Military Spending?" *American Economic Review* 72:2, pp. 296–303.

——— . 1973. "Military Spending and the U.S. Economy." In Steven J. Rosen, eds., *Testing the Theory of the Military-Industrial Complex,* pp. 85–104. Lexington, Mass.: Lexington Books.

Rotschild, Kurt W. 1973. "Military Expenditure, Exports, and Growth." *Kyklos* 26:4, pp. 804–813.

Russett, Bruce. 1969. "Who Pays for Defense?" *American Political Science Review* 63:2 (June), pp. 412–426.

——— . 1970. *What Price Vigilance?* New Haven: Yale University Press.

——— . 1982. "Defense Expenditure and National Well-being." *American Political Science Review* 76:4 (December), pp. 767–777.

Smith, Dan, and Ron P. Smith. 1980. "Military Expenditure, Resources, and Development." Report prepared for UN Group of Governmental Experts on the Relationship Between Disarmament and Development. Birkbeck College Discussion Paper no. 87.

——— . 1983. *The Economics of Militarism.* London: Pluto Press.

Smith, Ron P. 1977. "Military Expenditure and Capitalism." *Cambridge Journal of Economics* 1:1, pp. 61–76.

——— . 1978. "Military Expenditure and Capitalism: A Reply." *Cambridge Journal of Economics* 2:3, pp. 299–304.

——— . 1979. "The Resource Cost of Military Expenditure." In Mary Kaldor, Dan Smith, and Steve Vines, eds., *Democratic Socialism and the Cost of Defence,* pp. 262–280. London: Croom Helm.

——— . 1980a. "The Demand for Military Expenditure." *Economic Journal* 90:360 (December), pp. 811–820.

——— . 1980b. "Military Expenditure and Investment in OECD Countries, 1954–1973." *Journal of Comparative Economics* 4, pp. 19–32.

Smith, Ron P., and George Georgiou. 1983. "Assessing the Effect of Military Expenditure on OECD Economies: A Survey." *Arms Control* 4:1 (May), pp. 3–15.

Starr, Harvey; Francis W. Hoole; Jeffrey A. Hart; and John R. Freeman. 1984. "The Relationship Between Defense Spending and Inflation." *Journal of Conflict Resolution* 28:1 (March), pp. 103–122.

Stevenson, Paul. 1974. "A Defense of Baran and Sweezy." *American Journal of Sociology* 79:6 (May), pp. 1456–1458.

Sweezy, Paul. 1973. "Comments on Szymanski's Paper 'Military Spending and Economic Stagnation.' " *American Journal of Sociology* 79:3 (November), pp. 709–710.

Szymanski, Albert. 1973a. "Military Spending and Economic Stagnation." *American Journal of Sociology* 79:1 (July), pp. 1–14.

———. 1973b. "Reply to Sweezy." *American Journal of Sociology* 79:3 (November), pp. 710–711.

———. 1974. "A Reply to Friedman, Stevenson, and Zeitlin." *American Journal of Sociology* 79:6 (May), pp. 1462–1477.

Taylor, Charles Lewis, and Michael C. Hudson. 1972. *World Handbook of Political and Social Indicators.* 2d ed. New Haven: Yale University Press.

United Nations. 1972. *Economic and Social Consequences of the Arms Race and of Military Expenditure.* E.72.IX.16. New York: United Nations.

———. 1978. *Economic and Social Consequences of the Arms Race and of Military Expenditure.* E.78.IX.1. New York: United Nations.

———. 1981. *Reduction of Military Budgets: International Reporting of Military Expenditures.* E.81.I.9. New York: United nations.

———. 1982. *The Relationship Between Disarmament and Development.* Report of the Secretary-General. E.82.IX.1. New York: United Nations.

———. 1983a. *Economic and Social Consequences of the Arms Race of Military Expenditures.* E.83.IX.4. New York: United Nations.

———. 1983b. *Reduction of Military Budgets: Refinement of International Reporting and Comparison of Military Expenditures.* E.83.IX.4. New York: United Nations.

Weede, Erich. 1983. "Military Participation Ratios, Human Capital Formation, and Economic Growth: A Cross-national Analysis." *Journal of Political and Military Sociology* 11 (Spring), pp. 11–19.

———. 1986. "Rent Seeking, Military Participation, and Economic Performance in LDCs." *Journal of Conflict Resolution* 30:2 (June), pp. 291–314.

Woodbury, Nancy R., and Gary Zuk. 1984. "U.S. Defense Spending, Electoral Cycles, and Soviet-American Relations: A Time Series Analysis." Paper delivered at the Annual Meeting of the International Studies Association, Atlanta, Georgia. Also published in 1986 in *Journal of Conflict Resolution* 30:3 (September), pp. 445–468, with authors' names in reversed order.

Zeitlin, Maurice. 1973. "On Military Spending and Economic Stagnation." *American Journal of Sociology* 79:6 (May), pp. 1452–1456.

Zuk, Gary, and Nancy Woodbury. 1986. "U.S. Defense Spending, Electoral Cycles, and Soviet-American Relations: A Time Series Analysis." *Journal of Conflict Resolution* 30:3 (September), pp. 445–468.

9

Military R&D and Economic Growth in Industrialized Market Economies

Nils Petter Gleditsch, Olav Bjerkholt, and Ådne Cappelen

Economic Effects of Military Spending

In 1982 the world spent about US $674 billion on armaments,[1] which was 5.3 percent of the total global output and 19 percent of total public spending. Arms expenditure exceeded world spending on public education by 5 percent and health spending by 28 percent. Global arms spending was eighteen times higher than foreign aid and two and a half times higher than what was spent on international peacekeeping.[2] There is no question that the arms race remains one of the major projects of humankind, and as such, it is bound to have a number of economic effects.[3]

Like most other types of government consumption, military spending serves in the short run to stimulate demand, with favorable consequences for employment and other measures of economic activity. In a long-term perspective, military spending influences economic growth and development through different channels. The importance of this effect depends on the scarcity of the various resources. The financing of military spending may influence the overall savings rate in a negative way, and less saving means less growth. On the other hand, certain components of military expenditure may have nonmilitary benefits for economic growth. This situation might be true particularly in less developed countries for certain kinds of infrastructure (roads, airports) and for education of military personnel. In mature industrialized economies, technological progress might result from military R&D expenditure.

Because military spending is so centralized, it is sometimes suggested that it may be used as an instrument of economic policy. A significant economic *effect* may represent a possible *motive* for increasing or reducing arms spending. In the short term, arms spending may be used to boost an economy just before an election, to the advantage of the government in power. In the long term, arms spending may be used to promote the emergence of a national high-technology industry. This suggestion does not mean that there are not more effective national policy instruments for achieving the same ends, but the economic effects of arms spending—and particularly the beliefs about such effects—may influence defense policy decision making.[4]

The literature suggests that military spending may have a significant effect on a number of important economic variables: the level of employment, the savings rate, economic growth, inflation,[5] the volume of imports and exports, and the balance of payments. It is beyond the scope of this chapter to review all of these effects, but we will consider economic growth and in particular, R&D induced growth.

Effects of Military Spending on Economic Growth

The case for the harmful effect of military spending on economic growth rests on the premise that the arms sector is unproductive and that a reallocation of resources to the civilian sector is likely to improve the performance of the economy.[6] More specifically, military spending is likely to depress economic growth in at least three different ways. First, it may decrease investment and thus negatively affect the renewal and expansion of civilian industry. Second, if military spending leads to lower employment, labor resources will be utilized in an inefficient way. Third, military spending may create bottlenecks for highly qualified labor, R&D resources, etc., that are necessary for innovation and growth.

On the other hand, it has been claimed that military spending is conducive to economic growth. One basis for this claim is the "underconsumptionist" argument put forward by Baran and Sweezy that massive military spending is necessary to absorb surplus and to avoid depression. Another line of reasoning is that there are significant spin-off effects from military research and development that lead to innovation and improved productivity in the civilian sector. These effects are probably what Harold Brown had in mind when, as U.S. secretary of defense, he argued in 1980, "Our research indicates that [military expenditures] are beneficial to the civilian economy; since much of the additional spending promotes domestic production in our most capital and technology intensive sectors."[7]

Crossnational comparisons indicate that industrialized countries with high military spending tend to have lower economic growth.[8] On the other hand, country-by-country comparisons over time for the post–World War II period show that productivity growth has been higher in periods of high military spending.[9]

The longitudinal relationship seems more likely to be spurious. A positive correlation can come about by a "reversed" causal relationship: Economic expansion (or decline) may lead decision makers to increase (or cut back) public spending generally, including military spending. Besides, high military spending need not have an immediate negative effect on economic growth. The long-term effect is probably better measured by crossnational comparisons than by longitudinal comparisons without time lags from some countries.

Nevertheless, the contrast between the crosssectional and longitudinal results warrants a certain caution in interpreting the results of such simple comparisons. However a number of studies have gone beyond these comparisons to apply economic models to the relationship between military spending and economic growth. As far as industrialized market economies are concerned, the conclusion is fairly unanimous: High military spending competes with investment and thereby reduces economic growth.[10] In our own study of seventeen OECD countries for the period 1960–1980, we found, for instance, that military spending generally had a positive impact on manufacturing output but a negative effect on investment. These two effects have an opposite impact on economic growth. The net effect was that military spending had a negative influence on growth for the OECD area as a whole and for the subgroups of major powers and "other small countries" but not for the Mediterranean countries.[11]

A different approach was taken by Leontief and Duchin in using a model of the world economy.[12] Comparing a scenario for reduced growth in military expenditure to a base scenario that essentially continued present trends, they found that the former scenario led to increased growth in GDP in all of their seven regions of developed countries and in five out of their seven regions of developing countries. The additional GDP generated was modest (generally a few percent), but of course the degree of conversion envisaged in this scenario was also very modest.

To our knowledge, there are not many national studies that make use of economic models to study the growth effects of military spending. In a study of Norway, using the national growth model MSG-4, we found that scenarios involving modest levels of disarmament and conversion (15 percent reduction of military expenditure per ten years) yielded a slight increase in GDP (1 percent in twenty years) compared to the baseline.[13]

Growth Effects of Military R&D

Spin-off Effects

As already noted, there is a school of thought that argues that military R&D has significant spin-offs (or spillovers) into the civilian sector, that research in the military field yields civilian applications as a by-product. Radar, computers, and electronics are often cited as examples. Two scientists from the Massachusetts Institute of Technology have clearly stated the case for spin-offs:

> Missile guidance systems were an early source of support for integrated circuit developments; requirements for satellite-tracking radars have supported the development of surface acoustic-wave technology and charge-coupled devices, as well as modern signal-processing techniques. . . . Finally, we should mention such significant second-order developments as radio and radar astronomy, microwave spectroscopy, and instrumentation for earth resources satellites and for modern health care, all of which are heavily dependent on concepts and components derived from military electronics.[14]

Specific spin-off examples include commercial aircraft as the Boeing 707 was developed from the B-47 bomber, and the Boeing 747 was developed from the losing design for the C-5 cargo plane.[15]

A variant of the spin-off argument is that even when innovations are not made originally through military R&D, the military provides the extensive "first use" of a new technology that makes it commercially viable. The transistor has been mentioned as an example, as heavy purchases for military purposes led to an improved product and reduced price.[16]

Spin-off from the military to the civilian sector is also used as an argument for West European participation in the U.S. Strategic Defense Initiative (SDI).[17] It is argued that the SDI will produce goods directly useful to the civilian sector and, also, European participants would get an insight into modern U.S. technology that would be difficult to obtain otherwise. The latter point, it is argued, would strengthen the high-technology sectors in Western Europe. In recent years, the United States has been increasingly restrictive in releasing sensitive data from its R&D and in exporting civilian technology that could be exploited for military purposes. These restrictions have made it especially important to have good relations with the U.S. military-industrial establishment.

The evidence for such spin-offs is mixed, varying from one field to another. Bernhard Udis has interviewed professionals in Western European military R&D institutions and in firms producing military goods and found that their opinions were divided.[18] Some believed that military and civilian production are quite similar in many fields and that substantial spin-offs occur. Others were more skeptical and felt that the spin-off argument was frequently used as an excuse for high defense spending.

Lloyd J. Dumas quotes a 1974 report of a committee of the U.S. National Academy of Engineering. Although not commenting directly on military R&D, this report was very critical of the alleged spin-offs from federal R&D programs, of which military programs constituted a major share: "With a few exceptions the vast technology developed by federally funded programs since World War II has not resulted in widespread spin-offs of secondary or additional applications of practical products, processes and services that have made an impact on the nation's economic growth, industrial productivity, employment gains, and foreign trade."[19] The efficiency of publicly funded R&D projects has also been questioned in some econometric studies. Two U.S. studies indicate positive returns from privately financed R&D but no effect from federally funded R&D.[20] As a larger share of military R&D than civilian R&D is publicly funded, it is difficult to determine whether the lack of spin-offs from military R&D is owing to its being military or the funding. Other studies, however, have emphasized the role of Japan's Ministry of International Trade and Industry (MITI) in promoting the growth of knowledge-intensive industries. This role has been favorably compared to the role of the Department of Defense in the U.S. economy.[21]

There are a number of objections to the spin-off argument. First of all, the argument builds on selected examples. With military R&D after World War II absorbing at least 25 percent of all R&D, it would be surprising if no examples of benefits for the civilian sector could be found, but the civilian benefits seem to be in no proportion to this enormous amount of funding. Two case studies of the U.S. nuclear power and semiconductor industries seem to show that, in these areas, heavy military funding has been less than successful in promoting innovation. Commercial nuclear power was led down the wrong trail by pursuing a design developed by the U.S. Navy for submarines.[22] In electronics, the three military services—each with heavy funding—

backed three different approaches to the problem of miniaturizing electronic components. None was successful. Meanwhile, a commercial firm developed the integrated circuit—without military funding, and later, the development of a process for the mass production of silicon chips was also achieved without military funding. As with the transistor, the military provided a market for the mass production of these inventions. However, it is argued that military spending is now less necessary even in this respect since semiconductors have become so cheap and standardized that they can profitably be used in a wide array of civilian products. Hence, it is civilian rather than military demand that primarily stimulates further technological development.[23]

The importance of spin-offs has probably also decreased because military production has become more highly specialized and now has fewer civilian applications.[24] Cost considerations make the gap between engineering feasibility and operational practice much wider in the civilian than in the military sector, and the military sector is characterized by highly sophisticated production and small quantities while civilian products need to be inexpensive and are often produced in large quantities. Nuclear submarines and supersonic aircraft are examples of well-established military products with little, if any, promise of civilian use.

Spin-offs are sometimes discussed as if they occur only from military R&D to civilian products. However, spin-offs also occur the other way round—from civilian R&D to the military sector. An important example is the development of metallic paint to shield microwave ovens, which is now being exploited for the military purpose of creating a radar-absorbing surface for "stealth" aircraft and missiles.[25] Restrictions on selling militarily useful civilian technology to the other side in the Cold War is evidence for a belief in such "reverse" spin-off. The U.S. military establishment certainly benefits from that country's advanced civilian sector. Indeed, there are probably more spin-offs from the civilian sector because of a higher degree of free publication and openness; military research is more secret, which impedes institutional cooperation and the dissemination of knowledge.

Malcolm Chalmers has examined the spin-offs in the case of the United Kingdom and argues that at least for some military R&D, the spin-offs may actually be negative.[26] Spin-offs from military R&D have led to investments in civilian sectors that in themselves are uneconomic and need government subsidies—the major examples being the aerospace and nuclear power industries. Both have received large subsidies, and both are at least partly a result of Britain's strong emphasis on military R&D in these fields. In both industries, U.S. firms have a dominant position, and Chalmers concludes that military and military-

related production require a large amount of competition; these industries are probably better off researching in areas in which they have
a long-term comparative advantage. Japan and West Germany have
avoided the aerospace industry and have concentrated more on consumer
electronics—with impressive results.

Several studies emphasize the important role of small firms in the
process of innovation. These are not the firms that receive the greatest
support from military funding; large firms with major defense contracts
tend to be risk minimizers rather than innovators.[27]

The most fundamental objection to the spin-off argument, however,
is this: Spin-offs are uncertain, and when deciding on the desirability
of an R&D program, only the direct costs and benefits should be
evaluated. As Lester Thurow puts it, "Hoping that a solution for a
known problem will come from some project focused on a completely
different goal makes no sense at all."[28] As a general rule, it is more
efficient to use money directly for a civilian project instead of spending
money indirectly via military R&D. Military R&D is carried out for
military reasons: Chance by-products for the civilian sector cannot be
a justification for such programs.

Military R&D and military production would be most beneficial in
an economy with considerable unutilized resources as in such a case,
any alternative use of the resources has zero value. This situation
hardly exists, however. Military R&D competes with civilian R&D for
the best-qualified personnel. Even when unemployment is high, there
may be a shortage of personnel required in the military establishment,
for instance computer engineers or electrical engineers. Thus, an
expansion of military R&D may cause bottlenecks in the civilian sector.
Fewer of these people are left to teach in the universities or to work
on product innovations in civilian industries. To quote Thurow again,
"If the brightest engineers in Japan are designing video recorders and
the brightest engineers in the United States are designing MX missiles,
then we shouldn't find it surprising that they conquer the video recorder
market."[29] In addition to the competition for human resources, the
military sector of course also competes for other resources like energy,
raw materials, and land. These resources generally have alternative
uses in the civilian sector.

Dumas has commented on a deteriorating "patent balance" for the
United States in the 1966–1973 period.[30] Foreign patents in the United
States increased while U.S. patents abroad decreased, and this development seemed to continue in the 1970s. Dumas blames the high
share of military R&D for this situation. One problem with his argument
is that military R&D in the United States stagnated for the whole
period 1963–1980 and during 1966–1973, military R&D actually fell,

in absolute terms as well as in relation to civilian R&D. The patent trend may, however, be explained by a long-term deterioration of U.S. innovative capacity because of continuous high spending on military R&D.

Crossnational Comparisons

The economic performance of countries with different levels of military R&D spending can be compared crossnationally, as has been done for military spending generally. However, there is relatively little research as yet on the effects of military R&D spending, and we are aware of only a few crossnational assessments involving military R&D spending. DeGrasse does present data for productivity growth in manufacturing industries and military and civilian R&D efforts in relation to GDP, investigating six countries for the period 1970–1979.[31] His chart shows that the countries with the most military R&D (the USSR, the United States, and the United Kingdom) have the slowest productivity growth while the countries with less military R&D (West Germany, France, and Japan) have higher productivity growth. The relationship between civilian R&D and productivity is less clear-cut. DeGrasse argues that the negative relationship between military R&D and productivity growth can be explained partly by the low share of military R&D spent on basic research (this share was only 3 percent in the United States from the early 1960s to the early 1980s). He considers basic research important for broad innovations and productivity growth—a view that contradicts the view of most economists as generally, applied research is considered to have a stronger effect on productivity than basic research.

DeGrasse's empirical finding is borne out by our own data in studying eight OECD countries. Figure 9.1 shows a fourway classification of economic growth in 1964–1983 compared with the level of military R&D spending (as a percentage of manufacturing value added, [MVA]) for the same period. There is a clear negative relationship between the two variables although most of the correlation is accounted for by the four extreme cases: Japan, West Germany, the United States, and the United Kingdom.

The longitudinal relationship between R&D and economic growth was not studied by DeGrasse; for our study, the correlations are given in Table 9.1. For civilian R&D, five out of the eight correlations are positive, whereas for military R&D, the correlations with productivity growth are mostly negative (six out eight countries). The three negative (and, thus, anomalous) correlations for civilian R&D are smaller than those for military R&D for the same countries.

Figure 9.1. Publicly financed R&D as a percentage of manufacturing value added (MVA) by average growth of total factor productivity, 1964-1983.

Military R&D as Percentage of MVA

		Low	High
Average Annual Growth in Manufacturing Productivity	High	Japan West Germany Sweden	
	Low	Norway Finland Canada	United States United Kingdom

gamma = -1.0
r (ungrouped percentages) = -0.51

Note: The division into high and low on the two axes is done at the arithmetic mean of the extreme values. A scatter diagram of the relationship reveals that Japan, West Germany, Sweden, the United Kingdom, and the United States lie close to a regression line with a negative slope, whereas Finland, Canada, and Norway lie clustered together off to the side.

Sources: Total factor productivity and manufacturing value added: Arne Magnus Christensen and Asbjörn Torvanger, Military and Civilian Research and Development and Growth, (Oslo: International Peace Research Institute, 1985); Military R&D: Calculated from Table A.2.3., Appendix II in N.P. Gleditsch et al., "Economic Incentives to Arm," PRIO Report 21/86 (Oslo: International Peace Research Institute, 1986).

Thus, we do not find the same contradiction between the crossnational comparison and the longitudinal comparison as the studies on the effects on economic growth of military spending generally do. This finding strengthens our confidence in the empirical relationship. However, it is still a weakness of these analyses that they do not build on a theory-based model.[32]

Public Priorities

Discussion of defense policy frequently leaves the impression that "national security" is a nonnegotiable good that takes absolute priority. This impression is not always the case when it comes to actual budgeting. "Military spending seems quite simply to have lost out to social and political forces which are stronger in the competition for limited federal dollars" as Ted Goertzel says in an analysis of U.S. military spending

Table 9.1. R&D spending and growth; growth of factor
productivity over time, eight OECD countries, 1964-1981

	Correlation Between Growth of Total Factor Productivity and	
	Military R&D (in % of GDP)	Civilian R&D (in % of GDP)
United States	-0.91	-0.55
United Kingdom	0.48	0.25
West Germany	-0.76	0.87
Sweden	-0.87	0.77
Japan	-0.42	-0.33
Canada	-0.92	-0.43
Norway	0.77	0.64
Finland	-0.83	0.61

Source: See Fig. 9.1.

in the period 1951–1980.[33] As Hugh Mosley points out, the military share of the U.S. budget during President Truman's administration was arrived at residually, after essential domestic programs had been subtracted.[34] The testing of the first Soviet nuclear weapon and the outbreak of the Korean War changed that pattern dramatically: Military expenditure suddenly did receive top priority. This military expansion did not, however, occur at the expense of domestic programs. Rather, the rearming of the United States involved an expansion of the public sector of the economy. A "military Keynesianism" became prevalent: Rearmament, in addition to its role in checking perceived foreign aggression, also served to stimulate economic activity. The Reagan administration would seem to contradict this pattern in that it explicitly promised to "build up our military forces . . . , reduce federal spending . . . , significantly reduce business and personal taxes, . . . and balance the budget."[35] In fact, the Reagan administration, unable to fulfill all these goals simultaneously, largely financed the military buildup with increasing budget deficits. Thus, for the United States—at least up to the Reagan administration—there has been no clear competitive relationship between military and civilian spending with civilian spending invariably in the loser's role. But what about other countries?

Table 9.2 compares military spending and spending for public education by region for four years during the period 1970–1982. For most regions, public education spending at first grew more rapidly. However, a look at the data for the last two years considered indicates

Table 9.2. Military spending and spending for public education, 1970, 1975, 1980, and 1982 (in % of GDP)

		Military	Public Education	Military in % of Education
Africa	1970	3.3	4.7	60
	1975	3.4	4.8	75
	1980	3.4	4.9	72
	1982	4.1	4.3	94
America	1970	6.6	6.2	107
	1975	4.9	6.1	81
	1980	4.4	6.3	70
	1982	5.2	5.3	98
Asia	1970	5.4	3.6	72*
	1975	5.6	5.6	81*
	1980	4.5	5.4	72*
	1982	5.6	5.0	110
Europe	1970	6.7	5.3	127
	1975	6.7	6.1	110
	1980	5.1	5.7	90
	1982	5.6	5.0	110
Oceania	1970	3.2	4.3	74
	1975	2.5	6.1	41
	1980	2.4	5.8	41
	1982	2.7	6.0	45
World	1970	6.3	5.4	112
	1975	5.8	5.9	94
	1980	4.7	5.7	79
	1982	5.3	5.0	105
OECD area	1970	4.8	5.4	90
	1975	4.0	6.0	67
	1980	3.7	6.0	67
	1982	4.2	5.4	78

Source: For data country by country and sources, see Table A.1.1. in Appendix I of Gleditsch et al., "Economic Incentives to Arm," PRIO Report 21/86 (Oslo: International Peace Research Institute, 1986).

* The total for these years excludes China.

Table 9.3. Military and civilian R&D for thirteen OECD countries
(in percent except where noted)

	1983 Level of R&D Expenditure (US $ 1,000 million 1975 prices and p.p.p.)		Average Annual Growth of R&D Expenditure 1963-1984		% of Years Between 1963 and 1984 In Which R&D Expenditure Rose in Constant Prices	
	Mil.	Civ.	Mil.	Civ.	Mil.	Civ.
US	14	36	1.06	3.90	48	85
UK	2	5*	1.38	2.35	52	83
France	2	6	4.13	5.86	67	100
West Germany	0.4	10	1.80	6.79	62	95
Sweden	0.2	1	1.89	8.12	62	94
Italy	0.1	3	12.11	6.16	76	(85)
Japan	0.1	18*	7.18	9.80	90	100
Canada	0.07	2	0.00	6.26	45	85
Netherlands	0.02	2	3.06	3.33	67	90
Norway	0.02	0.4*	8.20	6.66	55	89
Spain	0.003	0.6*	-1.21	10.09	54*	(100)
Finland	0.004*	0.4	2.85	7.87	77	89
Belgium	0.001	0.8*	-8.39	5.78	38*	(100)
Total	19	85	1.36	5.42	61	89

Source: Calculated from the data in Table A.2-A.5 in Appendix II,
Gleditsch et al., "Economic Incentives to Arm," PRIO Report 21/86
(Oslo: International Peace Research Institute, 1986).
For the three countries without data for 1982-1983, the data were
set to equal 1981. For Finland, missing data for 1963-1969 were set
to equal 1970 and for 1982, to equal the average of 1981 and 1983.
Although more sophisticated estimating methods could have been used,
any differences would have been negligible.

* Latest year available
() Based on substantially fewer than twenty years

that this trend has been reversed. Nevertheless, for three out of the
five regions and for the world as a whole, military spending in percent
of public education spending was *lower* in 1982 than in 1970. Thus,
an important aspect of civilian spending had a higher priority than
military spending during this period.

We have examined in greater detail data on civilian and military
R&D spending for the period 1963–1984 for thirteen OECD countries,
and plotting these data over time for each country reveals two rather
striking points. First, the growth rates for civilian R&D were markedly
higher. Second, whereas the curves for military R&D had many ups
and downs, the curves for civilian R&D generally showed a steady
upward trend. Table 9.3 gives these average annual growth rates for
all thirteen countries as well as the percentage of years in which there
was real growth. The first of these measures indicates the size of the

Figure 9.2. Civilian and military R&D expenditures 1963-1984 for thirteen countries (US $ 1,000 million, 1975 prices and p.p.p.)

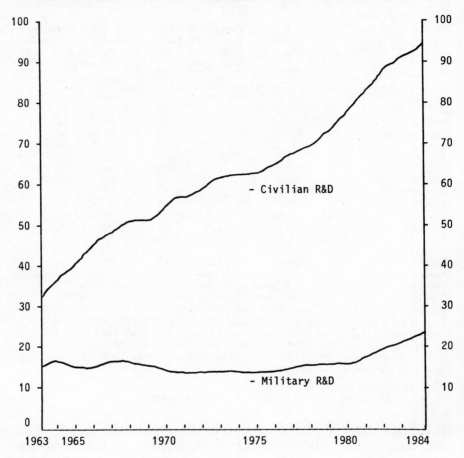

Source: Calculated from data in Tables A.2-A.5 in N.P. Gleditsch et al., "Economic Incentives to Arm," PRIO Report 21/86 (Oslo: International Peace Research Institute, 1986).

growth, the second its stability. Civilian R&D was higher on both for every country except Norway (where military R&D grew more rapidly but also more erratically and from a very low level) and Italy (where the initial level was also low).

Figure 9.2 shows the development of military and civilian R&D plotted over time for all thirteen countries together. This figure demonstrates the same relationship, even though the R&D curve for all countries together is less erratic than are the curves for each country—probably because the ups and downs occur at different times in the various countries.

A breakdown by subgroups within the OECD—not reproduced here—indicates that initially, the United States was very dominant within the OECD in terms of civilian R&D. But civilian R&D grew more rapidly in the other OECD countries, and by 1980, the other OECD countries (ten countries—Britain and France not included) had surpassed the United States. Britain is a deviant case in that it is ahead of all the other OECD countries, except the United States, in military R&D but has clearly fallen behind in civilian R&D. There is bit of the same picture in the data for France, but the situation is not as extreme as for Britain.

We have tried to examine the available data, country by country, to look for evidence of direct competition between military R&D and civilian R&D. Both types of R&D have had a long-term positive growth, although much more modestly for military R&D. Therefore, it is not reasonable to expect a negative correlation between the *levels* of military and civilian R&D, whether in absolute terms or in relative terms (as a fraction of the national product, public expenditure, etc.), but we might expect a negative correlation between the annual *changes* in military and civilian R&D: When one increases, it is at the expense of the other. In fact, a negative relationship of any size holds only for a small number of countries so no very clear evidence of a competitive relationship emerges from the data.[36]

Alternative Uses

We conclude from the previous sections that releasing resources from the unproductive arms race would put industrialized market economies in a position to improve their economic performance with regard to key indicators such as economic growth. Whether disarmament measures in fact would lead to such desirable results would depend on the economic policy carried out by the country in question. Moreover, since arms spending in peacetime accounts for a relatively limited share of the economies of the industrialized countries, any reduction in arms spending would also have a limited impact.

Recent international debate on conversion has focused particularly on the link between disarmament and development, the idea being that the resources currently wasted on the arms race could be used for development purposes. The idea is politically appealing. As already noted, global arms spending was eighteen times higher than foreign aid in 1982. Even the smaller states in Western Europe, which approach

1 percent of GNP in development aid, spend about three times as much on arms. Studies of the development effects of military spending indicate that disarmament may have a significant impact on development if a substantial portion of the released resources is allocated to development aid.[37] However, conversion is by no means a sufficient condition for overcoming the development gap. And as Faye Duchin has argued, structural change is essential to achieve sustained development in less developed countries, regardless of the amount of outside aid received.[38]

If we look beyond the proportion of resources spent on arms, it is of course possible that the arms race may have other and more serious effects on an economy than appear at first glance. For instance, military research and development may capture the best brains. In that case, it is possible that the diversion of brainpower to essentially unproductive endeavors may carry a disproportionate cost in terms of lost growth. The opposite could also be the case, but as far as we know, there have been no major studies of this question. This is an obvious task for further research, although the lack of reliable data will provide a major stumbling block.

In the absence of such studies, it seems reasonable to conclude that although the economic effects of the arms race are likely to be detrimental, these effects are relatively minor. They are obviously overshadowed by the threat that the arms race may contribute to war, which could threaten the very existence of entire countries or civilizations.

Notes

This is a revised version of a report commissioned by the UN Department of Disarmament Affairs in connection with the International Conference on the Relationship Between Disarmament and Development. Financial support for the work was also provided by the Norwegian Ministry for Development Cooperation through the Ministry for Foreign Affairs. Research assistance, including data collection, programming, and word processing, is gratefully acknowledged from Totto Befring, Arne Magnus Christensen, Håvard Hegre, Kristen Nordhaug, Enrique Perez-Terron, Agnete Schjönsby, Rolf Skomsvold, Asbjörn Torvanger, and Knut Öygard. We have also benefited from the use of computer resources at the University of Oslo and in the Central Bureau of Statistics, where two of the authors (Bjerkholt and Cappelen) are employed. The third author (Gleditsch) works at the International Peace Research Institute, Oslo (PRIO), where the project was carried out. The full text of the UN report is available as publication X-41/86 from PRIO. The UN published the report without the Appendix tables as A/CONF.130/PC/INF/14 April 29, 1986. The UN document is also available in French. Another early version of this report was presented to the eleventh general conference of the International Peace Research Association, University of Sussex, Brighton, England, April 13–18, 1986. We are grateful to Göran Lindgren and other participants of the IPRA session for comments.

1. We use the 1982 figure here for the purpose of comparison with other available data. The SIPRI *Yearbook on World Armament and Disarmament 1986* (Oxford: Oxford University Press, 1986), gives the 1985 figure as US $850–$870 billion (p. 211).

2. Ruth Leger Sivard, *World Military and Social Expenditures 1985* (Washington, D.C.: World Priorities, 1985), and *World Military Expenditures and Arms Transfers 1985* (Washington, D.C.: Arms Control and Disarmament Agency, 1985).

3. The existing literature on the economic effects of military spending is large and growing rapidly. For some reviews of the academic literature, see Ådne Cappelen, Nils Petter Gleditsch, and Olav Bjerkholt, "Military Spending and Economic Growth in the OECD Countries," *PRIO Report*, no. 6 (1984); Steve Chan, "The Impact of Defense Spending on Economic Performance: A Survey of Evidence and Problems," *Orbis* 29:2 (1985), pp. 403–434, and Göran Lindgren, "Armaments and Economic Performance in Industrialized Market Economies," Chapter 8 in this book.

4. See Chapter 8.

5. Harvey Starr et al., "The Relationship Between Defense Spending and Inflation," *Journal of Conflict Resolution* 28:1 (1984), pp. 103–122, and H. C. Mosley, *The Arms Race: Economic and Social Consequences* (Lexington, Mass.: Heath, 1985), chap. 6.

6. This view can be traced back to classical economists such as Smith, Ricardo, and Say. See Ted G. Goertzel, "Militarism as a Sociological Problem," in Richard Braungart and Philo Washburn, eds., *Research in Political Sociology* (New York: JAI Press, 1985), pp. 119–139.

7. Harold Brown in testimony before the U.S. Senate Budget Committee, February 27, 1980, cited Robert W. DeGrasse, Jr., *Military Expansion—Economic Decline;* (New York: M. E. Sharpe for the Council on Economic Priorities, 1983), p. 55. DeGrasse cites similar statements by one of Brown's predecessors (Schlesinger) and by his successor (Weinberger).

8. For a review of the evidence, see Chapter 8 by Lindgren; Cappelen, Gleditsch, and Bjerkholt, "Military Spending"; and Chan, "Impact of Defense Spending."

9. Congressional Budget Office, *Defense Spending and the Economy* (Washington, D.C.: CBO, 1983), p. 38; Cappelen, Gleditsch, and Bjerkholt, "Military Spending," p. 17.

10. Ron Smith: "Military Expenditure and Investment in OECD Countries 1954–73," *Journal of Comparative Economics* 4:1 (1980), pp. 19–32.

11. Cappelen, Gleditsch, and Bjerkholt, "Military Spending," pp. 17 ff.

12. Wassily Leontief and Faye Duchin, *Military Spending: Facts and Figures, Worldwide Implications, and Future Outlook* (New York: Oxford University Press, 1983).

13. Ådne Cappelen, Olav Bjerkholt, and Nils Petter Gleditsch, *Global Conversion from Arms to Development Aid: Macroeconomic Effects on Norway* (Oslo: PRIO, 1982), sect. 5.

14. G. P. Dineen and F. C. Frick, "Electronics and National Defense: A Case Study," in P. Abelson and A. Hammond, eds., *Electronics: The Continuing Revolution* (Washington, D.C.: American Association for the Advancement of Science, 1977), pp. 82–83, cited in Robert DeGrasse, "The Military and Semiconductors," in John Tirman, ed., *The Militarization of High Technology* (Cambridge, Mass.: Ballinger, 1984), p. 100.

15. John Tirman: "The Defense-Economy Debate," in Tirman, ed., *Militarization*, pp. 1–32.

16. DeGrasse, "Military and Semiconductors," pp. 77 ff.

17. A moderate version of this argument is stated in "Forsvar mot ballistiske raketter: De tekniske og vitenskapelige sider ved USAs strategiske forsvarsinitiativ [Defense against ballistic missiles: The technical and scientific aspects of the U.S. Strategic Defense Initiative; in Norwegian] (report prepared for the Office of the Prime Minister, Oslo, June 1985); reprinted in *Aktuelle utenrikspolitiske spörsmål* (Norwegian Ministry of Foreign Affairs, September 1985).

18. Bernhard Udis, *From Guns to Butter: Technology Organizations and Reduced Military Spending in Western Europe* (Cambridge, Mass.: Ballinger, 1978).

19. Cited in Lloyd J. Dumas, "Disarmament and Economy in Advanced Industrialized Countries—the US and the USSR," *Bulletin of Peace Proposals* 12:1 (1981), p. 3.

20. Nestor E. Terleckyj, *Effects of R&D on the Productivity Growth of Industries: An Exploratory Study* (Washington, D.C.: National Planning Association, 1974), and Zvi Griliches and Frank Lichtenberg," R&D Productivity Growth at the Industry Level: Is There Still a Relationship?" in Zvi Griliches, ed., *R&D, Patents, and Productivity,* National Bureau of Economic Research Conference Report (Chicago and London: University of Chicago Press, 1984), pp. 465–501.

21. DeGrasse, "Military and Semiconductors," p. 95, and John Tirman, "Conclusions and Countercurrents," in Tirman, ed., *Militarization,* p. 221.

22. Gordon Thompson, "The Genesis of Nuclear Power," in Tirman, ed., *Militarization,* pp. 63–75.

23. DeGrasse, "Military and Semiconductors," pp. 90–93.

24. Malcolm Chalmers, *Paying for Defence: Military Spending and British Economic Decline* (London: Pluto, 1985), p. 120.

25. SIPRI *Yearbook 1983,* p. 215.

26. Chalmers, *Paying for Defence,* pp. 120 ff.

27. Jacques Gansler, *The Defense Industry* (Cambridge, Mass.: MIT Press, 1980), p. 101, and Tirman, ed., *Militarization,* p. 19. A Norwegian leader in industry-oriented R&D also comments favorably on the role of small firms in innovation (see Johannes Moe, "Forskningens rolle i vår industrielle utvikling," *Bergen Bank kvartalsskrift,* no. 3 [1985], pp. 119–145, 137).

28. Lester Thurow, "Eight Imperatives for R&D," *Technology Review* (January 1978), pp. 64–71.

29. *Los Angeles Times,* July 10, 1983; quoted from Chalmers, *Paying for Defence,* p. 122.

30. Lloyd J. Dumas, "Military Spending and Economic Decay," in Burns H. Weston, ed., *Toward Nuclear Disarmament and Global Security: A Search for Alternatives* (Boulder, Colo.: Westview Press, 1984), p. 184.

31. DeGrasse, *Military Expansion,* p. 126.

32. Christensen and Torvanger have applied an econometric model to these same data and have performed separate analyses for the longitudinal, the cross-sectional, and the pooled data sets (Arne Magnus Christensen and Asbjörn Torvanger, *Military and Civilian Research and Development and Growth* [Oslo: International Peace Research Institute, 1985]). In the time-series analysis, their first model yielded significant positive influence for two countries and negative influence for two. Their second model yielded mixed results: a negative correlation for four countries. In the cross-sectional analyses, there were also few significant coefficients. Using the second model, military R&D was found to have a significant positive influence on growth in the periods 1964–1969 and 1974–1976 and a negative influence in the period 1977–1980. Surprisingly, the coefficients for civilian R&D were largely negative. One possible explanation for this finding is that civilian R&D data include both basic and applied research while military R&D is overwhelmingly concentrated on applied research. Thus the comparison is biased in favor of military R&D; a more "fair" comparison would be between the applied parts of civilian and military R&D. However, the available data do not permit such disaggregation. Some authors discuss "growth-oriented" R&D as a separate category, excluding not only military R&D but also, e.g., medical R&D, and it has been shown that such growth-oriented R&D has stagnated in the United States (see Mosley, *Arms Race,* pp. 75 ff. for a review of such studies). Data are not available for enough countries to permit a comparative study. On the whole, the results of the Christensen and Torvanger study are not very conclusive.

33. The quotation is from Goertzel, "Militarism," p. 128.

34. Mosley, *Arms Race,* p. 6.

35. Richard A. Vigurie, *The New Right: We're Ready to Lead* (Falls Church, Va.: Vigurie Company, 1980), pp. 226–229; quoted from Goertzel, "Militarism," p. 133.

36. Asbjörn Eide, Nils Petter Gleditsch, Arne Magnus Christensen, Asbjörn Torvanger, Magnus Haavelsrud, and Marek Thee, "Impact of the Arms Race on Education, Science and Technology, Culture, and Communication" (study prepared for UNESCO, Division of Human Rights and Peace; to be published in *UNESCO Yearbook of Peace and Conflict Studies*).

37. Cappelen, Bjerkholt, and Gleditsch, *Global Conversion,* and Nils Petter Gleditsch et al., "Economic Incentives to Arm?" PRIO Report no. 21/86 (Oslo: PRIO, 1986), sec. 7.

38. Faye Duchin, "Economic Consequences of Military Spending," *Journal of Economic Issues* 27:2 (1983), pp. 543–553.

PART FIVE

Challenges to
Peace Research

10

Emancipatory Empiricism: Toward the Renewal of Empirical Peace Research

Hayward R. Alker, Jr.

Harold Guetzkow has long cautioned about empirical peace research becoming too "data bound." Without claiming to have captured exactly his intentions, I wish to develop the positive side of this injunction. How can we recognize the actualities in our data without hiding the underlying, more or less just and peaceful possibilities? Assuming that there are various truths in our data, are there ways to find those special truths that can help unbind us from past falsehoods, possibility-distorting representations, continuing oppressions, even war itself? In this chapter, I shall answer these questions in terms of a research orientation I call "emancipatory empiricism." Although this research orientation is more general than peace research itself, I shall argue that it fits peace research well because the latter's disciplinary distinctiveness derives from an emancipatory knowledge interest.

One can conceptualize that social scientific research orientations in general, and those of peace research in particular, exist on three increasingly comprehensive and concrete levels:

ontology: their (metaphysical) doctrines of being—reality, actuality, necessity, and possibility in the realms of human action and experience

epistemology: their philosophies of scientific knowledge generation and the methodologies (applied epistemologies) developed to discern reality

disciplinarity: the institutionalized disciplinary matrices (including research sponsors, professional organizations, research programs, and knowledge interests) guiding research, teaching, and applications of a field of knowledge

After some beginning remarks about the relevance of peace research's emancipatory knowledge interest for the field's distinctive disciplinary self-understanding, I shall characterize emancipatory empiricism somewhat more generally. Then I offer twelve epistemological guidelines, or lessons, for emancipatory peace research and conclude with a call for nonemancipatory empiricists to rethink their social ontologies.

During a period when quite a few younger researchers are skeptical about, or disillusioned with, the empirical methodologies pioneered by Burton, Deutsch, Galtung, Guetzkow, Haas, Lasswell, Rapoport, Richardson, Singer, and Wright, I hope this contribution will serve to reawaken interest in those methodologies. My practical purpose is to help renew and develop a style of peace research that is both empirical and emancipatory.

How Emancipatory Knowledge Interest Distinguishes Peace Research

I believe, and shall argue, that peace research's inherent, emancipatory knowledge interest—more strongly evident in some contexts than in others—forms a most important basis for the disciplinary distinctiveness of peace research. What, then, is an emancipatory knowledge interest? Habermas has described it as "an attitude which is formed in the experience of suffering from something man-made, which can be abolished and should be abolished." Habermas believes that emancipatory interest is more than a mere "subjective attitude which may or may not guide this or that piece of scientific research"; rather, it is something profoundly ingrained in certain of our social structures, the "calling into question, and deep-seated wish to throw off, relations which repress . . . without necessity."[1]

Let us accept for now a provisional characterization of peace research both as research in the service of war avoidance and as research organized in the interest of coercion-minimizing social justice (including the avoidance of what Galtung has called structural violence). How does peace research qualify for such an emancipatory knowledge interest? First of all, by demonstrating, as Margaret Mead long ago argued, that war is evidently "man-made," an invention rather than a necessity.[2] Second, by arguing that war—and the coercive, militaristic way of life it supports—should be abolished. Third, by attempting to establish that, like slavery, war and its way of life, and its most deleterious consequences, can be ended. Indeed, to the extent that the work of peace researchers is consistent with these efforts, peace research is an appropriate, partly institutionalized, increasingly global embodiment of such a knowledge interest and thus an apt candidate for emancipatory empiricism.

Accepting this characterization of the focus of peace research points one toward the distinctiveness of such an orientation vis-à-vis alternative research traditions. Consider peace research's major alternative with a similar focus, the realist tradition of international relations research. With varying degrees of critical distance, the realist tradition defines itself in terms of state interest, conceived of in enhanced or maintained levels of power. Order (not peace) is given precedence over justice, domestically and internationally.

Even when made more "rigorous" by the adoption of scientific practices borrowed from the natural sciences, mathematical economics, or statistics, behavioral "neorealism" suffers directly or indirectly from difficulties similar to those of its realist progenitor. Claims of scientific neutrality with respect to policy issues may or may not be justified, but they get in the way of explicit criticisms of realism's too comfortable relationship with powerholders and inhibit the reasoned advocacy for the elimination of war, militarism, structural violence, ecological exploitation, and other forms of social or natural injustice that are constitutive of the openly avowed commitment of emancipatory peace research to social change.

Similarly, despite this commitment, there are actual and potential conflicts of interest between peace research and Marxian scholarship defined entirely in terms of the interests of a particular coalition of classes, if that coalition excludes many others. Despite the emancipatory thrust of Marxist analysis and its optimistic view about the possibility of achieving more just, prosperous, and peaceful communities, Marxist theory can (and has) become a justification for unnecessary violence and repression on much too large a scale to be considered easily compatible with peace research's emancipatory interest. Consistent, determinate intellectual bases for judging what is "good" and what is "bad" about the peace-bringing capacities of existing institutions are very hard to come by within that tradition.

Finally, consider the alternative candidate tradition concerned with war and peace that is perhaps even closer to peace research than Marxism per se, viz., international law. Its interests are mixed with respect to conflict resolution. Surely its contributions to social justice and peaceful conflict settlement need recognition, but its use (and abuse) by rationalizers unwilling or unable to submit matters at hand to a legal settlement process seems quite distant from peace research's distinctive knowledge interest. Private and state interests can easily transcend peaceful ones in the shaping and application of genuinely shared normative standards, which themselves often embody historical biases.

None of these oppositions need be conceived of as total or non-negotiable. There are variants of liberal realism, behavioral neorealism, Marxian peace research, and international law that have made significant contributions to knowledge and practices recognized by many peace researchers. Nor is peace research itself devoid of the problems of conforming to its interests in peace, justice, and academic viability that the above characterization is designed to help clarify. But the above sketch represents, I believe, a prima facie case for peace research's disciplinary distinctiveness.

Given peace research's distinctive emancipatory interest, which sometimes places it in an uneasy relationship with certain other disciplinary orientations within the behavioral, social, and ecological sciences, it is indeed appropriate to ask whether there is anywhere else outside of academia that one can find that same emancipatory interest. Are there possible allies in the social and political contexts of contemporary peace research with which peace researchers might or should make common cause? Were there no other peace-promoting movements or institutions, the practical import of the emancipatory task would be overwhelmingly difficult, and one would have grounds for suspecting the bona fides of peace researchers.

Late in what Raymond Aron has called "the century of total war,"[3] however, peace movements are widespread—some with state support, some without. Moreover, I believe that some of the other social institutions—the global collective security system of the early post–World War II years, the defensive military establishments of certain nonaligned states—have rightly called war into question in a similar way. Domestically, the "welfare state," to the extent that it has eclipsed the "warfare state"[4] and promotes the dignity and mutually compatible well-being of its citizens, is another positive development.

Another such domestic institution, perhaps, is the law-abiding, conflict-managing police force.[5] The international instances of legitimate police practice are also, on the whole, positive remnants of the UN collective security system.[6] The tougher question, and one on which Realists, Marxists, international lawyers, and peace researchers are likely to disagree, concerns the extent to which the modern, Western state system is itself necessarily or unnecessarily war prone, and this question must remain central to the agenda of emancipatory peace research, especially because of the growth in this century of overly coercive militarized and police states.

How Emancipatory Empiricism Connects to Peace Research

The above line of reasoning points toward a broader epistemological stance for peace research, one that is grounded in the field's distinctive emancipatory knowledge interest. I call such a stance "emancipatory empiricism" and intend now to show how it gets that name.

Institutionally, empiricism is widely identified with the heavily inductive, externally funded collection of scientific data that is followed by statistical analysts who are searching for timeless and universally valid probabilistic laws. Philosophically, such empiricism is often contrasted with the "rationalist" philosophies of science that emphasize natural possibilities more than quantitative probabilities, the role of human intensionality in the shaping of experience, or the importance of theoretical reasoning in scientific analysis.

Sometimes empiricism is understood to be one of several research programs within a larger discipline, or the argument is made (as Karl Deutsch and Harold Lasswell have done) that at a particular period in its history a discipline needs renewal through extensive data-making efforts. More exclusively, the view is sometimes argued (or assumed) that only this inductive style of research is truly scientific and deserving of the disciplinary privileges of tenured appointments, research grants, etc.

Conceived of as especially relevant to the behavioral, social, and ecological sciences, emancipatory empiricism is more rationalist than empiricist, but I keep (and redefine) the empiricism label because emancipatory empiricism pays very serious attention to the data of experience and its proper collection, practical interpretation, and reconstructive analysis. Thus, emancipatory empiricism is especially interested in practical possibilities that can be hidden by "normal" regularities, in transformations that cannot always be captured by statistical probabilities in emergent breakthroughs to preferable, sometimes novel, psychological, social, and ecological orders.

Institutionally, emancipatory empiricism aligns its knowledge-generating activities and its disciplinary self-understanding with historically changing and spatially contingent emancipatory knowledge interests. That such knowledge interests have influenced and can shape the disciplinary activities and self-understandings of peace researchers has just been argued. A more detailed epistemological exposition is offered by the guidelines below.

Epistemological Guidelines for Emancipatory Peace Research

The following twelve epistemological (and methodological) guidelines, or lessons, distill some of my own learning from a fairly lengthy period of empirical research on the successes and failures of the UN collective security system, as buttressed conceptually and methodologically by related work on sequential prisoner's dilemma games.[7]

One may begin a sequential exposition of guidelines for a peace research governed by emancipatory empiricism by asserting that the data of human experience should continually be reinterpreted and respecified in the emancipatory interest of discovering and improving upon determinative possibilities for conflict management and conflict resolution that justly avoid civil and international wars. Taking seriously rationalist critiques of empiricism and the call for ontological depth of emancipatory realism,[8] one can recast the empirical thrust of creative data making, interpretation, and analysis. Basically, one must look for peaceful possibilities *within* the data, always remembering that data recordings are nothing but manufactured traces of history. These actualities of practical human experience have complex relationships with real, but not directly observable, alternative possibilities—with a past, present, and future of their own. Among such possibilities are movements beyond power politics toward peace and community.

Lesson 1: *Data-coding procedures should be considered key dependent variables in an emancipatory peace research because they often (sometimes unconsciously) reflect just those social and political forces affecting war and peace that are supposed to be the objectives of investigation.*

Let me begin with a true story, which is all the more important because it apparently has nothing to do with the content of coding operations, only their procedural implementation. In the pioneering article by Lincoln Moses, Richard Brody, et al. on the quantification of levels of cooperation and conflict in international events data,[9] one graduate student coder (out of about five) was a non-American, a citizen of a Third World country, a woman. Her codings did not "reliably" agree with those of the others and were discarded for most purposes. She then went on to cofound a new paradigm of international conflict research, lateral pressure theorizing, which redefined the meaning and significance of imperialism as it has been experienced by domestic populations within the great powers, their unequal allies, and Third World countries.[10]

Because of Thomas Kuhn's writings, it is easier to argue that "new ways of seeing" can become scientifically significant. Distinguishing them from "random error," as some naturalistically inclined behavioralists might label deviations, is more difficult. The differences one might expect are paradigmatic, orientational, and nationalistic. The necessity of regularly choosing coders from among the informed citizenry of differently aligned world countries seems as evident a precaution as it is difficult to realize in practice. Orientational differences, e.g., those between men and women or among different occupational or ethnic groupings, may be subtler biases, harder to detect and requiring corrections not as easily prescribed. Paradigmatic differences, e.g., among liberal realists, structural Marxists, and dialectical peace researchers, should be more familiar to interdisciplinary scholars, even if an appropriate response to such differences is also controversial. Relevant methodological research requires the new dependent variables here mentioned.

Lesson 2: *Always include the case inclusion and exclusion rules in the (augmented if necessary) specification of the coding rules for a conflict/cooperation data set.*

Now let us consider the definition of cases, the units of data included in a particular collection. The most remarkable difference among the definition of conflict cases I have experienced in studies of conflict management precedent logics came in discussions of Akihiko Tanaka's thesis.[11] In (re)coding data from the Chinese *People's Daily*, he noted a tendency for episodic conflict cases to be conceptualized in terms of longer-term, essential, ongoing conflicts. Nonviolent periods of moderate duration, the stuff of Western coders' case of phase distinctions, were less likely to be treated as evidence of hostility or conflict termination. Although this editorial practice clearly fits (and can be justified by) the scholarly Marxist understanding of the continuing reality of (sometimes) unobservable social contradictions, the Chinese press's practice has merit for a variety of other reasons as well. Thus, the Haas-Butterworth tradition tends to define case boundaries according to the international lawyer's dispute management practice of separating out manageable "cases," an operational practice that tends to obscure what Azar might call "the underlying protracted social conflicts."[12] One could add the behavioral scientist's dubious tendency to increase the sample size of purportedly "independent" cases (in Stanley Hoffman's language, treating history as if it were a field of daisies waiting to be stripped).

Another issue immediately related to case definitions concerns the extent to which universes of data collection consciously or unconsciously reproduce partitions of a larger reality than a more emancipatory empiricist would want to directly investigate. J. David Singer and Melvin Small initially focused on major power wars and then on wars among central system members. Civil (and colonial) wars came later. Certainly their initial focus can be justified on the grounds of data availability and resource limitations, but the theoretical justifications for continuing the earlier focus are more slippery.

Why should a peace researcher consider as valuable what great-power leaders think is important? Should we accept either the Cold War or the anti-imperialist characterization of the principal international post-1945 conflict just because one of the superpowers officially condones such labeling?

Beyond the analytically important distinction loosely suggested by the distinction between cold and hot wars, there are deep issues concerning structural displacements of central system conflicts into peripheral, more overt areas of competition, such as occurred before World War I. In frequency terms, there is a rich variety of evidence suggesting a greater incidence of what might be called North-South conflicts in post-1945 conflict patterns. There is similar evidence of diminished UN conflict management activities outside the areas and issues of direct interest to the major powers.[13]

Since exemptions from international scrutiny and accountability concerning imperial/colonial affairs have in the past two centuries often been legally argued in terms of "domestic jurisdiction," and the executive branches of major-power governments have all sought secrecy concerning the conduct of foreign affairs on the grounds of national security, must not we be especially on our guard not to be affected by correlated data nonavailabilities in identifying the root causes of war? To put it in discourse analysis language, do not the "silences" in the data speak as powerfully as the observations we have been able to gather? In a paper "Can the End of Power Politics Be Part of the Concepts with Which Its Story Is Told?"[14] I referred to the "bloody ordination" that great powers confer on new system members with their acts of diplomatic recognition. Should not the standards of conduct implicit in related scholarly definitions (by Singer and his associates) of their universes of investigation be equally carefully and critically scrutinized for tendencies that unreflectively reproduce a repressive status quo?

Perhaps the most dramatic finding along these lines that I have been associated with is contained in Frank Sherman's dissertation.[15] Whereas Alker and Sherman together identified the possibility of easily observing agenda nondecisions in UN conflict management activities, Sherman's effort to code domestic quarrels and international disputes by relying primarily on sources other than the international organizations themselves doubled or tripled what might be argued to be internationally relevant conflicts. The gestalt flip encouraged by this finding—the silences in the Haas-Butterworth data that my research team had recoded, specifying actors, actions, conflict phases, and outcome—is to see conflict management practices by the extended UN system (including both regional and ad hoc management agents) as more like the tip of an iceberg of internationally unrecognized and unmanaged conflicts.

One should also note that the critique of inclusion or exclusion rules can have politically relevant consequences. Not only do "success batting averages" change, one may also find more sense in views one previously held suspect. I now see, for example, my own partially latent dissatisfaction with the watered-down, conflict management research program that Ernst Haas originated[16] as having a certain resonance with much harsher criticisms of the United Nations from U.S. academic ambassadors like Daniel Moynihan and Jeane Kirkpatrick. Indeed, the emphasis on the UN's failure to resolve conflicts—they have claimed that it exacerbates some of them—is related to the criticisms that John Burton would make from a much more antistatist conflict resolution perspective.[17]

Lesson 3: *Collect, try to reproduce, compare, confront, and match different "scientific" treatments of the same conflict events or episodes (cases, disputes, crises, wars, agreements, peace breakthroughs).*

If one recognizes the strong, if sometimes unconscious, tendency of scholars to reflect the biases of their research-originating traditions and contexts, then the obvious first step for the empirically minded is to check for such biases by undertaking a comparative and synthetic investigation of paradigmatic, orientational, and political perspectives. Scholars on all sides of the Cold War need each other, as do those from different research traditions and orienting perspectives.

If one allows that differences in scholarly perspectives are not simply private, unbiased conceptual or topical preferences of the "sovereign" research scholar, then the discovery and operational definition of international realities is more complicated. The more data sets of good quality one can find that embody different scholarly perspectives, the more one can learn from the data about these reality-assessing perspectives. I have tried, when honest and reproduceable differences among serious scholars of different research traditions could be found, to think of a larger, more coherent, yet often contradictory totality of conflict descriptions that could be synthesized from the sometimes contradictory perspectives of these scholars. The totality includes the interplay of perspectives, the range of possibility/actuality relationships discursively implied by alternative coding schemes, and the inner relations of participants and observers (who can never be totally disinterested) of the conflict itself.

There are several, even deeper ontological issues here, seen from an emancipatory, dialectical-hermeneutic perspective. First of all, a dispute description is not completely separable from the cognitive practices or procedures that produced it. The real contenders for the "social scientific construction of international reality" are the different coding procedures, which, according to Lesson 1, are for this and other purposes appropriately treated as dependent variables.

Coding practices (including case exclusion rules) can best be compared operationally by incorporating both them and the raw data texts they were applied to into a software system, like the RELATUS system Gavan Duffy and John Mallery are developing, that can both interpret and apply coding rules to textual information sources.[18] Such a comparison would amount to a rigorous yet dialogical examination of complementary and contradictory scholarly practices, a necessary step on the way to a socially achieved (rather than simply posited) scholarly universality.

A related ontological issue concerns the existence (and reliable discovery) of emergent social relationships of a collaborative or conflictful sort. New social emergents occur when previous determinations break down and when emancipatory restructurings of social relationships are possible. They emerge out of, and can be found within, overlapping perspectives. Dag Hammarskjöld's role as UN secretary-general in eliciting support from the superpowers and General Assembly majorities for UN interventions in the Suez and Congo crises would be such an example. Belated Soviet and U.S. groping in 1987 for some coordinated ways of containing the impacts of the Iran-Iraq war on their naval and commercial interests would be another. But for such evolutions to take place, they must be shared across a range of international actors.

Lesson 4: *Progress toward genuine scholarly universalism can be achieved by making explicit the normative bases, procedural preferences, or political allegiances that inform coding practices.*

Obviously, such differences in orientation are major factors affecting differences in coding practices. Surely it will help the empiricist to delineate the different, value-relevant dependent and independent variables that are of concern. For me, normative clarification has had a much greater impact than just a modest clarification of research hypotheses. It has changed the paradigmatic ways I have tried to study alternative pasts and futures for international conflict management practices.

Twenty years ago, after my empirical study of UN voting patterns, prompted by Ernst Haas's pioneering empirical studies of the UN collective security system, I became especially interested in the evolutionary development and decay and the organizational learning, ossification, and decay of the United Nations with respect to peacemaking activities. The attempt to use econometric time-series models and/or Markov learning models of UN management actions eventually led me to a double discovery of heuristic significance. First of all, it turned out that the Congo crisis, which helped precipitate the most serious UN constitutional crisis of that period, was more than a deviant case in the tracking of these models. Indeed, Christensen found statistically significant "breakpoints" before and after that episode in my causal models. What did this fact signify?

The UN operation in the Congo was everywhere compared with the UN emergency force deployed at the time of the Suez crisis. This debatable "precedent," creatively deployed by the secretary-general and his supporters, suggested the emergent possibility of decisive action by the United Nations on the basis of superpower agreement with General Assembly majorities, even when other veto powers (Britain and/or France) disagreed. Trying to model that kind of relationship— i.e., to match the conflict phases of the Congo crisis with those of the Suez crisis in a search for relevant actions that might be taken and, similarly, to explain why the United Nations seemed to know what actions to try in 1945 and 1946 without any directly relevant previous experience—was not working. Using the most advanced system for computerizing social science data analysis I then knew of (SPSS, TROLL, ESP, Ithiel Pool's ADMINS), it was impossible to code and include in my analysis (the search for) precedential similarities without writing my own rather lengthy programs for that purpose. It turned out that these search algorithms, which evolved into a precedential seeking and applying simulation model, roughly paralleled organizational memory processes. Not only did I invent for political scientists and international lawyers the subfield of formalized "precedent logics," through an analysis of residuals, I operationally rediscovered a normative level of political engagement theretofore only implicit in the data I was (re)analyzing.

Let me talk about precedent logics first.[19] When I found (in my work with Christensen) that there was an "operational charter" implicit in my early set of post-1945 conflict management cases, I knew that it would be better to model explicitly the norm application and revision process. To do so meant shifting to a research tradition, artificial intelligence, with appropriate representation, modeling, and analysis techniques. It turned out that these (oversimplified) precedent-seeking "procedures" (modeled in PL1), when included in the analysis, generated outcome-involvement residuals with no statistically significant breakpoints near the Congo crisis as well. I soon noticed that Herbert Simon (in his work with Gregg on concept attainment and his work with March and Newell on organizational problem solving) had been there before me: Simon largely stopped writing about causal modeling, path analysis, structural modeling, and conventional econometric methodologies more generally when many others were just beginning to do so because he found—what many sociological and political scientific methodologists have yet to discover—something more intellectually challenging, and empirically appropriate for the problems he was interested in, viz., psychologically and organizationally relevant artificial intelligence, or cognitive science.

There was also an ontological shift implicit in this rejection of conventional behavioral scientific methodology, my going from causal modeling to artificial intelligence. In doing so, I recognized a deeper level of reality and a new kind of scientific data relevant to it—the diplomatic debates about charter revision that were at the center of international attention as the Congo- and Suez-related UN financial crisis matured.

As I was helped to see by Harold Lasswell's invitation to report my work with Christensen and Greenberg to the American Society of International Law, the negotiated, legal-normative aspect of conflict management is not merely instrumental searching for excuses, it may be constitutional politics as well. And it has a crucial parallel at the levels of practical reasoning and institutional learning about policy alternatives.

Lesson 5: *Precedential reasoning about the relevant past is an integral part of diplomatic realities; to ignore the normative-empirical dynamics of defining a "case" (e.g., in charter terms), or those of norm-based precedential learning ("drawing a lesson"), in one's data making is seriously to diminish the likelihood that practical, significant lessons can be drawn from one's data.*

The rationale here is both profound—concerning the difficulties behaviorally minded scholars have in getting at the constitutive level of political relationships in their data—and obvious. Have you tried to talk to diplomats about the lessons you have learned from behavioral research? They always want to relate your lessons to theirs. Unless you have already juxtaposed and simulated how your findings relate to their collective, practical self-understanding, you will talk past one another. Habermas might say that the realm of discursive, practical will formation must be distinguished from the world of adaptive or maladaptive systemic functioning of the sort causal modelers are used to modeling.

But there is another lesson, which I illustrated in my "Polimetrics" chapter in the *Handbook of Political Science* (Reading, Mass.: Addison-Wesley, 1975). There I applied Larzarsfield-Sills's reason analysis to the dialectical process whereby a remarkable consensus was achieved in the Security Council for coercive UN intervention in the Congo. In my econometric data residuals, I had rediscovered metapolitics, constitutional politics, the fundamental, discursively mediated, dialectical process of structuring and restructuring international political institutions toward (and, as it happened, away from) supranationality.

Noting in passing the ontological character of this claim about the multiple layers of reality within my data, let me state two important additional lessons.

Lesson 6: *In the construction of new data sets on international conflict, be sure to include the reasons actors give for the actions they take (or avoid) and the precedents they cite (or avoid) for justifying such (in)actions.*

Lesson 7: *If you have not coded conflict resolution efforts (and their successes and failures) as part of your conflict data, get such information or include such information from other studies.*

Here we have a crucial difference between those people who follow realist categories of analysis and those who derive theirs from the communitarian tradition. Following in Richardson's footsteps, but failing to rethink Richardson's injunction that his differential equation models were only adequate for projecting behavior if statesmen "did not stop to think," Singer and Small have not coded such efforts in any of their data making concerning wars or militarized international disputes. The Haas tradition and Azar's COPDAB project, on the other hand, like the Behavioral Correlates of War project (to which Singer and Russell Leng made early contributions), are more inclusive in this regard, collecting rich data on conflict and cooperation activities. The reasons for my preferences on this matter are obviously related to my emancipatory interest in war avoidance and conflict resolution. Peace researchers have very few reasons for continuing to replicate "war only" data making. As communitarians, they are paradigmatically predisposed to see any war short of total war as only a partial breakdown of normally nonantagonistic forms of social communication and interaction, which they are trying to discover how to reinvigorate.

Lesson 8: *Going beyond the idea of deviant case analysis, and approaching case data from what Habermas calls a reconstructive perspective, take the best or the worst cases of conflict resolution* *outcomes and use them to uncover the practical "grammars" of action (and habit) making such outcomes possible.*

The work on the successes and failures of UN conflict management has only looked intensively at a few cases, in particular the Congo crisis, which was an important turning away from UN supranationality. But the sequential prisoner's studies are going further: In a forthcoming dissertation, Roger Hurwitz will look at player-generated protocols (and, one hopes, also at the narrative game histories players were asked to write) for two exceptional classes of sequential prisoner's dilemma games, those evolving into stable cooperative patterns and those degenerating into stable defection relationships. These outcomes represent, if you will, historically contingent evolutions (or devolutions) of community and anarchy, not naturalistic or inevitable outcomes as some realists and some extreme idealists like to think. Hurwitz is looking for those reflective redefinitions of the other player, his or her actions, and the game situations that account for turning points in the overall, cumulative trajectories in game payoffs.

The major behavioral generalization from Haas's and Sherman's most recent studies is the decline in the effectiveness of the UN system, including its reformulation and weakening through the use of regional and ad hoc conflict management agents. Indeed, Sherman concludes his dissertation rather apocalyptically. The deep causes of this regime decay require investigation in an analytical/empirical mode; surely they include the rise of protracted social conflicts, of domestic, multiethnic, recognition, or identity conflicts as Burton might describe them. Even the globalization of superpower conflict, since it has catalyzed the remilitarization of the Third World, must be carefully investigated. But I have no doubt that selective (perhaps situationally matched) studies of exceptional successes and failures in conflict management or conflict resolution by the UN conflict management system will shed new light on possibilities for, and conditions of, significant improvements in that system.

There is an equally important methodological conclusion implicit here. I believe the amount of information lost by quantitative attempts to code such qualitative accounts of conflict initiation and termination successes and failures to be tremendous. Compared to Butterworth's coding of his two-page narrative account of UN failures to manage the 1956 Hungarian crisis, information summarized quantitatively on two or three computer cards worth of bits, John Mallery's highly structured semantic representation takes something like a half a megabyte of LISP encoded storage. The moral is given in Lesson 9.

Lesson 9: *Structured narrative accounts of conflict developments are crucial and necessary components of any data set on conflict* *(and its resolution attempts); when integrated accounts can be constructed from partially convergent interpretive perspectives, they are especially valuable representations of the contradictory, yet social, nature of political reality, including its emergent conflict resolution possibilities.*

The values of narrative accounts of conflict developments—structured and retold from the multiple perspectives of the key participants, mentioning their practical understandings of their (and others') actions, and incorporating the multiple sets of theoretically significant phenomena attended to by the relevant paradigms of empirical research—are numerous. First, they can be behaviorally recoded in the future in different ways with far less work. Second, the significant meanings of key events are much more clearly conveyed in partial story forms. Third, precedential analogies are more holistically discussable in such terms. Fourth, process modeling methods are now becoming available that treat entire narrative accounts operationally, as data. Fifth, there is the practical, hermeneutic process of building consensual understandings of collective political actions, described and analyzed (both causally and reconstructively) on the basis of such narrative accounts. The "reason analysis" of partially convergent practical understandings of the Congo crisis, mentioned above, crudely exemplifies such possibilities.

Can one be more specific and rigorous about such possibilities? What do greatly enriched semantic encodings allow?[20] John Mallery is constructing his formalized account of the Hungarian crisis so that it can be metaphorically matched with other accounts of the same intervention and other great-power interventions. He wants to compare the case descriptions in the manner that Pat Winston has compared Shakespearean plots, a subject of similar interest to me in my Abelson and Lehnert–inspired work on story summarizations. James Bennett talks about the artificial intelligence modeling of precedential "data stories" as part of the history of the Vietnam War and the evolution of the strategy of "extended deterrence." Dwain Mefford is collaborating with Alex Hibel in a precedential model of coercive U.S. interventions in Latin America and using a similar computational approach, deriving his narrative accounts of interventions from history books. He sees such stories as potentially usable, quasi-legal (non-)intervention precedents.

Lesson 10: *Think of conflict and cooperation case descriptions as LISP encodable data stories; these descriptions are then executable programs, situation specific practical accomplishments, procedural enactments that constitute the cases, analogous to, but possibly different* *from, the practical actions constituting the observed realities they refer to.*

At last, we are directly at the ontological level of discussion. I think it helpful here to emphasize the formal properties of LISP encoded descriptions. LISP is a computer language in which each description is procedurally executable. Each conflict and cooperation case description is then a context specific program, or recipe, of action and interaction, potentially available in individual or institutional memories for subsequent modification and implementation.

Ontologically, I think of data stories as cell-like organisms, interacting monads, pieces of world history often externally revealing traces of the historical processes that internally or constitutionally generated them. As cited in my "Fairy Tales" article, V. Propp had the same vision when he said that "if any call of a tale organism becomes a small tale within a larger one, it is built . . . according to the same rules as any fairy tale."[21]

Once the identity of a case description with its constitutive and engendering processes is recognized, learning from the data inductively becomes searching its external, visible traces for its internal and constitutive, yet contradictory, essences. It is very important to recognize the multiple possibilities according to which that episodic case history (or tale) might have unfolded. Otherwise the freedom to intervene, to change, to avoid "that which represses without necessity" is obscured. Emancipatory empiricism requires that the end of power politics be a possibility within the concepts with which its stories are told.

Lesson 11: *More generally, think of historical events data as external traces of internal contents: the multiple layerings of contradictory and complementary determination to which they owe their hidden unities, multiple meanings, and possible futures.*

One must conceptualize one's codings to reveal the multiple practical perspectives and institutional relationships that determine them. Here Marxist research can do much more than just problematize liberally oriented neorealists' definitions of international reality. It challenges their avoidance of ontological issues by offering a more potent alternative to the skeptical, conventionalist—or probabilistic—empirical realism they are wont to retreat to. I shall try to respond constructively to this challenge.

An ontologically robust reading of the Marxist tradition suggests that present and past class conflicts have generated multiple layerings of directly or indirectly observable reality. The ontological sharpness of this tradition, with its emphasis on identity-constitutive "internal" relations, was epitomized for me when John O'Neill gave a lecture at M.I.T. in the mid-1970s, arguing that "this cup of coffee contains the history of imperialism!" How much more true that would be for comprehensive narrative accounts of U.S. interventions in Vietnam or Central America and Soviet invasions of Hungary or Afghanistan.

Not to be sensitive to these layerings (and others) is to miss the historical impact of the multiplicity of psychological, social, political, and ecological structures that determine and constitute contemporary reality, including its emancipatory constraints and possibilities. **The sensitized observer can see traces of prior class dominations everywhere, but there are also traces of multiclass collaborations and other social solidarities.** Classical "idealism," the Grotian realism of Hedley Bull, and behavioral peace research all attest to such achievements.

When both internal and external relations affect case relationships, case-matching or precedent-seeking efforts become more complicated and historically more interesting. Similarity matching and dissimilarity contrasting of procedurally specified data stories are external comparisons unless the attributes used in such efforts are in some sense essential, characteristic, and case-identifying ones. Obviously one wants to relate essential characteristics. The analytical problem, for which statistics can be only moderately helpful, is to develop ontologically cogent distinctions between essential and inessential properties of the case descriptions.

One might think of actor identities either in terms of the self-symbols that are important in their cognitive processing or in terms of their characteristic action propensities, such as the defense of dominance or exploitation relationships in crisis. In more complex multiactor events or episodes, one looks for storylike significances, holistic descriptions in terms of key conflict or cooperation variables, and plotlike structures that take actor identities and key interaction propensities into account.

Sometimes, indeed often, data stories are internally related. One cannot properly appreciate a case unless its constitutive inner relationships with other cases are appreciated. Hammarskjöld's creative, personally tragic role in precedentially connecting the Suez and Congo crises is one such inner relationship. The strange mixture of external and internal features of the Tibet and Korean conflicts is one of Sherman's most distinctive contributions to the Alker-Sherman article.[22] A related point is his insistence that the Dominican intervention by the United States must be seen—as indeed Lyndon Johnson said—as negative learning from the Cuban Missile Crisis, which Johnson did not want repeated. Within such intensional relationships one can find the true and imperfect historicities that bind together our larger political societies and communities.

International histories, written in an ecologically sensitive way, are the largest such stories yet recorded about our species. I have been debating with Robert Keohane, Stanley Hoffman, and others about the historical constitution of international society, the "anarchical society" as Hedley Bull has brilliantly described it. I have argued that game-theory representations of international interactions have too often ahistorically obscured the dynamic sociality—the continuous extension, stretching, tearing, and repairing of the practical/normative fabric of society. Peace researchers should be able to display ways in which pluralistic security communities arise and decline within and through the reproductive-transformative processes of that society. Hence, Lesson 12.

Lesson 12: *Code conflict/cooperation case descriptions in instrumental and expressive ways that reveal their internal and external connections; otherwise, historicities in the development of international society that point toward peace and community, rather than the renewal and extension of power politics, will never be related.*

I can restate, and perhaps crystallize, the perspective of emancipatory empiricism in the interest of just war avoidance with a concrete data-making question. How would, or how should, one code a piece of text from the mouth or pen of a foreign minister of a major power, which is privately associated with a new Third World coercive intervention, a statement that reads, "The strong do what they can, and the weak suffer what they must"? With fatalistic acceptance; as ahistorical, instrumental metatalk; as the overriding of contrary recommendations (if discoverable); or as ironic and tragic, a remediable failure?

Toward Emancipatory Ontology

Both my deepened understanding of constitutional metapolitics during and after the Congo crisis, the tracking of imperialism's powerful reproductive mechanisms, and my arguments for the precedential historicity of international community formation reflect a slowly growing awareness of the importance of ontological depth in empirical peace research. My emphasis in this chapter on the possibilities of emergent social orders, of peace breakthroughs and regime decays, reflects this concern. Perhaps it can be generalized.

When major changes in scientific thinking occur, they are sometimes associated with changes in the understood reality of things. The Reformation and the Renaissance brought an end to Medieval Aristotelianism, replacing spiritual understanding with mechanical understandings of the nature of the physical world. Such a transformation is needed now if we are to escape the defeatist, flat, empiricist, naturally exploitive conception of reality that underlies too much of contemporary behavioral science and empirical peace research.

One can take from Roy Bhaskar's brilliant book, *Scientific Realism and Human Emancipation,* a very clear statement of the guiding motivation of such a newer conception: Emancipatory peace research epistemologically directs its "learning from the data" toward the emancipatory "uncoupling (of) the present from the causality of the past," replacing "depotentialising (disempowering, oppressive)" psychological, social, and ecological structures by "potentialising (empowering, enhancing)" ones. Conceiving of emancipation as a "special qualitative kind of becoming free" that consists in the self-directed "*transformation . . . from an unwanted and unneeded to a wanted and needed source of determination.*" Bhaskar argues that it "is both causally presaged and logically entailed by explanatory theory, but that it can only be effected in *practice.*"[23]

Notes

Written while the author was a Fellow at the Swedish Collegium for Advanced Studies in the Social Sciences, Uppsala, and on sabbatical leave from the Department of Political Science at M.I.T., this chapter reflects both discussions of social ontology sponsored by the Swedish Collegium and investigations of data development possibilities in the area of conflict management funded in part by a grant from the John and Catherine MacArthur Foundation, administered by the Center for International Studies at M.I.T. This chapter is an expanded version of a presentation given to the Department of Peace and Conflict Research of Uppsala University; I am grateful to Peter Wallensteen for his suggestive comments. The title is intended to transcend the style of empirical sociology and political science described in D. Willer and J. Willer, *Systematic Empiricism* (Englewood Cliffs, N.J.: Prentice-Hall, 1973). It reflects both the emancipatory impulses often evident in Karl Deutsch's systematic empiricism (which recognizes both inductive and deductive moments of social scientific development) and Johan Galtung's more dialectical conceptions of social research, spelled out most explicitly in his *Essays in Methodology,* 2 vols. (Copenhagen: Ejlers, 1977–1979).

1. Jurgen Habermas, "Life Forms, Morality, and the Task of the Philosopher," in Habermas, *Autonomy and Solidarity: Interviews,* edited and introduced by Peter Dews (London: Verso, 1986), p. 198. The classic account of "surplus repression" by an earlier member of the Frankfurt school is Herbert Marcuse, *Freudian Eros and Civilization* (Boston: Beacon Press, 1966).

2. Margaret Mead, "Warfare Is Only an Invention—Not a Biological Necessity," *Asia* 40:8 (August 1940), pp. 402–405; this essay has been widely reprinted. Given her view, Mead does not subscribe to the genetic-necessity arguments involving male sexual hormones. Jean Bethke Elshstain, *Women*

and War (New York: Basic Books, 1987), is a more recent, thoughtful feminist account of the roles contemporary women play (or can play) in sustaining (or undermining) war as a contemporary institution.

3. Raymond Aron, *The Century of Total War* (Boston: Beacon Press, 1955).

4. An empirically disciplined account of special relevance here is Ted Robert Gurr's impressive, but overly pessimistic, "War, Revolution, and the Growth of the Coercive State," *Comparative Political Studies* (forthcoming). Rewriting Lasswell's "garrison state" construct, Gurr elaborates two empirically discernible developments, externally oriented "militarized states" and domestically oriented "police states." both of which clearly overrely on coercive state capacities. His suggestive conclusion that "only homogenous democracies with low power capabilities and limited alliance obligations are insulated from the development of the institutions and political culture of militarized and police states" is tempered by the sobering reflection that "chronic international conflict undermines the maintainance of non-coercive means of managing internal conflict both in specific countries and in the international system as a whole." His final remark that " 'idealistic' paths to a national and global future with diminished reliance on violence for the management of conflict . . . do not follow from the realistic propositions and models advanced here" belies the "mixed message" of these two generalizations, which broadly might be said to be consistent with Richard Falk's structural reform proposals for the interstate system and Anthony Gidden, *The Nation-State and Violence,* vol. 2 of *A Contemporary Critique of Historical Materialism* (Berkeley and Los Angeles: University of California Press, 1985), especially chap. 11.

The inadequate "realism" evident here appears to be the all too influential conjunction (found in many other behavioral peace researcher's works) of Morgenthau's (anti-"idealist") "realism" and Hume's probabilistic "empirical realism." Roy Bhaskar's *Scientific Realism and Human Emancipation* (London: Verso, 1986), may be read as a 300-page constructive critique of the "empirist ontology" at the root of this version of empiricism, the Humean notion that "the objects of sense-experience are atomistic events constantly conjoined in determinate ways" (see especially pp. 39 and 96).

5. News reports on American Public Radio from Haiti in the spring of 1987 suggested that the existence of a more civilized, post-Duvalier regime should include the restoration of police functions to a domestic police force rather than the partly secret armies theretofore involved in domestic security operations. The unevenly reciprocated patterns of social expectation concerning "domestic," "terrorist," and "international" violence are obviously of great scholarly interest in an era in which "sovereign" states no longer have a monopoly on "legitimate" coercion.

6. Relevant discussions of the UN collective security system include H. R. Alker, Jr., and Frank Sherman, "Collective Security-seeking Practices Since 1945," in Daniel Frei, ed., *Managing International Conflict* (Beverly Hills, Calif.: Sage, 1982); Hedley Bull, *The Anarchical Society: A Study of Order in World Politics* (New York: Columbia University Press, 1977); Ernst B. Haas, "Regime Decay: Conflict Management and International Organizations, 1945–

1981," *International Organizations* 37:2 (Spring 1983), pp. 189–256; Raimo Väyrynen, "Is There a Role for the United Nations in Conflict Resolution?" *Journal of Peace Research* 22:3 (1985), pp. 189–196; Edward E. Azar and John W. Burton, *International Conflict Resolution: Theory and Practice* (Sussex, Eng.: Wheatsheaf Books, and Boulder, Colo.: Lynne Rienner Publishers, 1986).

7. In particular, see H. R. Alker, Jr., James Bennett, and Dwain Mefford, "Generalized Precedent Logics for Resolving Insecurity Dilemmas," *International Interactions* 7:2 (1980), pp. 165–206, and H. R. Alker, Jr., "From Quantity to Quality: A New Research Program on Resolving Sequential Prisoner's Dilemmas" (Paper delivered at the annual meeting of the American Political Science Association, New Orleans, August 1985).

A second source of these reflections is my involvement over the last several years in the Data Development in International Relations project, led by Richard Merritt and Dina Zinnes, which is both renewing and rethinking data collection efforts in the international relations and foreign policy field. Merritt and Zinnes are themselves preparing a review tentatively entitled "Data Development in International Relations."

A third source of these ideas is the arguments and conversations I have had with Stanley Hoffman, Robert Keohane, Joseph Nye, and others in a Harvard-M.I.T. seminar on international institutions and cooperation, led by Keohane and funded by the Ford Foundation. See the more qualitative and historical discussions in H. R. Alker, Jr., and Richard Ashley, eds., *After Neorealism: Anarchy, Power, and International Collaboration* (in preparation).

8. David A. Sylvan and Barry Glassner, *A Rationalist Methodology for the Social Sciences* (Oxford: Blackwell's, 1985). See also Bertell Ollman, *Alienation* (New York: Cambridge University Press, 1971); Jean Bethke Elshtain, "Methodological Sophistication and Conceptual Confusion: A Critique of Mainstream Political Science," in J. Sherman and E. T. Beck, eds., *The Prison of Sex: Essays in the Sociology of Knowledge* (Madison: University of Wisconsin Press, 1979), pp. 229–252; and Bhaskar, *Scientific Realism.*

9. Lincoln Moses, Richard Brody, et al., "Scaling Data on Inter-Nation Action," *Science,* May 26, 1967. The source of the information I have used here, but not my interpretation of it, is Nazli Choucri, the coder whose work was discarded.

10. Nazli Choucri and Robert North, *Nations in Conflict* (San Francisco: W. H. Freeman, 1975), and Richard K. Ashley, *The Political Economy of War and Peace* (London: Frances Pinter, 1980). Choucri and North have just completed a new application of their theory to Japanese experiences in the twentieth century.

11. Akihiko Tanaka, "Chinese International Conflict Behavior, 1949–1978," (Ph.D. dissertation, Department of Political Science, M.I.T., 1981). An English-language summary was published in Tanaka "China, China Watching, and CHINA-WATCHER," in Donald A. Sylvan and Stephen Chan, *Foreign Policy Decision-Making: Perception, Cognition, and Artificial Intelligence* (New York: Praeger, 1984).

12. See Edward E. Azar, "Protracted International Conflicts: Ten Propositions," in Azar and Burton, *International Conflict Resolution,* chap. 2. E. Azar

and Thomas N. Havener, "Discontinuities in the Symbolic Environment: A Problem in Scaling," *International Interaction* 2 (1976), pp. 231–246, poses the related sociological measurement question of how to tap those often unobservable integrative/disintegrative processes whereby social objectives are created and dissolved, processes that events-data research in particular does not adequately (or continuously) reflect.

One of Azar's students, Craig Murphy of Wellesley College, has shown me an unpublished paper entitled "After Hegemony" that takes the events-data-analysis approach pioneered by Lincoln Moses, Richard Brody, Robert North, Charles McClelland, and Edward Azar into the transgovernmental realm of UN programmed activities. Murphy is able to show that such activities (in those program areas he has looked at) more often reinforce interstate relations and capacities than attempt to transcend them.

13. Three empirical studies emphasize conflictful North-South interaction patterns in various parts of the twentieth century from very different paradigmatic perspectives: Istvan Kende, "Wars of Ten Years (1967–1976)," *Journal of Peace Research* 15:3 (1978), pp. 227–241; Peter Wallensteen, *Structure and War: On International Relations, 1920–1968* (Stockholm: Rabén and Sjögren, 1973); and Michael Doyle, "Liberalism and World Politics," *American Political Science Review* 80:4 (December 1986), pp. 1151–1170.

14. This paper was given at the 1977 meeting of the American Political Science Association; it will be included in a collection of my papers tentatively entitled, *Reformulations: Formal Modeling Alternatives for International Relations Researchers* (in preparation). The role of great-power diplomacy in defining systems members is evident in J. David Singer and Melvyn Small, *The Wages of War: A Statistical Handbook* (New York: Wiley, 1972), and M. Small and J. D. Singer, *Resort to Arms: International and Civil Wars, 1816–1980* (Beverly Hills, Calif.: Sage, 1982). That such definitional practices have continued is clear from a reading of Charles S. Gochman and Zeev Maoz, "Militarized Interstate Disputes, 1816–1976," *Journal of Conflict Resolution* 28:4 (December 1984), pp. 585–617, which also reports more evidence supporting the exceptional dispute involvement role of the major powers (see especially Tables 2, 3, 5, and 8).

15. Frank L. Sherman, "Part-Way to Peace: The United Nations and the Road to Nowhere?" (Ph.D. dissertation, Department of Political Science, Pennsylvania State University, May 1987). The study of UN "non–decision making" is preliminarily thematized in Alker and Sherman, "Collective Security-seeking Practices Since 1945."

16. The first empirical report is Ernst B. Haas, *Collective Security and the Future International System* (Denver: University of Denver, 1968); see also Haas's "Types of Collective Security: An Examination of Operational Concepts," *American Political Science Review* 49 (March 1955), and Haas, "Regime Decay."

17. See in Azar and Burton, *International Conflict Resolution,* Burton, "The History of International Conflict Resolution," pp. 40–55; Burton, "The Procedures of Conflict Resolution," pp. 92–116; and Azar and Burton, "Lessons for Great Power Relations," pp. 117–125.

18. A useful overview of the RELATUS system and its application to data from sequential prisoner's dilemma games conducted at M.I.T. is G. Duffy and J. C. Mallery, "Relatus: An Artificial Intelligence System for Natural Language Modelling" (Paper presented to the meeting of the International Studies Association, March 1986); see also Appendix in G. Duffy, "Language, Politics, and Method: Grounding a Computational Hermeneutic" (Ph.D. dissertation, Department of Political Science, M.I.T., August 1987).

19. This paragraph recalls my "Are There Structural Models of Voluntary Structural Action?" *Quality and Quantity* 8 (1974), pp. 199–246, an article that evoked considerable resistance from conventional empirical methodologists at the time of its authorship and eventual publication in a European journal: It argues that the positive answer to the title's question implies following the paradigmatic shift of Herbert Simon's own career. In now making a similar, explicit methodological challenge to quantitative peace researchers, I am suggesting that those people who consider formal operationalization and measurement a *necessary* condition of science need to make such moves for cogent analytical (and representational) reasons. Since teaching methodology in Chile in 1971 and 1972, I have come to more fully appreciate the "techno-rational domination" aspects of very rigorous and expensive standards of scientific practice. Epistemologically, historically oriented dependencia theorizing was much more mature and sophisticated scientifically than the quantitative SPSS approaches to survey data analysis then being introduced (and funded) from the United States.

20. Beyond unpublished work by John Mallery and Dwain Mefford, relevant citations for this paragraph include my "Fairy Tales, Tragedies, and World Histories: Towards Interpretive Story Grammars as Possibilist World Models," *Behaviormetrika,* no. 21 (1987), pp. 1–28 (which had existed in draft form since 1975); James P. Bennett, "Data Stories: Learning About Learning from the U.S. Experience in Vietnam," in Sylvan and Chan, *Foreign Policy Decision-Making;* and Hayward R. Alker, Jr., Wendy Lehnert, and Daniel K. Schneider, "Two Reinterpretations of Toynbee's Jesus: Explorations in Computational Hermeneutics," in Graziella Tonfoni, ed., *Artificial Intelligence and Text Understanding, Quaderni di Ricerca Linguistica,* no. 6 (1985), pp. 49–94. "Data stories," Bennett's phrase, encapsulates nicely many aspects of my earlier suggestion that the end of power politics (as well as other possibilities) should be part of the operational concepts with which peace researchers, at least, map the history of power politics.

21. Alker, "Fairy Tales, Tragedies, and World Histories," p. 1.

22. Alker and Sherman, "Collective Security-seeking Practices Since 1945."

23. Bhaskar, *Scientific Realism,* pp. 142, 171 (italics in the original). This book agrees to a remarkable extent with Galtung's *Essays in Methodology,* which Bhaskar does not cite. Chapters 2 and 3 of Galtung's vol. 1 also provide a rich summary of the ways in which scientific reasoning is more than purely ("Teutonically," Galtung would say) deductive.

11

The Next Twenty-five Years of Peace Research: Tasks and Prospects

Johan Galtung

The Eightfold Path

Is peace research, or peace studies as it is now often referred to,[1] in any way related to Buddhism as the above heading might indicate? The eightfold path of Buddhism is based on the *right* view, thought, speech, action, livelihood, effort, mindfulness, and concentration; all of them heavy words of problematic interpretation. To many this path has a ring of the metaphysical. To others it is highly practical, and to me, it is surprisingly similar to peace research.

The point of departure is the "right view," in the broad sense, varying from rational understanding to total permeation. This right view is informing or imprinting thought, speech, and action, yielding a rather classical threefold division of what an actor can do and should do. From there the view spreads into praxis as livelihood, effort, mindfulness, and concentration.[2] In short, the concrete human being is a bridge between fundamental, deep insights and the actions he or she engenders, as well as the inner and outer structures in which he or she is embedded. Of course, as in most oriental thought, the focus is on inner life and the microspaces around the individual, not on the local, national, and global politics that certainly have to be a major concern of peace researchers. But that difference is less important than the insistence, predominant in Buddhism, on the deep connection between the struggle to develop deeper insight and the struggle to do what is right, in any context.[3]

What a distance between this insistence and what is so often found in the Occident, and also in oriental practice for that matter! The "struggle for deeper insight" is left to science and its search for knowledge and *know-how*. The "struggle for the right action" is seen as a question of values, of morality, of religion and ideology, of church and party, which presumably inform us about the *know-why*. The bridge is unclear, lost in the midst of a tragic dichotomy that is said to exist between facts and values. It is considered perfectly normal to be high on facts and low on values, or vice versa. In the United States, I might even offer the observation that there seems to be some kind of division between East Coast and West Coast intellectual milieus in this regard, the former high on knowledge and low on morality, the latter much lower on concrete knowledge but also much higher on practical morality.[4] That the exceptions are numerous, on either coast, goes without saying. But the combination of "high on knowledge, high on morality" is rare.

I have chosen this point as a point of departure for another eightfold path, one that is possibly useful in discussing the coming twenty-five years in peace research.[5] The Buddhist point of departure is too broad. I have to take as a point of departure the peace researcher as an intellectual; it is to that community that this chapter primarily is addressed. And the question naturally arises, What do intellectuals in general do, and what do we think peace researchers qua intellectuals could usefully do in the coming twenty-five years? In my experience, intellectuals tend to do four things, all of them more or less well.[6]

First, there is the *exploration of the underlying paradigms,* or intellectual frameworks, to try to understand better the underlying assumptions, making them explicit, criticizing them; making them irrelevant, or more relevant, but certainly not trying to deny their existence. Some of these assumptions take the form of values; some of these values may be closely related to the concrete interests of the researcher or the age, gender, race, nation, class, or community from which he or she originates. One type of critical thinking in the scientific enterprise as a whole finds its focus in this paradigm exploration, but there are other kinds to be explored.

Second, there is the effort to arrive at a *description* of empirical reality, through the collection of data, even data banks; in other words, highly empirical activity. Third, there is the effort to arrive at an *explanation,* to weave more or less rich fabrics of verbal constructions to provide the basis for an understanding of why the empirical reality is the way the descriptive activity leads one to believe. The what is seen in the light of the why.

Fourth, there is the *commentary* on how other intellectuals are carrying out paradigm exploration, description, explanation, and commentary. Just as one can explore paradigms underlying paradigm explorations, one may also comment on the commentaries, construct theories about theory formation, and collect data about data collection. In other words, there is more than enough work for intellectuals to do, as is testified by the sheer size of libraries today. And the library is the ideal base for commentary.

It will be noted that what has been said so far constitutes a relatively complete description of what intellectuals as we know them, or us, from universities and similar institutions, do. Depending on where the points of gravity are located in this quadrangle, we can get different intellectual styles, which are more or less lopsided.[7] However, rather than exploring that theme, let me turn to the incompleteness of this paradigm for understanding intellectuals, which is already implicit in the difference between the number eight in the section heading and the number four we have arrived at so far.

If we return to the eightfold path of Buddhism for a moment, it may be noted that what has been said is a verbal description not only of a purely verbal activity but even of an activity that does not at any point equip human beings, or their environment, or the interaction between the two, with any kind of *arrow* in the sense of saying what is better and what is worse.[8] Put very simply, the rather important word "right" in the Buddhist eightfold path is at no point implicit in this standard four-point model of intellectual activity: rational under-standing yes, right views no, or at best as a by-product. Hence, we have to continue to list, not so much what the activity of intellectuals consists of, as of what it might, or even should, consist of in order to come closer to something bearing on the day-to-day reality of a peace researcher. The problem is how to weave values in general, and the broad family of values referred to as "peace" in particular, into the paradigm of intellectual activity, not as a detachable prologue or epilogue, but as an indelible part of intellectual activity itself. The next four points are devoted to that effort.

The fifth point is the effort to engage in *criticism,* viewing empirical reality with the perspective provided by (peace) values and exploring the connections between data and values. The sixth is *constructivism,* in the sense of exploring the connections between values and theories, constructing a future (as opposed to merely criticizing the present) that is seen as "right," not only because the right values are embedded in the verbal construction, but also because that future is seen as viable, even as attainable ("transition strategies") in the light of theory. The seventh consists of *peace education,* the effort to broaden both the range and the depth of those who have the "right views," the insight about peace, in a peaceful manner; and the eighth, *peace action,* is the basic translation of all into a concrete, peace-promoting praxis.

I propose to discuss the activities of peace researchers under these eight headings—no doubt other people can come up with equally good or better schemes. In a sense, the first six points refer to peace research as it has developed; the addition of peace education and peace action results in a division into three parts that has become relatively commonplace.[9]

But if one compares this eightfold path with the Buddhist one, the correspondence is, of course, somewhat less clear. The rightness of what is "right" certainly refers to peace, a concept that may be said to harbor within itself some deep interconnection to enlightenment (*sartori*) and nirvana in the Buddhist sense.[10] Stretching the concept a little, one could perhaps say that the first two on the Buddhist list, view and thought, correspond to the first six on the present list for peace research. The view is the paradigm, the thought the others. Then, there is a relationship between right speech and peace education, just as there is a relationship between right action and peace action. But even so, the remaining four elements on the Buddhist list are missing, or at least not made explicit, with their increasing subtlety as to what peace praxis might imply. I just mention this point: It may be good to know that there is a long way to go in order to catch up with insights developed 2,500 years ago, in a very distant place.[11]

Let me add that in Buddhist thought any list of eight elements, or of any number of elements for that matter, is usually seen, not as a linear progression, but as a wheel.[12] In other words, one may start at any point, proceed to any point, and keep the process moving as the point of gravity changes from one point to the other, but in no particular order. This concept is important because it sensitizes us to the rather obvious idea that there are many roads not only to but in peace, and also not only to but in peace research. Some people might start exploring the foundations of peace research and end up going deeper and deeper into the matter until they disappear and are not heard from ever again.[13] Others might start with peace action and be guided by some intuitions they might like to explore further. Still others, to me often surprisingly so, feel they can jump right into peace education without really knowing what to teach but certainly do so with much energy and perseverance. But what then happens is that they start exploring other aspects of this octagonal wheel, until after some time they have spun a rather rich web of interconnections that makes their paradigms much more significant.[14]

I feel one should enter into such activity with an open mind, with no a priori conviction as to where any such process starts or ends. A

Brownian movement might be better both as a descriptive and as a normative model than any linear order. Also, any trajectory obviously crosses itself, even overlaps itself, many times. And that is perhaps the most important insight that can be derived from this introductory comparative study of eightfold paths.

Peace Research: An Agenda

Let me now make use of these eight points fully, and try to see for each point what might be particularly useful pursuits for a period bringing us into the twenty-first century, conscious of the fact that this also means the third millennium of the era initiated by a person sometimes referred to as the Prince of Peace.[15]

Paradigm Exploration

I see peace research as an effort to explore the conditions of peace in a wholistic and global manner. Wholistic (I prefer this spelling because the word refers to a "whole," not a "hole") means more than transdisciplinary, and much more than interdisciplinary; global means more than transnational, and much more than international. According to this view, there are three relatively clear but also unending tasks.

I think we shall never come to anything like a final conclusion as to what "peace" might mean. Nor do I think we should ever hope for that to happen: The moment we arrive at a consensus within, and even without, the peace research community as to the meaning of "peace," the basis is already laid for the ossification of peace research and practice and the creation of one more technocratic production line, presumably producing peace.

Rather, I think it is our task to continue to draw on the richness of that concept in the geography and history of civilization and culture, exploring more and more facets of that diamond.[16] Nor do I think we should limit ourselves to peace concepts already manifested in the past, some of which are still on the agenda of the present, but also dedicate ourselves to the exploration of the possible future manifestations of peace. Maybe the future is in the past; maybe the future consists of bringing together components of a richer peace concept that history has kept apart because of particular characteristics of particular civilizations.[17] It looks as if each civilization has a peace concept that is compatible with its unwritten code, which then might lead us to explore the possibility of a joint human code, that famous "global civilization" so many people are talking about,[18] for its implications in terms of peace concepts and a global consciousness.

Obviously, any such concept can only be explored in a relatively wholistic and global manner. These are problematic words, indeed, but they strike at the very roots of the epistemology of peace research. I see them as programmatic, not only as problematic. One can easily see what they exclude: a narrow disciplinary perspective and a narrow national (or regional) perspective, as when some people try to make us believe that the problem of peace is merely a problem of military (nuclear) balance between two occidental powers, East and West. But it is more difficult to see what these concepts imply positively. I can see links between wholism and such ancient disciplines as philosophy and theology, and links between globalism and a compassion for humankind as a whole. All point in the direction of some type of spiritualism that certainly is not on the surface of any typical Western social science discipline, and probably not to be found deeper down either. On the other hand, I am also afraid that the invocation of such terms as *wholism* and *globalism* will serve as an invitation for everybody to utter his or her blah-blah with no concern for such tested and important canons of scientific activity as falsifiability of hypotheses and/or possible confirmation through praxis.[19]

However, this contradiction may also be a fruitful one to live with: on the one hand, the spiritual quest for peace, which is considerably more rooted in all human civilizations than what is found; on the other hand, the research/scientific approach of our age. What I am suggesting is simply to see this as another fascinating domain to be explored by peace researchers, who usually consider themselves more scientific than spiritual, *and* by people who think they have the opposite profile. Taking on the challenge to explore the conditions of peace, researchers in the field are already in the thick of values they should continue to make more explicit. But we could also try to make them deeper, in the sense of relinking with much older traditions in this field. The road is paved with wholistic and global approaches.

One point, however, should be taken very seriously. For a person well trained in one discipline, it may be very painful to take on the perspectives of other disciplines, gradually evolving a transdisciplinary, even wholistic, perspective. But the process may also be highly liberating—a caterpillar-turned-butterfly-type of liberation—in the sense of having more dimensions at one's disposal in viewing the world. However, the delights of wholism are available only to those people who have suffered the distortions of excessive disciplinary discipline (this is not a pun, the double meaning of the term "discipline" is certainly not by chance). And exactly the same point applies to the transition from a more or less narrow nation-state perspective on the world to a global perspective, trying to apply what Picasso did with cubism, to view the world from many angles at the same time: a great sense of liberation not easily communicated to people with a more narrow vision.

There is a dialectic at work here, between the narrow and the broad and then back to the narrow again because of a need to specialize in something, but now from a higher point of departure—from a degree in economics via exposure to, and immersion in, peace research to a sociocultural study of the (dis)economies of the arms race? But the basic problem remains: Can the same feeling of delight/liberation be obtained if peace research starts from the dizzying heights of wholism and globalism instead of going through the arduous struggle to arrive at those altitudes through personal effort, rather than being parachuted from above from helicopters built by others? What attracted so many bright students to peace research in the 1960s was, in my view, less peace than wholism/globalism.[20] Today this attraction is more commonplace—witness the rise of development, environment, future, women's, and black studies. What I propose is that this dialectic itself is to be seen as a field of study.

Data

As a point of departure, I am not so sure that we are desperately in need of much more in terms of data. I have a feeling that the problem is more a question of digesting and understanding what we have than to give top priority to further data production. We know an enormous amount about the inequality in power and privilege. Thanks to J. David Singer's and his collaborator's painstaking and path-breaking research on correlates of war,[21] I think we know by now that arms races, when combined with confrontations, tend to lead to wars and that wars occur more frequently to members of alliances than to nonmembers. I think we also know a lot, for instance because of the very important documentation provided by the Stockholm International Peace Research Institute, about the arms race.[22]

At some point it is a good idea to say, this much we know, let us put the data in perspective. There is a particular reason for that view: In my experience, data in and by themselves do not produce any major social change, although some revealing data may precipitate change. I do not even think data change theories however much this is supposed to be the case from the point of view of normative scientific methodology.[23] Theories more than data change society and other theories, and that calls for constructivism that relates values to theories; not just for empiricism relating data to theory and for criticism relating data to values. Data are indispensable. Seen through values, they provide the second basis[24] for critical thinking: Society does not work and a theory does not work if they are contradicted by data. But this observation is at most necessary, certainly not sufficient, for social or theoretical change. Rather, power elites are only moved by data, however critical the implications, the moment two conditions are fulfilled: They think there is a solution to the problem posed, and they think that the solution will not seriously challenge the social paradigms which vest them with power and privilege.[25] The same goes for theories or intellectual paradigms: Critical data are acknowledged only when an essentially paradigm-preserving solution has been found. But minimum theory change is still change and may also be undertaken for other reasons (e.g., compatibility with deeper values and beliefs than data). Breakthroughs, with breakdowns of the old social and/or intellectual paradigms, are rare.[26]

On the other hand, data collection should of course be continued. And I am not even sure that it should always be guided by theory and value. It is like perusing the shelves of a good library: When you know what you are looking for, you may find exactly that but nothing more; when you do not know, you might find the unexpected, the unknown that might release something in you so far unborn. So, all I am saying is that I am not sure that data collection is the top priority for the coming peace research generation; the preceding and succeeding points on the list are more important, for instance.

Theory

I am convinced that theory formation is a top priority. My personal bias in this field is to see the manifestations of antipeace, direct and structural violence, not so much in the light of concrete political events, or in the light of general theories of "human nature" in general and social biology in particular,[27] but in the light of those two middle-level factors between the most general and the most specific: structure and culture. Much has been done to relate the phenomenon of war to the structure of capitalism; we now also know a lot about nonpeaceful behavior between socialist states.[28] We might turn our attention to industrialism as such, and that is useful in order to understand environmental degradation. But it may very well be that the structure we should now focus on would be the state as such, and that the military should be seen as its inevitable concomitant for internal and external purposes. I think the approach taken by Ekkehart Krippendorff in this direction is extremely important.[29]

This approach also leads to a new type of international relations theory, viewing world politics as something much broader than interstate politics.[30] For some time, states will probably still continue to think of themselves not only as having ultimate power, power over power in the territory over which they have "jurisdiction," but also as having monopoly over basic aspects of foreign policy. They will try to link domestic and foreign policy through the nebulous concept of national interests, which are usually left for self-appointed elites to define, perhaps even in such a way that national interests have a global reach.[31] Evidently some states and some military organizations are more antipeace than others: I would prefer states with a defensive rather than an offensive military doctrine, and a military organization that has clearly understood and implemented this doctrine to those states with the opposite profile.[32] But it may also well be that future explorations will increasingly pose the question whether there is something flawed in the very conceptualization of the state as an organization found within all countries, and that the concept simply has to come up for serious review because of intrinsic links between the state and the military as organizations.

If some states are more antipeace than others, the same certainly applies to cultures.[33] Maybe one reason why we have tended to stay away from comparative culture and civilization theory in the field of peace research has been the doctrine of cultural relativism, meaning that all cultures are equally to be respected.[34] This doctrine was important in giving dignity to cultures and civilizations (I use the latter term in the sense of macroculture, the culture of big and related chunks of social geography and history)—even when they are all ranked according to how similar they are to the northwestern corner of the world. This type of ranking was, and is still, ethnocentrism,[35] pure and simple, itself an important aspect of the civilization of that corner. But I do not think cultural relativism should stand in the way of permitting us also to rank cultures in terms of their peace potentials. Nor should it stand in the way of regarding cultures as changeable, even if we do not know today how a civilization can uproot and discard unfortunate elements in its civilizational code and substitute for those elements something more compatible with our common desire to continue staying alive on this planet.[36]

We are also badly in need of *general conflict theory* and *general peace theory;* with general conflict resolution theory as a part of the former, and general theory of how wars end as a part of the latter.[37] Needless to say, the four are closely related and should present the social scientist with extremely difficult and fascinating problems. I do not think we are helped very much in this endeavor by contemporary efforts to delineate "schools" in the field of international relations studies, such as structuralism and functionalism; the realist school (balance of power?) and the idealist school (world order?); and actor-oriented (liberal) and structure-oriented (Marxist, neo-Marxist, dependencia) schools.[38] I think we should be guided by the *problem,* not by allegiance to any school, and pick what we need wherever we can find it. There is such a thing today as peace research/peace studies, but within that field let hundreds of schools bloom.[39] One day we may transcend all the schools; maybe we already have—in that case, the transcendence of that transcendence should already be on the agenda. There is no final state of affairs in human enterprise in general, nor in world politics or in peace, and certainly not in peace research.

Commentary

The first efforts to write histories of peace research, from within the peace research community and from without, are already visible.[40] These commentaries are certainly useful, particularly if they serve to pinpoint limitations in the peace research paradigms by studying their origins, and if they serve to point out how the effort could be improved. In the chronicle of events, I would tend to put commentary in the category of data collection and give it, in its present phase, somewhat lower priority. Maybe I should also note—in passing—how easy it is to engage in this kind of activity: All that is needed is a good library and a visit to some peace research conferences in order to get into direct touch with that type of reality; meaning peace researchers, singly and combined. At no point does one have to touch upon the problems of peace. There is even the danger that there might be people who think that studying peace research is the same as studying peace,[41] just as there certainly are many people who think that to study books about world politics is the same as to study world politics.

Criticism

I believe criticism to be a very important activity: documenting what happens in the world in the perspective of peace values. In so doing, we are helped by an important concept that bridges data and values, the type of value dimension known as an "indicator." The concept of indicator has to some extent come into disrepute because of the way it has been abused by the establishment, focusing on aggregate indicators for a country as a whole (such as the gross national product) at the expense of focusing on internal differences and the external impact, sometimes negative, sometimes positive, of the country on its surroundings in the world space and in nature, on the total system in which it is embedded. In order to do this work well, peace values must be made even more explicit and to some extent they must be operationalized, and at this point it would be excellent if such indicators could not only be of or about people (as opposed to such abstractions as states and countries) but also be developed by people and be for people in the sense that people can understand them and use them.[42] One can easily see that this idea presupposes a world system that is seen less as an interstate system and more as a, say, interperson system, intermunicipality system, or an interpeople's organization system. (I am avoiding the negative expression "nongovernmental organization" because it suggests only one more way in which governments try to make themselves important, by defining people as "nongovernments"— one might try referring to governments as "nonpeople organizations" in order to realize more clearly how unfortunate this negative terminology actually is.)[43]

Critical research should also be used for prognosis, for the type of political meteorology that is so needed. And here, of course, peace researchers should not feel second to geophysical meteorologists, which is not to suggest that our endeavors should be geopolitical—a term that was destroyed a long time ago.[44] But political meteorology should be macropolitical, global. The formulation "what does that mean to us" is perfectly acceptable as long as "us" stands for humankind and the natural environment, not for any limited part (such as, for instance, the United States). In doing this work we would have to be guided not only by theory but also by some of those analytical tools that may make more global and wholistic prognosis possible; I am thinking particularly of dynamic matrix and graph analysis, with the hope that something much better might also soon be available.[45]

Constructivism

It is in the particular area of constructivism, or visioning, that I think the point of gravity of peace research activity should be in the coming twenty-five years. More particularly, the task is to go much beyond the current concern with alternative security policies, which are based on such ideas as defensive rather than offensive defense and deterrence, on transarmament rather than disarmament, and on the possible integration of conventional military, paramilitary, and nonmilitary defense, however important those policies may be.[46] To put the idea bluntly, I think nothing short of the abolition of war as a social institution should be our goal.[47] And in order to reach that goal, images of a peaceful world are not only a conceptual tool but in and of themselves a strategy of major significance. Once in the not too distant past, some people had abolition of poverty as their goal, and they had images of a welfare state. In some parts of the world this goal has to a large extent been attained, and well maintained. In still some other parts the goal was attained, but the welfare state is now to some extent being dismantled. In still other parts of the world that goal remains a compelling image for the future. We could think in terms of the "peacefare state" if it were not for the circumstance (see under "Theory" above) that this may be a *contradictio in adjecto* ("contradictory expression"). If a slogan is needed, perhaps one should settle for "from welfare to peacefare." Humankind designs new agendas for itself all the time; the task of peace researchers is to contribute not only to the exploration of the points on the agenda but to the agenda itself.

Abolition of war as an institution is by no means more a priori impossible than the abolition of slavery or the abolition of colonialism.[48] The defenders of all three of these institutions have always invoked the idea that slavery/colonialism/war is intrinsic to "human nature," without ever really contemplating whether the institution is equally intrinsic to the persons bought and sold (the slaves), the peoples possessed and sometimes dispossessed (the colonials), or the countless victims of war. That there is a potential in human nature for horrid institutions we know extremely well; that that potential is acted out more under some structural and cultural conditions than under others we also know (although we may discuss which ones).

Given certain structural and cultural conditions, it is also true that "if we/I stop doing it" (having slaves, having colonies, waging wars), "somebody else will do it—and why should they get the benefits rather than us/me, when nothing changes anyhow?" But then it is also true, under some conditions, that "if we/I stop doing it, somebody else might follow." Moreover, some types of colonialism served as substitutes for slavery (it was more profitable to exploit black laborers in situ, on the plantation in Africa, than to transport them across the ocean), and in the wake of colonialism came neocolonialism, possibly less political/ military but equally or more cultural/economic in its exploitation profile. And that, of course, raises the terribly important questions that any researcher with a minimum sense of dialectics will pose from the very beginning, If we should succeed in abolishing war as an institution, what would come in its place? and What would be the successor state of affairs, and how can we anticipate it, in order to prevent something equally bad or worse becoming part of the antithesis to war?

I do not think these questions can be answered without due consideration of two classical fields of inquiry: What would be the institutions of peacefare in a world in which war is eliminated as an institution? and What would be the minimum metaphysical/spiritual requirements of a global consciousness? Many people do have and should have ideas about those questions; we are in need of as many good ideas as possible in trying to focus on the twin problems of abolition of war and a peacefare world.[49]

Peace Education

Something new has happened relatively recently in the field of peace education as a result of resolutions from UNESCO and the First Special Session on Disarmament of the United Nations General Assembly in 1978: Governments are encouraged to engage in peace education/ disarmament education. I think there are good reasons to believe that this new development is a major cause of the U.S. withdrawal from UNESCO since almost any such curriculum, even any statement about peace and disarmament education, can be interpreted as having a certain edge against a country with the biggest war machine in human history.[50] That edge is also directed against the Soviet Union, but the Soviet Union has followed a wiser course, in a sense pretending that it does not feel the cut of the edge and for that reason feels comfortable in organizations launching such efforts to educate humankind (watching closely the exact wording of the resolutions, however).

These education efforts are unproblematic.[51] In a dictatorship, the situation is simple. The leadership knows exactly what messages it would like the population to believe in, and the task of the education is to serve as a conveyor belt, filling people like empty bottles with those messages. In a democracy matters are more complicated. We, as peace researchers, would of course insist on being heard in these matters, but equally we would insist that we are not the only ones to be heard, mindful as we are of the multiplicity of views in this difficult *problématique* of peace.

A course of action that I believe useful would be to call for a broadly based committee of people who can design a textbook for schools of all levels (primary, secondary, tertiary) on the problems of peace and war. This textbook would contain the type of information that everybody finds useful and relatively noncontroversial, material about the wars in this century (when and where; who were the participants; what were the causes, dynamics, and consequences), the nature of governments in various parts of the world, the nature of disarmament conferences and treaties, and so on. As for the material that is considered controversial, we are in the fortunate position that we know what to do in a democracy: We put the issues to the people, and let them discuss them. Concretely, the task of the teacher would be to bring such material to his or her class, distribute it to the pupils, and then discuss it without the teacher's feeling that the discussion has to end with the views of the pupils being identical or more similar to his or her own. Peace education, in short, is a question of practicing democracy in the most consequential—to democracies, to all of us— area: peace and war.

But there is another aspect of peace education that in a sense is more difficult, and also more fascinating, than the designing of curriculums for all possible levels and for all possible groups. I am thinking of the *forms* of presentation of insights, of the Buddhist "right view." More particularly, I do not think oral and written presentations in the forms of lectures and articles or books, possibly with some pictures and tables and graphs, should be seen as exhausting the possibilities at our disposal.[52]

The theater is an extremely powerful form of presentation and has not been used at all by social scientists in general, or peace researchers in particular, the way it should. The theater is so powerful because it portrays a live interaction among human beings, possibly also involving spectators, and above all because it permits simultaneous synchronic and diachronic presentations of phenomena. What a way of portraying the key problems of our age—the workings of direct and structural violence in space and time, the groups that try to fight against the machineries of war and exploitation, the power of the forces of violence and the apparent powerlessness of the forces against it! All of these problems are, I think, dramas in search of authors. But I must confess that when authors feel called upon to delve into these difficult matters, what comes out is very bad social science in general and very bad peace research in particular. If peace researchers were to try to write drama, the result might be good social science but miserable theater. There must be ways of overcoming this dilemma, and I think we should push forward in that direction, under the heading of education. New forms of presentation might also give a fresh impetus to the whole research enterprise.[53]

Peace Action

Peace action is a question of the choice of the appropriate strategies for a more peaceful world. In this field also something new has happened: Peace researchers have achieved a relatively clear role as experts/ consultants of the peace movement, of course doing so openly, not protected by secrecy like security experts.

It is not by chance that these two phenomena, the peace movement and the peace research movement, now coincide in time: They have been created by the urgency of avoiding an impending holocaust.[54] And yet the relationship between the two is not without problems.

There are peace researchers who feel they are much above the peace movement, seeing the movement as essentially stupid and misguided in its insistence, usually expressed in slogans, on simple factors. And there are peace researchers who take the opposite stance, of being the servants of the peace movement, believing that the leadership should state the course of action and the peace researcher should elaborate the rationale. In short, we have the old attitudes of the ivory-tower intellectual, who does not want to get his or her hands dirty, and the willing servant, who works for a peace movement that does not even pay the servant but in other regards is similar to the establishment's making use of the intellectual.

The task of a peace researcher is to steer clear of these two aberrations. In a democracy we should always have deep respect for a popular movement, even if we do not like what it stands for.[55] If we feel the peace movement is by and large going in the right direction, our task is to help and guide, and that is not done by being aloof or subservient. The dialogue model is much better, if one constantly keeps in mind the fact that peace researchers have had the privilege of studying some things in more detail than the members of a popular movement can possibly have done. What movements might do for the researcher, however, is to point out that he or she has been studying in the wrong direction or in the right direction but without practical conclusions[56]— a challenge that should make any peace researcher very grateful, because it implies being taken seriously as opposed to the establishment's attitudes, which are characterized by disdain, fear, or both for peace researchers.

But there are also other role model possibilities for the peace researcher. I am thinking of Amnesty International, which is doing an excellent job in the field of human rights, for instance, in working for the abolition of torture. Why should there not be a War Abolition International,[57] to some extent staffed by peace researchers, which would be in contact with relevant government and popular committees and organizations to see to it that the right items are being considered and pursued with an energy proportionate to their urgency? In fact, many such organizations are needed, such as Environment International, and the better they cooperate, the more they might create pressure for a peacefare world.

The same need exists for the other side of the peace research coin, structural violence, and a related science, development studies.[58] We also need a Development International; what we have is too scattered, too fragmented.[59] The codification of human rights has served to crystallize our efforts in that direction. Similar codifications for abolition of war and the abolition of worldwide misery might be useful provided we are willing to see all such codes as parts of a rolling agenda, with no beginning and no end.

Conclusion

There is enough to do. I have chosen the analogy of Buddhist thought deliberately to indicate an unending agenda. I do not believe in occidental sectarianism. I do not think there is a god somewhere, watching our painful endeavors, deciding to exterminate us *or* to save us from the scourge of war—not because we deserve it, but out of His grace. Peace, if attained, is possible only through intense human effort. And peace research has an important role to play in that effort.

To summarize, peace research should delve much deeper into the basics of peace, of wholism and globalism, perhaps even in the search for a new spiritualism. Somewhat lower priority should be given to data collection than to making sense of the data we already have. The search for better theory should go on unabated, particularly with a view to theorizing about the world politics of peace and war, not merely about occidental, big-power models. The focus should be on conflict resolution and how wars end—that is where our knowledge deficit is most obvious. Commentary on the work of other intellectuals in general and of peace researchers in particular could have lower priority. The thrust should rather be in the direction of critical predictions and positive constructions, and on peace education and peace action guided by these explorations.

We are still left with the last four items on the Buddhist eightfold path: livelihood, effort, mindfulness, and concentration. These points touch the inner person and are not usually the concern of scientific epistemology in general or of methodology in particular. A researcher is judged on the basis of scientific production regardless of how the producer looks on the inside. There is a universalism to the scientific community as it is open to everybody who produces according to the rules. Maybe the situation should stay like that. Research, like a universal church, makes a great contribution to the never-ending task of weaving humankind together simply by being open and universal—a place where you can meet your antagonist along value and/or interest lines.

But there is something else that can be and should be done. In a very important article,[60] Glenn D. Paige challenges not only the types of research that end up legitimizing state-supported violence but even his own book, which, in an agonizing reappraisal, he decided had done exactly that. Paige rejects his own book, and with it a complete tradition in political science: "In an age of unprecedented potential for violence, the supreme task of political science becomes the creation and application of non-violent knowledge." I agree, certainly—hence, peace research and my own involvement in the efforts to explore how peace can be obtained through *peaceful* means.

However, I could also go one step further and suggest a Hippocratic oath for peace researchers.[61] Merely trying to draft such an oath would be more than a difficult and fascinating task; it might start dialogical processes that in themselves could be not only revealing and educational but also peace building. And it might bring the two eightfold paths somewhat closer to each other, to the benefit of both.

Notes

This chapter was first presented as a lecture at the Department of Peace and Conflict Research, Uppsala University, in connection with the inauguration of the Dag Hammarskjöld Professor of Peace and Conflict Studies, Peter Wallensteen, November 15–17, 1985; then at the universities of Toronto, Hawaii, and California at Berkeley; Stanford University; University of Missouri, Kansas University; and other places. I am indebted to the discussants in all places.

1. The term *peace science* is also used in the United States, e.g., by the Peace Science Society founded by Walter Isard. In my view, that term is much too pretentious and also misleading, giving the impression that solutions are found rather than created.

2. A useful introductory book to Buddhist thought is Christmas Humphreys, *The Buddhist Way of Life* (London: Mandala Books, 1980).

3. Thus, in Buddhism, the distinction between descriptive and normative, between "is" and "ought," so dear to Western thought, is much less sharp.

4. See Johan Galtung, "Visioning a Peaceful World—from the US Mid-West" (Keynote address to the Iowa State Initiative for a U.S. Institute for Peace, May 1986), in which this idea is developed in more detail. From East to West, knowledge increases and morality (international affairs) decreases; from North to South in the United States, politics becomes increasingly conservative, bordering on the reactionary—Florida, Hawaii, and Alaska being exceptions.

5. See Johan Galtung, "Twenty-Five Years of Peace Research: Ten Challenges and Some Responses," *Journal of Peace Research* 22:2 (1985), pp. 146–159.

6. See Johan Galtung, "Culture, Structure, and Intellectual Style: Saxonic, Teutonic, Gallic, and Nipponic Approaches Compared," *Social Science Information* (1981).

7. Ibid. This article develops only four such styles; no doubt there are more, and more can be imagined—and then there are any number of typologies to describe styles.

8. Except one possibility, of course: the accumulation of knowledge, presumably a change for the better. Given the ability of the human race to abolish itself through weapons of mass destruction, now including laser beams, amelioration is at least not obvious. Nor is it obvious that there is an accumulation

of knowledge if we assume that each new item of knowledge makes us more aware of the ignorance surrounding that knowledge.

9. This combination was, not by change, the title of the first volume of Johan Galtung, *Essays in Peace Research, Peace: Research, Education, Action* (Copenhagen: Ejlers, 1975).

10. See Johan Galtung, "Peace Theory: An Introduction," *World Encyclopedia of Peace* (Oxford: Pergamon Press, 1986)—or Johan Galtung, "Entropy and the General Theory of Peace," in *Peace: Research, Education, Action,* chap. 2.

11. For an effort to indicate in what direction the four missing Buddhist roads may be located, relative to where peace research is today, see the conclusion of this chapter.

12. A linear order is diachronic, if there is a direction. The points on a wheel are synchronic, and all of them can be related to each other directly without passing through other points. But there is also diachrony if the wheel starts rolling with one point after the other "coming up."

13. This is the danger of digging too deep, one might say, getting lost in problems for which there may be no "solution," at least not today, and in problems that later on may evaporate as uninteresting, being based on false dichotomies, etc. Research presupposes some (intuitive?) ability to distinguish between significant and insignificant.

14. Thus, in the many interesting publications from the Peace Education Committee of the International Peace Research Association, there is a continuous lack of advances built on new developments in the field of education.

15. This reference, however, has a very ambiguous message—see the last chapter, on the role of Christianity, in Johan Galtung, *Hitlerism, Stalinism, Reaganism: Three Variations on a Theme by Orwell* (in Norwegian, Spanish, and German editions; forthcoming in English).

16. For one such effort, see Galtung, *Essays in Peace Research,* Vol. 5, *Peace Problems* (Copenhagen: Ejlers, 1980), chap. 15 on peace concepts around the world.

17. This theme is developed in Johan Galtung, "Peace and the World as Inter-Civilization Interaction," in R. Väyrynen, D. Senghaas, and C. Schmidt, eds., *The Quest for Peace,* pp. 330–347 (Beverly Hills, Calif.: Sage, 1987).

18. I am skeptical of this idea. There may be an inner logic to the codes of civilization, but we cannot just combine all kinds of good characteristics and call it a global civilization.

19. A solid dose of Popperism harms no one when not taken too seriously: Popper is far too limited when it comes to the possibilities of transcending social orders.

20. Peace research was a new way of doing research. In my own case, I learned a great deal from a little encounter at the Department of Sociology, Columbia University, in the late 1950s, at that time a stronghold of sociology. Discussing reactions of the unemployed in certain situations, somebody brought up the idea that one explanation might be that they were poor. This reasonable idea was, however, immediately rejected, the variable being economic rather

than social. "Try to arrive at a sociology explanation" was the advice from higher up.

21. I am thinking particularly of the research by Michael Wallace in "Arms Races and Escalation," *Journal of Conflict Resolution* 23:1 (1979), pp. 3–16.

22. One of the directors of SIPRI, Frank Blackaby, explains the basic assumptions of policy research: "The problem-oriented researcher is not concerned to identify the 'basic' causes—whatever they might be. The concern is to separate the 'malleable' and 'non-malleable'—those that can be shifted and those that cannot. To put it in another way, the purpose of the research is to try to find, in the system, levers which might be pulled in order to improve the outcome" (Frank Blackaby, "Peace Research and Disarmament: A Problem-oriented Approach" (Paper presented at conference, Peace Research: Retrospect, Prospect, Uppsala, November 1985), p. 2. Others might feel that we unfortunately have to identify "basic" causes as only at that level can the system be improved.

23. For an alternative approach, see Johan Galtung, "Empiricism, Criticism, Constructivism: Three Approaches to Scientific Activity," in Galtung, *Methodology and Ideology* (Copenhagen: Ejlers, 1977), chap. 2.

24. The first basis is, of course, paradigm critique.

25. Thus, as Schumacher used to point out, when somebody says that most of humankind is doing essentially deadly boring work, and documents this, nothing happens because nobody has any idea what to do about it. When such ideas come around and they do not threaten the status quo, the data can be safely admitted.

26. Thus, there may also be a tendency to "accept" an alternative that is known not to work, such as disarmament, which is easily rejected yet always up for discussion again, precisely for that reason.

27. It is interesting to note that two of the theories projecting human beings as inherently aggressive have been produced in two of the most aggressive countries in the world, Germany (Konrad Lorentz) and the United States (E. Wilson).

28. The number of cases in which violence aggression has been directed against socialist states that wanted a change in the status quo is proverbial: Yugoslavia, Albania, Hungary, Czechoslovakia, Poland, China (but here the Soviet Union did not dare attack, China presumably being too big), Vietnam (from China), and Afghanistan. Such cases look very much like ordinary relations inside any hegemonic system; it is difficult to see anything particularly socialist about them.

29. See his impressive book *Staat und Krieg: Die historische Logik politischer Unvernunft* (Frankfurt am Main: Suhrkamp, 1985). However, it may be pointed out that in using Prussia as a point of departure, the linkage state-military-war becomes more clear than if the reference country were, say, Norway.

30. See the excellent article by Chadwick F. Alger, "Bridging the Micro and the Macro in International Relations Research," *Alternatives* 10 (1984-1985), pp. 319–344.

31. One little story sometimes catches more than long theories. At a meeting of the Palme Commission with politicians and researchers in Stockholm in

September 1983, I had the occasion to ask Richard Perle, U.S. assistant secretary of defense, what he thought of a country that saw its national interests as something located far outside the borders of the country. His answer was, "The United States decides herself where her national interests are located." His Soviet opposite number had a more clever, less revealing answer: "A very important question that requires some deep deliberation."

32. This is the basic thesis of my book, Johan Galtung, *There Are Alternatives!* (Nottingham, Eng.: Spokesman, 1984)—also in Norwegian, Swedish, Dutch, German, Italian, Spanish, and Japanese editions.

33. See Galtung, "Peace and the World as Intercivilization Interaction."

34. Of course, it would be exceedingly strange if of all the distributions of an inclination toward belligerence of the world civilizations the distribution with zero dispersion were the one realized in this world of ours. But UNESCO, which should take up this issue, has encountered enough problems with the issues already tackled, such as press and other media, and accusations of politicization.

35. The most important researcher in the field of ethnocentrism as a force shaping our perception of development alternatives is probably still the late Roy Preiswerk.

36. The remarkable thing is that peoples with very different cultures are nonetheless adjusting to each other around our tremendously mobile globe all the time, by and large through migration.

37. Peter Wallensteen is, I think very rightly, pointing to the need to continue the work done in the 1960s on conflict theory (see Chapter 1 and Chapter 6 in this book). Axelrod's work, based on computer simulation, suffers from the shortcoming of almost all work originating from the United States in this field, insufficient attention to conflicts among actors endowed with highly unequal resources. For one effort, see Donald Wittman, "How a War Ends: A Rational Model Approach," *Journal of Conflict Resolution* 23:4 (1979), pp. 743–763.

38. In the United States in 1986, the number was grotesquely simplified to three schools only: realists, liberals, and Marxists.

39. As any observer at an IPRA meeting will find, it is definitely not correct that all peace researchers think alike. But most of them do share the goal of obtaining peace through peaceful means.

40. At the tenth IPRA conference (1983), efforts by Håkan Wiberg and by Mario Borelli and Magnus Haavelsrud were visible. Wiberg's excellent work is published as Chapter 2 of this book.

41. I would see this way of thinking as characteristic of much of Japanese peace research, in line with the sad tendency of Japanese social scientists to focus on commentary—see the article referred to in note 6.

42. Ruth Sivard's work on indicators is classic—in the best tradition of the Abraham Lincoln slogan for democracy.

43. See the article by Alger, "Bridging the Micro and the Macro," for a good review of how much more is involved in "international relations" than just approximately 160 states.

44. And yet there is such a thing as macropolitics, which refers to the relations among big chunks of humankind, each one of them with more or less explicit geopolitical projects. For one example of this approach, see Johan Galtung, *World Politics of Peace and War* (forthcoming).

45. The basic point about matrices and graphs is that they permit subdivisions in rows and columns, points and lines, and yet also lend themselves to global characterizations, matrices using determinants and other types of parametrization and graphs, a host of parameters.

46. In a sense, I am talking here in opposition to my own book, *There Are Alternatives!*, but that book is only about a possible project for the small peace movement, not about the abolition of war, which is the project of the large peace movement.

47. For a forceful argument that this is the task, see Anatol Rapoport, "Can Humanity Eliminate War?" *Soka Gakkai News* (September 1985), pp. 2–12. Volker Rittberger, in "Ist Frieden möglich?" *Universitas* 40 (1985), pp. 1139–1149, argues that an alliance like NATO is perhaps more effective in bringing about (negative) peace among its members, and he is very careful in trying to answer the question. Peter Wallensteen, in work on ongoing armed conflicts and in his survey "Regional Conflicts and Strategic Confrontation: Some Crucial Links" (Department of Peace and Conflict Research, Uppsala University, Working Paper, 1985), certainly warns against excessive optimism and presents an impressive/depressive array of ongoing conflicts.

48. This argument is pursued in some detail in chap. 10 of Galtung, *World Politics of Peace and War.*

49. This discussion is a reformulation in more evocative terms of the old problem formula for peace research: negative peace versus positive peace.

50. It is reported that a U.S. ambassador told (not very effectively) a closed meeting of UNESCO: "We do not want the UNESCO to publish data that can make young Americans have doubts about their own country."

51. See Johan Galtung, "Peace Education: How to Succeed in Peace Education Without Really Trying" (Jackson Lecture, Ontario Institute for Studies in Education, Toronto, 1987).

52. See Johan Galtung, "Forms of Presentation," in *Methodology and Development* (Copenhagen: Ejlers, 1987), chap. 5, for a discussion of exactly this issue.

53. For instance, what would it do to the whole research process if the social scientist knew the end product was going to be a theater piece for the general public, not a paper for a professional meeting?

54. See my paper for END IV, Amsterdam, June 1985, on the peace movement and the role of scientists, *Bulletin of Peace Proposals,* "Scientists and the Peace Movement," 17:1 (1986), pp. 79–85.

55. Example: I certainly dislike what right-wing, populist evangelists of the Jerry Falwell/Pat Robertson type stand for, yet I must admit respect bordering on admiration for their ability to establish contact with people by visiting them and taking them seriously. They have much to teach us for the peace movement.

56. Thus, the only concrete policy proposal I know from the enormous U.S. production in the field of peace research is the rightly famous GRIT (gradual reduction of international tension) proposal by Charles Osgood.

57. The closest there is, War Resisters' International (WRI), is more modest in its name, giving a free harbor to conscientious objectors of all kinds.

58. Björn Hettne, professor of peace research at Gothenburg University in Sweden, is doing excellent work on the linkage between peace and development studies. He does much of the work within the framework provided by the European Association of Development Institutes (EADI).

59. The Society for International Development tends in that direction, but perhaps it is too elitist. A better example is provided by Marc Nerfin's important network, International Foundation for Development Alternatives in Nyon, Switzerland, which publishes the *IFDA Dossier.*

60. Glenn D. Paige, "On Values and Science: The Korean Decision Reconsidered," *American Political Science Review* 71 (1977), pp. 1603–1609. The book by the same author, *The Korean Decision: June 24–30, 1950* (New York: Free Press, 1968), is a high-quality, mainstream work.

61. Maybe it should be pointed out that such an oath would never admonish the researcher not to take a stand, only that he or she should always look for nonviolent (nonkilling, as Glenn Paige would have said) solutions.

About the Contributors

Hayward R. Alker, Jr., is currently Professor of Political Science, MIT, Cambridge, Mass. He has a background in mathematics and is presently completing a book on *The Dialectics of World Order*.

Olav Bjerkholt is Assistant Director-General of the Central Bureau of Statistics of Norway and has a background in economics.

Ådne Cappelen is a Senior Research Fellow at the Central Bureau of Statistics of Norway and has a background in economics.

Johan Galtung is founder and former director of the International Peace Research Institute, Oslo, Norway. He was editor of the *Journal of Peace Research* 1964–1974 and Professor of Peace and Conflict Research at the University of Oslo, 1969–1978. Until 1987 he was Professor of World Politics at Princeton University, and he is now Professor of Peace Studies at the University of Hawaii.

Nils Petter Gleditsch is Senior Research Fellow, International Peace Research Institute (PRIO) and editor of *Journal of Peace Research* (1976–1977 and since 1983). He has a background in sociology.

Göran Lindgren is Research Fellow and Computer Manager at the Department of Peace and Conflict Research, Uppsala University, Uppsala, Sweden.

Volker Rittberger is Professor of Political Science, University of Tübingen (FRG), and Special Fellow of the United Nations Institute for Training and Research (UNITAR).

Bruce Russett is the Dean Acheson Professor of International Relations and Political Science, Yale University. He is also Editor of the *Journal of Conflict Resolution*.

Raimo Väyrynen has been Professor of International Relations at the University of Helsinki, Finland, since 1978. He was Visiting Professor of War and Peace Studies, Princeton University, 1986–1987. Previously he was Director of Tampere Peace Research Institute (TAPRI), Tampere, Finland, and Secretary General, International Peace Research Association (IPRA).

Peter Wallensteen is the first holder of the Dag Hammarskjöld Chair of Peace and Conflict Research, Uppsala University, Uppsala, Sweden. He has previously published *Global Militarization* (1985) with Westview Press.

Håkan Wiberg is Professor of Sociology, Lunds University, Lund, Sweden, and also holds degrees in mathematics and philosophy.

Index